IFRS Explained

First edition 2010

ISBN 9780 7517 8545 6

British Library Cataloguing-in-Publication Data
A catalogue record for this book
is available from the British Library
Published by
BPP Learning Media Ltd
BPP House, Aldine Place
London W12 8AA

www.bpp.com/learningmedia

Printed in Malta

Printed on paper sourced from sustainable,
managed forests.

Contents

Contents

Introduction

v

Introduction

Introduction

This book is intended for those with basic accounting knowledge who now wish to get familiar with IFRS. We have dealt with the standards under topic headings and the aim has been to show how the provisions of the standards are applied in practice. Rather than detailed cross-references to sections and sub-sections, we have concentrated on bringing out the key points and showing examples and workings where applicable.

We have explained in some detail the preparation of IFRS financial statements including consolidated financial statements. Many readers will already be familiar with consolidation procedures, but may find it useful to go through the basics before taking account of those issues peculiar to IFRS, such as non-controlling interest at fair value.

We have omitted two standards dealing with financial reporting by financial institutions:

*   IAS 26 – *Accounting and Reporting by Retirement Benefit Plans*
*   IFRS 4 – *Insurance Contracts*

These are complex standards and knowledge of them is not required by most preparers of financial statements.

1 Impact of globalisation

The current reality is that the world's capital markets operate more and more freely across borders. The impacts of rapid globalisation are epitomised by the words of Paul Volker, Chairman of the IASC Foundation Trustees in November 2002, in a speech to the World Congress of Accountants.

> 'Developments over the past year and more have strongly reinforced the logic of achieving and implementing high-quality international accounting standards. In an age when capital flows freely across borders, it simply makes sense to account for economic transactions, whether they occur in the Americas, Asia, or Europe, in the same manner. Providing improved transparency and comparability will certainly help ensure that capital is allocated efficiently. Not so incidentally, generally accepted international standards will reduce the cost of compliance with multiple national standards.'

As the modern business imperative moves towards the globalisation of operations and activities, there is an underlying commercial logic that also requires a truly global capital market. Harmonised financial reporting standards are intended to provide:

- A platform for wider investment choice
- A more efficient capital market
- Lower cost of capital
- Enhanced business development

Globally, users of financial statements need **transparent** and **comparative information** to help them **make economic decisions**.

From 2005 EU listed companies have been required to use IAS/IFRS in preparing their consolidated financial statements. This is an important step towards eventual harmonisation with the US.

2 International Accounting Standards Board (IASB)

The International Accounting Standards Board is an independent, privately-funded accounting standard setter based in London. Contributors include major accounting firms, private financial institutions, industrial companies throughout the world, central and development banks, and other international and professional organisations.

In March 2001 the IASC Foundation was formed as a not-for-profit corporation incorporated in the USA. The IASC Foundation is the parent entity of the IASB.

From April 2001 the IASB assumed accounting standard setting responsibilities from its predecessor body, the International Accounting Standards Committee (IASC). This restructuring was based upon the recommendations made in the Recommendations on Shaping IASC for the Future. In essence, the restructuring was driven by the need to increase the level of resourcing owing to an increasing workload.

The 15 members of the IASB come from nine countries and have a variety of backgrounds with a mix of auditors, preparers of financial statements, users of financial statements and an academic.

The formal objectives of the IASB are to:

(a) **Develop**, in the public interest, a **single set** of high quality, understandable and **enforceable global accounting standards** that require high quality, transparent and comparable information in financial statements and other financial reporting to help participants in the various **capital markets** of the world and other users of the **information** to make **economic decisions**

(b) **Promote** the use and **rigorous application** of those standards

(c) Work actively with national standard-setters to bring about **convergence** of national accounting standards and IFRSs to **high quality solutions**

Structure of the IASB

The structure of the IASB can be illustrated by the following diagram:

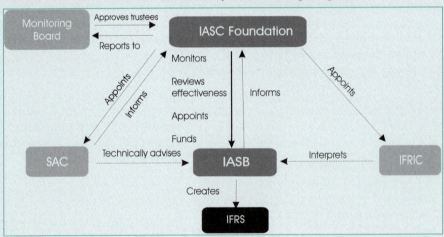

IASC Foundation

The IASC Foundation is made up of 22 Trustees, who essentially monitor and fund the IASB, the SAC and the IFRIC. The Trustees are appointed from a variety of geographic and functional backgrounds according to the following procedure:

(a) The International Federation of Accountants (IFAC) suggested candidates to fill five of the Trustee seats and international organisations of preparers, users and academics each suggested one candidate.

(b) The remaining Trustees are 'at-large' in that they were not selected through the constituency nomination process.

Standards Advisory Council (SAC)

The SAC is essentially a forum used by the IASB to consult with the outside world. It consults with national standard setters, academics, user groups and a host of other interested parties to advise the IASB on a range of issues, from the IASB's work programme for developing new IFRSs, to giving practical advice on the implementation of particular standards.

International Financial Reporting Interpretations Committee (IFRIC)

IFRIC provides guidance on specific practical issues in the interpretation of IFRSs. The IFRIC is discussed in more detail below.

Scope and authority of IFRSs

The IASB achieves its objectives primarily by developing and publishing IFRSs and promoting the use of those standards in general purpose financial statements and other financial reporting.

IFRSs set out **recognition, measurement, presentation and disclosure requirements** dealing with transactions and events that are important in general purpose financial statements. IFRSs are based on the IASB Framework, which:

- Addresses the **concepts** underlying the information presented in general purpose financial statements
- Facilitates the **consistent** and logical formulation of IFRSs
- Provides a basis for the use of judgement in resolving accounting issues.

IFRSs are designed to apply to the general purpose financial statements and other financial reporting of all profit-oriented entities.

General purpose financial statements are directed towards the common information needs of a wide range of users, for example, shareholders, suppliers, employees and the public at large. The objective of financial statements is to provide information about the financial position, performance and cash flows of an entity that is useful to those users in making economic decisions.

A complete set of financial statements includes:

- A statement of financial position
- A statement of comprehensive income
- A statement of all changes in equity, showing only owner changes in equity (Non-owner changes are in the statement of comprehensive income)
- A statement of cash flows
- Accounting policies and explanatory notes

The term 'financial statements' includes a complete set of financial statements prepared for an interim or annual period, and condensed financial statements for an interim period. In the interest of timeliness and cost, and to avoid repeating information previously reported, an entity may provide less information in its interim financial statements than in its annual financial statements. IAS 34 Interim financial reporting prescribes the minimum content of complete or condensed financial statements for an interim period.

Many of the IASs produced by the old IASC allowed entities to make a choice between 'benchmark treatments' and 'allowed alternatives'. By contrast, the IASB has shifted the emphasis away from allowing entities a choice between accounting treatments, and is reconsidering all those IASs where choices are permitted. Its objective is either to reduce the number of options available to choose from, or to eliminate the element of choice altogether. This is in line with the IASB's emphasis on reporting like transactions and events in a like way, and reporting different transactions and events differently.

Any limitation of scope of an IFRS will be made clear in the standard.

IFRS due process

IFRSs are developed through an international due process that involves accountants, financial analysts and other users of financial statements, the business community, stock exchanges, regulatory and legal authorities, academics and other interested individuals and organisations from around the world. The IASB consults the SAC in public meetings on major projects, agenda decisions and work priorities, and discusses technical matters in meetings that are open to public observation.

The overall agenda of the IASB will initially be set by discussion with the SAC. The process for developing an individual standard would involve the following steps.

Step 1   During the early stages of a project, IASB may establish an **Advisory Committee** to give advice on issues arising in the project. Consultation with the Advisory Committee and the Standards Advisory Council occurs throughout the project.

Step 2   IASB may develop and publish **Discussion Papers** for public comment.

Step 3   Following the receipt and review of comments, IASB would develop and publish an **Exposure Draft** for public comment.

Step 4   Following the receipt and review of comments, the IASB would issue a final **International Financial Reporting Standard**.

The period of exposure for public comment is normally 90 days. However, in exceptional circumstances, proposals may be issued with a comment period of 60 days.

Interpretation of IASs/IFRSs

The International Financial Reporting Interpretations Committee (IFRIC) assists the IASB by improving existing Standards. It was established in March 2002 by the IASC Foundation to replace the Standing Interpretations Committee (SIC). Where before SIC Interpretations were issued, now IFRIC Interpretations are issued.

The IFRIC has two main responsibilities:

*   Review, on a timely basis, newly identified financial reporting issues not specifically addressed in IFRSs
*   Clarify issues where unsatisfactory or conflicting interpretations have developed, or seem likely to develop in the absence of authoritative guidance, with a view to reaching a consensus on the appropriate treatment.

The IFRIC also helps the IASB move towards international harmonisation by working with its equivalent national-level bodies (such as the UITF in the UK).

The IFRIC, like the IASB itself, adopts a **principle-based approach**. Its intention is to provide guidance that is in line with the rest of the IFRSs. It therefore bases itself, like each of the individual Standards, first and foremost on the IASB Framework. It will then look at any relevant IASs for principles applying the Framework to that particular area. It is absolutely essential to the work of the IFRIC that its interpretations are in line with IASB Framework principles, rather than any other accounting principles.

The IFRIC then in turn informs the IASB of any inadequacies that it finds in the Framework or in existing IFRSs. If it believes that they should be modified or that a new Standard should be developed, the IFRIC informs the IASB so that it can consider whether or not to do so. This helps to ensure that the Framework and existing IFRSs are kept up to date for the actual financial reporting issues that the IFRIC has found with them.

The IFRIC develops its interpretations through a due process of consultation and debate which includes making Draft Interpretations available for public comment. The IFRIC Interpretations that it makes publically available are the consensus views that it has reached as a result of this process.

Authority and application of IFRIC Interpretations

IFRIC Interpretations carry the same authority as IFRSs, in the sense that they set out consensus views that entities must adhere to if they describe their financial statements as being prepared in accordance with IFRS.

IFRIC Interpretations are applicable from the date of issue or if they specify one, from their effective date. Some Interpretations may contain 'transitional provisions' that apply to their first application.

An Interpretation then ceases to apply when it is overridden by a new IFRS (or other authoritative IASB document). When this happens, this would be mentioned in the Exposure Draft of the new, overriding IFRS (or other document). The IASB would then inform the IFRIC when this happens.

Comment periods

The IASB issues each Exposure Draft of a Standard and discussion documents for public comment, with a normal comment period of 120 days. In certain circumstances, the Board may expose proposals for a much shorter period. However, such limited periods would be used only in extreme circumstances. Draft IFRIC Interpretations are exposed for a 60-day comment period.

Co-ordination with national standard setters

Close co-ordination between IASB due process and due process of national standard setters is important to the success of the IASB's mandate.

The IASB is exploring ways in which to integrate its due process more closely with national due process. Such integration may grow as the relationship between IASB and national standard setters evolves. In particular, the IASB is exploring the following procedure for projects that have international implications.

(a)   IASB and national standard setters would co-ordinate their work plans so that when the IASB starts a project, national standard setters would also add it to their own work plans so that they can play a full part in developing international consensus. Similarly, where national standard setters start projects, the IASB would consider whether it needs to develop a new Standard or review its existing Standards. Over a reasonable period, the IASB and national standard setters should aim to review all standards where significant differences currently exist, giving priority to the areas where the differences are greatest.

(b)   National standards setters would not be required to vote for IASB's preferred solution in their national standards, since each country remains free to adopt IASB standards with amendments or to adopt other standards. However, the existence of an international consensus is clearly one factor that members of national standard setters would consider when they decide how to vote on national standards.

(c)   The IASB would continue to publish its own Exposure Drafts and other documents for public comment.

(d) National standard setters would publish their own exposure document at approximately the same time as IASB Exposure Drafts and would seek specific comments on any significant divergences between the two exposure documents. In some instances, national standard setters may include in their exposure documents specific comments on issues of particular relevance to their country or include more detailed guidance than is included in the corresponding IASB document.

(e) National standard setters would follow their own full due process, which they would ideally choose to integrate with the IASB's due process. This integration would avoid unnecessary delays in completing standards and would also minimise the likelihood of unnecessary differences between the standards that result.

3 Generally Accepted Accounting Practice (GAAP)

The expression GAAP may or may not have statutory or legal authority or definition, depending on the country involved, eg it does not have statutory authority in the UK, but does so in the USA.

GAAP is in fact a **dynamic concept** and changes constantly as circumstances alter through new legislation, standards and practice.

The problem of what is 'generally accepted' is not easy to settle, because new practices will obviously not be generally adopted yet. The criteria for a practice being 'generally accepted' will depend on factors such as whether the practice is addressed by financial reporting standards or legislation, and whether other companies have adopted the practice. Most importantly perhaps, the question should be whether the practice is consistent with the needs of the users and the objective of financial reporting and whether it is consistent with the 'true and fair' concept.

True and fair view (or presented fairly)

It is a requirement of both national legislation (in some countries) and International Standards on Auditing that the financial statements should give a **true and fair view of** (or **'present fairly, in all material respects'**) the financial position of the entity as at the end of the financial year.

The terms 'true and fair view' and 'present fairly, in all material aspects' are not defined in accounting or auditing standards. Despite this, a company's managers may depart from any of the provisions of accounting standards if these are inconsistent with the requirement to give a true and fair view. This is commonly referred to as the **'true and fair override'**. It has been treated as an important **loophole** in the law in different countries and has been the cause of much argument and dissatisfaction within the accounting profession.

4 Other international influences

European Commission (EC)

The EC regulations form one part of a broader programme for the harmonisation of company law in member states. The commission is uniquely the only organisation to produce international standards of accounting practice which are legally enforceable, in the form of directives which must be included in the national legislation of member states.

However, the EC has also acknowledged the role of the IASB in harmonising world-wide accounting rules.

Prior to the EU adoption of IFRS in 2005 the IASB undertook an improvements project, dealing with revisions to IAS, for example in the area of materiality, presentation, leases, related parties and earnings per share. This has been matched in, for example, the UK, by a convergence project, bringing UK GAAP into line with IASs/IFRS where these are better.

United Nations (UN)

The UN has a Commission and Centre on Transnational Reporting Corporations through which it gathers information concerning the activities and reporting of multinational companies. The UN processes are highly political and probably reflect the attitudes of the governments of developing countries to multinationals.

International Federation of Accountants (IFAC)

The IFAC is a private sector body established in 1977 and which now consists of over 100 professional accounting bodies from around 80 different countries. The IFAC's main objective is to co-ordinate the accounting profession on a global scale by issuing and establishing international standards on auditing, management accounting, ethics, education and training.

Organisation for Economic Co-operation and Development (OECD)

The OECD supports the work of the IASB but also undertakes its own research into accounting standards via ad hoc working groups. For example, in 1976 the OECD issued guidelines for multinational companies on financial reporting and non-financial disclosures. The OECD appears to work on behalf of developed countries to protect them from the extreme proposals of the UN. The OECD has also entered the debate on corporate governance.

International Organisation of Securities Commissions (IOSCO)

IOSCO is the representative of the world's securities markets regulators. High quality information is vital for the operation of an efficient capital market, and differences in the quality of the accounting policies and their enforcement between countries leads to inefficiencies between markets. IOSCO has been active in encouraging and promoting the improvement and quality of IASs over the last ten years. Most recently, this commitment was evidenced by the agreement between IASC and IOSCO to work on a programme of 'core standards' which could be used by publicly listed entities when offering securities in foreign jurisdictions.

The 'core standards' project resulted in fifteen new or revised IASs and was completed in 1999 with the issue of IAS 39 Financial instruments: recognition and measurement. IOSCO spent a year reviewing the results of the project and released a report in May 2000 which recommended to all its members that they allow multinational issuers to use IASs, as supplemented by reconciliation, disclosure and interpretation where necessary to address outstanding substantive issues at a national or regional level.

IASB staff and IOSCO continue to work together to resolve outstanding issues and to identify areas where new IASB standards are needed.

Financial Accounting Standards Board (FASB)

The US standard setter, the FASB and the IASB have been undertaking a project of harmonisation between US GAAP and IFRS.

In September 2002, both parties acknowledged their commitment to the process of developing accounting standards that can be used for domestic and international purposes. Both the FASB and the IASB have worked together to make amendments to current accounting standards in the short term, and to work together on a long term basis to ensure new standards issued are compatible.

The FASB is a important influence on the current and future work of the IASB.

5 Scope and application of IASs/IFRSs

Any limitation of the applicability of a specific IAS/IFRS is made clear within that standard. IASs/IFRSs are **not intended to be applied to immaterial items, nor are they retrospective**. Each individual IAS/IFRS lays out its scope at the beginning of the standard.

Within each individual country **local regulations** govern, to a greater or lesser degree, the issue of financial statements. These local regulations include accounting standards issued by the national regulatory bodies and/or professional accountancy bodies in the country concerned.

The IASs/IFRSs **concentrate on essentials** and are designed not to be too complex, otherwise they would be impossible to apply on a worldwide basis.

IASs/IFRSs do not override local regulations on financial statements. Members of the IASB should simply disclose the fact where IASs/IFRSs are complied with in all material respects. Members of the IASB in individual counties will attempt to persuade local authorities, where current regulations deviate from IASs/IFRSs, that the benefits of harmonisation make local change worthwhile.

6 Progress towards global harmonisation

Close co-ordination between IASB due process and due process of national standard setters is important to the success of the IASB's mandate.

The IASB is exploring ways of further integrating its due process with that of national standard setters. This integration may grow as the relationship between IASB and national standard setters evolves. In particular, the IASB is exploring the following procedure for projects that have international implications.

(a) IASB and national standard setters would co-ordinate their work plans so that when the IASB starts a project, national standard setters would also add it to their own work plans so that they can play a full part in developing international consensus. Similarly, where national standard setters start projects, the IASB would consider whether it needs to develop a new Standard or review its existing Standards. Over a reasonable period, the IASB and national standard setters should aim to review all standards where significant differences currently exist, giving priority to the areas where the differences are greatest.

(b) National standards setters would not be required to vote for IASB's preferred solution in their national standards, since each country remains free to adopt IASB standards with amendments or to adopt other standards. However, the existence of an international consensus is clearly one factor that members of national standard setters would consider when they decide how to vote on national standards.

(c)   The IASB would continue to publish its own Exposure Drafts and other documents for public comment.

(d)   National standard setters would publish their own exposure document at approximately the same time as IASB Exposure Drafts and would seek specific comments on any significant divergences between the two exposure documents. In some instances, national standard setters may include in their exposure documents specific comments on issues of particular relevance to their country or include more detailed guidance than is included in the corresponding IASB document.

(e)   National standard setters would follow their own full due process, which they would ideally choose to integrate with the IASB's due process. This integration would avoid unnecessary delays in completing standards and would also minimise the likelihood of unnecessary differences between the standards that result.

IASB liaison members

Seven of the full-time members of the IASB have formal liaison responsibilities with national standard setters in order to promote the convergence of national accounting standards and International Accounting Standards. The IASB envisages a partnership between the IASB and these national standard setters as they work together to achieve convergence of accounting standards worldwide.

The countries with these liaison members are Australia and New Zealand, Canada, France, Germany, Japan, UK and USA.

In addition all IASB members have contact responsibility with national standards setters not having liaison members and many countries are also represented on the Standards Advisory Council.

World-wide effect of IASs and the IASB

The IASB, and before it the IASC, has now been in existence for around 25 years, and it is worth looking at the effect it has had in that time.

As far as Europe is concerned, the consolidated financial statements of many of Europe's top multinationals are already prepared in conformity with national requirements, EC directives and IASs. These developments have been given added impetus by the internationalisation of capital markets. As discussed, IASs/IFRSs have been implemented in EU since 2005.

In Japan, the influence of the IASB had, until recently, been negligible. This was mainly because of links in Japan between tax rules and financial reporting. The Japanese Ministry of Finance set up a working committee to consider whether to bring national requirements into line with IASs/IFRSs. The Tokyo Stock Exchange has announced that it will accept financial statements from foreign issuers that conform with home country standards, which would include IFRS.

The Japanese standpoint was widely seen as an attempt to attract foreign issuers, in particular companies from Hong Kong and Singapore. As these countries base their accounting on international standards, this action is therefore implicit acknowledgement by the Japanese Ministry of Finance of IAS/IFRS requirements.

Part
A

The regulatory and conceptual framework

In America, the Securities and Exchange Commission (SEC) agreed in 1993 to allow foreign issuers (of shares, etc) to follow IAS/IFRS treatments on certain issues, including cash flow statements under IAS 7. The overall effect is that, where an IAS/IFRS treatment differs from US GAAP, these treatments will now be acceptable. The SEC is now supporting the IASB because it wants to attract foreign listings.

In certain countries, the application of IASs/IFRSs is **mandatory** for all domestic listed companies. The following provides an example of some of the countries, but the schedule is not exhaustive: Barbados, Cyprus, Georgia, Jamaica, Jordan, Kenya, Kuwait, Malawi, Mauritius, Nepal, Peru, Serbia and Trinidad and Tobago.

Countries that implemented IFRS for the 2005 European ruling in respect of the consolidated financial statements of public listed companies include Austria, Belgium, Czech Republic, Denmark, Estonia, Finland, France, Germany, Greece, Hungary, Iceland, Ireland, Italy, Liechtenstein, Lithuania, Luxembourg, Netherlands, Norway, Poland, Portugal, Slovenia, Slovak Republic, Spain, Sweden and the United Kingdom.

Many non-European counties also require their listed companies to adopt IFRS. These include Australia, Bahamas, Bahrain, Chile, Costa Rica, Egypt, Hong Kong, Kenya, Kuwait, Mauritius, New Zealand, and South Africa.

There are some countries where the implementation of IASs/IFRSs is **not mandatory but discretionary**. These include Aruba, Bermuda, Bolivia, Botswana, Cayman Islands, Dominica, El Salvador, Gibraltar, Laos, Lesotho, Swaziland, Switzerland, Turkey, Uganda, Zambia and Zimbabwe. In December 2009 the Japanese FSA announced that Japanese listed companies would be allowed to use IFRS from 31 March 2010.

However, there are several countries where the **use of IASs/IFRSs is not currently permitted**. The following are some of the countries, but the list is not exhaustive: Bangladesh, Cuba, Indonesia, Iran, Saudi Arabia, Senegal, Taiwan, Thailand, Tunisia and Vietnam.

Harmonisation in Europe

The objective of the European Commission (EC) is to build a fully integrated, globally competitive market. A key element of this is the harmonisation of company law across the member states. In line with this the **EC aims to establish a level playing field for financial reporting**, supported by an effective enforcement regime. The commission is uniquely the only organisation whose accounting standards are legally enforceable, in the form of directives which must be included in the national legislation of member states. However, the directives have been criticised as they might become constraints on the application of world-wide standards, and might bring accounting standardisation and harmonisation into the political arena.

The EC adopted a regulation under which from 2005 consolidated financial statements of listed companies were required to comply with IFRS. The implications of this measure are far reaching. However, member states currently have the discretion to extend the implementation of IAS/IFRS to include non-listed companies. In the UK, for example, small companies report under UK GAAP, with many taking advantage of the reduced disclosure requirements of the FRSSE (Financial Reporting Standard for Smaller Entities). The IASB has recently issued the IFRS for SMEs (Small and Medium-sized entities) and this is an important step toward the introduction of IFRS for all companies.

Many commentators believe that in the light of the EC's commitment to IFRS it is only a matter of time before national standard setting bodies like the ASB in the UK are, in effect, replaced by the IASB, with national standards falling into disuse. However, the IASB will continue to need input and expertise from valued national standard setters like the ASB.

IFRS in the USA

Convergence between IFRS and US GAAP is **one of the bigger issues** in the global implementation of IFRS. At present, all US entities must file accounts prepared under US GAAP. However, in 2002 the IASB and its US equivalent, the FASB (Financial Accounting Standards Board) did agree to harmonise their work plans, and to work towards reducing the differences between IFRS and US GAAP.

In **2008 the Securities and Exchange Commission (SEC) issued a 'roadmap'** for the use of IFRS, proposing the eventual mandatory use of IFRS for all US public companies by 2014. At present, only overseas issuers of securities are allowed to file accounts under IFRS (without having to provide a reconciliation to US GAAP).

The SEC's 'roadmap' would allow some companies the option of using IFRS from 2010. It envisages phasing in IFRS by requiring companies to file accounts under both IFRS and US GAAP for the two years 2012-2014, after which accounts would be prepared under IFRS alone. The SEC has said that it will make its final decision on timings in 2011.

Rules-based versus principles-based financial reporting standards

US GAAP is an example of a rules-based approach. It consists of a large number of specific accounting standards, and each standard contains a large number of rules (as well as exceptions to the rules), attempting to prescribe treatments for every possible situation that might arise. However, in 2002 the incoming chairman of the **FASB** signalled his support for a **shift to a principles-based approach**:

> 'I understand the US environment where there has been such a proliferation of rules. I like the principles-based approach but some people have exaggerated the differences. You are always going to have rules but the question is: 'Where do I start?' You can never have a rule for everything and at that point you have to go back to principles.'

> Bob Hertz, FASB Chairman (*Financial Times, 27 May 2002*)

The US has accordingly begun to develop a principles-based approach, which coincides with its move toward adoption of IFRS, which are themselves principles-based.

A principles-based approach then, is one where the individual standards can be clearly seen to be applications of the approach to accounting adopted by the standards as a whole. Thus each individual IAS/IFRS applies the IASB Framework, and each standard is an individual reflection of the whole. Specificity at the level of detail is sacrificed for clarity in terms of the overall approach.

Accountants working under **IFRS** are required, then, to use **more professional judgement** than under a rules-based approach. There may not be a specific rule that applies to the event that they need to report, so they need to use judgement in applying the principles contained in the relevant IFRS. It is the view of the IASB that this will result in better quality financial reporting. Accounts will have to be **true to the overall principles of IFRS**, rather than to an individual rule that may not be appropriate for the event being reported, and which may therefore end up with an accounting treatment that is not true to the intentions of IFRS as a whole.

Brief comparison of IFRS v UK GAAP v US GAAP

To provide you with some practical perspective, here is a very brief comparison between IAS, UK GAAP and US GAAP requirements regarding two financial reporting areas.

Subject	UK GAAP	US GAAP	IFRS
Inventory valuation	The **LIFO** method is **not** permitted under UK GAAP, so inventory must be valued using a method such as FIFO (first in first out).	In the USA inventory may be valued using the **LIFO** (last in first out) method. Under this method, assuming prices are rising, closing inventory has a lower value than using FIFO.	IAS 2 (revised) requires use of FIFO or the weighted average method for ordinarily interchangeable items.
Development expenditure	Development expenditure should be written off in year of expenditure, except in certain circumstances where it may be deferred.	Development expenditure must be written off to profit or loss under all circumstances.	Under IAS 38 (revised) development costs are capitalised if certain criteria are met.

UK Accounting Standards Board Convergence Approach

In the UK a detailed comparison has been carried out between international and UK accounting standards which has been documented in what is called The Convergence Handbook.

The following statement is taken from The Convergence Handbook.

'The ASB is working with the IASB and other national standard setters in order to seek improvements in IFRS and convergence of national and international standards. The ASB is one of several national standard setters that have a formal liaison relationship with the IASB. This relationship involves regular meetings and other consultations as well as several joint standard setting projects, including the ASB's joint project with the IASB on reporting financial performance.

The ASB intends to align UK accounting standards with IFRS whenever practicable. It proposes to do this, in the main, by a phased replacement of existing UK standards with new UK standards based on the equivalent IFRS.'

This is from an article by Sir David Tweedie, Chairman of the IASB.

'The UK is part of an increasingly global economy, and its prosperity depends upon inward and outward capital flows to facilitate investment and promote economic growth. Adopting international standards will remove a hurdle in the way of developments that offer the prospects of benefits for the UK investor and for UK business as a whole.'

7 Benefits of and barriers to global harmonisation

Benefits of global harmonisation

The benefits of harmonisation will be based on the benefits to users and preparers of accounts, as follows.

(a) Investors, both individual and corporate, would like to be able to compare the financial results of different companies internationally as well as nationally in making investment decisions.

(b) Multinational companies would benefit from harmonisation for many reasons including the following.

    (1) Better access would be gained to foreign investor funds.

    (2) Management control would be improved, because harmonisation would aid internal communication of financial information.

    (3) Appraisal of foreign entities for take-overs and mergers would be more straightforward.

    (4) It would be easier to comply with the reporting requirements of overseas stock exchanges.

    (5) Preparation of group accounts would be easier.

    (6) A reduction in audit costs might be achieved.

    (7) Transfer of accounting staff across national borders would be easier.

(c) Governments of developing countries would save time and money if they could adopt international standards and, if these were used internally, governments of developing countries could attempt to control the activities of foreign multinational companies in their own country. These companies could not 'hide' behind foreign accounting practices which are difficult to understand.

(d) Tax authorities. It will be easier to calculate the tax liability of investors, including multinationals who receive income from overseas sources.

(e) Regional economic groups usually promote trade within a specific geographical region. This would be aided by common accounting practices within the region.

(f) Large international accounting firms would benefit as accounting and auditing would be much easier if similar accounting practices existed throughout the world.

Barriers to harmonisation

(a) Different purposes of financial reporting. In some countries the purpose is solely for tax assessment, while in others it is for investor decision-making.

(b) Different legal systems. These prevent the development of certain accounting practices and restrict the options available.

(c) Different user groups. Countries have different ideas about who the relevant user groups are and their respective importance. In the USA investor and creditor groups are given prominence, while in Europe employees enjoy a higher profile.

(d) Needs of developing countries. Developing countries are obviously behind in the standard setting process and they need to develop the basic standards and principles already in place in most developed countries.

(e) Nationalism is demonstrated in an unwillingness to accept another country's standard.

(f) Cultural differences result in objectives for accounting systems differing from country to country.

(g) Unique circumstances. Some countries may be experiencing unusual circumstances which affect all aspects of everyday life and impinge on the ability of companies to produce proper reports, for example hyperinflation, civil war, currency restriction and so on.

(h)   The lack of strong accountancy bodies. Many countries do not have strong independent accountancy or business bodies which would press for better standards and greater harmonisation.

8 IFRS 1: First-time adoption of International Financial Reporting Standards

IFRS 1 sets out the precise way in which companies should implement a change from local accounting standards (their previous GAAP) to IASs and IFRSs. One of the main reasons for issuing a new standard was that listed companies in the EU were required to prepare their consolidated financial statements in accordance with IFRSs from 2005 onwards.

The standard is intended to ensure that an entity's first IFRS financial statements contain high quality information that: is transparent for users and comparable over all periods presented; provides a suitable starting point for accounting under IFRSs; and can be generated at a cost that does not exceed the benefits to users.

> **Date of transition to IFRSs.** The beginning of the earliest period for which an entity presents full comparative information under IFRSs in its first IFRS financial statements.
>
> **Deemed cost** An amount used as a surrogate for cost or depreciated cost at a given date.
>
> **Fair value** The amount for which an asset could be exchanged, or a liability settled, between knowledgeable, willing parties in an arm's length transaction.
>
> **First IFRS financial statements** The first annual financial statements in which an entity adopts International Financial Reporting Standards (IFRSs), by an explicit and unreserved statement of compliance with IFRSs.
>
> **Opening IFRS statement of financial position** An entity's statement of financial position (published or unpublished) at the date of transition to IFRSs.
>
> **Previous GAAP** The basis of accounting that a first time adopter used immediately before adopting IFRSs.
>
> **Reporting date** The end of the latest period covered by financial statements or by an interim financial report.   *(IFRS 1)*

IFRS 1 **only applies** where an entity prepares IFRS financial statements **for the first time**. Changes in accounting policies made by an entity that already applies IFRSs should be dealt with by applying either IAS 8 or specific transitional requirements in other standards.

Making the transition to IFRS

An entity should:

(a)   Select accounting policies that comply with IFRSs at the reporting date for the entity's first IFRS financial statements.

(b)   Prepare an opening IFRS statement of financial position at the date of transition to IFRSs. This is the starting point for subsequent accounting under IFRSs. The date of transition to IFRSs is the beginning of the earliest comparative period presented in an entity's first IFRS financial statements.

(c)   Disclose the effect of the change in the financial statements.

Example: reporting date and opening IFRS statement of financial position

A listed company has a 31 December year-end and will be required to comply with IFRSs from 1 January 2009.

What is the date of transition to IFRSs?

The company's first IFRS financial statements will be for the year ended 31 December 2009.

IFRS 1 requires that at least one year's comparative figures are presented in the first IFRS financial statements. The comparative figures will be for the year ended 31 December 2008.

Therefore the date of transition to IFRSs is 1 January 2008 and the company prepares an opening IFRS statement of financial position at this date.

Preparing the opening IFRS statement of financial position

IFRS 1 states that in its opening IFRS statement of financial position an entity shall:

(a)   Recognise all assets and liabilities whose recognition is required by IFRSs
(b)   Not recognise items as assets or liabilities if IFRSs do not permit such recognition
(c)   Reclassify items that it recognised under previous GAAP as one type of asset, liability or component of equity, but are a different type of asset liability or component of equity under IFRSs
(d)   Apply IFRS in measuring all recognised assets and liabilities

This involves restating the statement of financial position prepared at the same date under the entity's previous GAAP so that it complies with IASs and IFRSs in force at the first reporting date. In our example above, the company prepares its opening IFRS statement of financial position at 1 January 2008, following accounting policies that comply with IFRSs in force at 31 December 2009.

The accounting policies that an entity uses in its opening IFRS statement of financial position may differ from those it used for the same date using its previous GAAP. The resulting adjustments are recognised directly in retained earnings (in equity) at the date of transition. (This is because the adjustments arise from events and transactions before the date of transition to IFRS.)

Exemptions from other IFRSs

A business may elect to use any or all of a range of exemptions. These enable an entity not to apply certain requirements of specific accounting standards retrospectively in drawing up its opening IFRS statement of financial position. Their purpose is to ensure that the cost of producing IFRS financial statements does not exceed the benefits to users.

Business combinations

IFRS 3 need not be applied retrospectively to business combinations that occurred before the date of the opening IFRS statement of financial position. This has the following consequences.

(a)   Combinations keep the same classification (eg acquisition, uniting of interests) as in the previous GAAP financial statements.

(b)   All acquired assets and liabilities are recognised other than:

   (i)   Some financial assets and financial liabilities derecognised under the previous GAAP (derivatives and special purpose entities must be recognised);

   (ii)   Assets (including goodwill) and liabilities that were not recognised under previous GAAP and would not qualify for recognition under IFRSs.

   Any resulting change is recognised by adjusting retained earnings (ie equity) unless the change results from the recognition of an intangible asset that was previously subsumed within goodwill.

(c)   Items which do not qualify for recognition as an asset or liability under IFRSs must be excluded from the opening IFRS statement of financial position. For example, intangible assets that do not qualify for separate recognition under IAS 38 must be reclassified as part of goodwill.

(d)   The carrying amount of goodwill in the opening IFRS statement of financial position is the same as its carrying amount under previous GAAP. However, goodwill must be tested for impairment at the transition date.

1 The need for a conceptual framework

A **conceptual framework**, in the field we are concerned with, is a statement of generally accepted theoretical principles which form the frame of reference for financial reporting. These theoretical principles provide the basis for the development of new accounting standards and the evaluation of those already in existence.

Although it is theoretical in nature, a conceptual framework for financial reporting has highly practical final aims.

The **danger of not having a conceptual framework** is demonstrated in the way some countries' standards have developed over recent years; standards tend to be produced in a **haphazard and fire-fighting way**. Where an agreed framework exists, the standard-setting body acts as an architect or designer, rather than a fire-fighter, building accounting rules on the foundation of sound, agreed basic principles.

The lack of a conceptual framework also means that fundamental principles are tackled more than once in different standards, thereby producing **contradictions** and **inconsistencies** in basic concepts, such as those of prudence and matching. This leads to ambiguity and it affects the true and fair concept of financial reporting.

Another problem with the lack of a conceptual framework has become apparent in the USA. The large number of highly detailed standards produced by the Financial Accounting Standards Board (FASB) has created a financial reporting environment governed by **specific rules rather than general principles**. This would be avoided if a cohesive set of principles were in place.

A conceptual framework can also bolster standard setters **against political pressure** from various 'lobby groups' and interested parties. Such pressure would only prevail if it was acceptable under the conceptual framework.

Advantages and disadvantages of a conceptual framework

Advantages

(a) The situation is **avoided** whereby standards are being developed on a **patchwork** basis, where a particular accounting problem is recognised as having emerged, and resources were then channelled into standardising accounting practice in that area, without regard to whether that particular issue was necessarily the most important issue remaining at that time without standardisation.

(b) As stated above, the development of certain standards (particularly national standards) have been subject to considerable political interference from interested parties. Where there is a conflict of interest between user groups on which policies to choose, policies deriving from a conceptual framework will be **less open** to criticism that the standard-setter buckled to **external pressure**.

(c)   Some standards may concentrate on the **income statement** whereas some may concentrate on the **valuation of net assets** (statement of financial position).

Disadvantages

(a)   Financial statements are intended for a variety of users, and it is not certain that a single conceptual framework can be devised which will suit all users.

(b)   Given the diversity of user requirements, there may be a need for a variety of accounting standards, each produced for a different purpose (and with different concepts as a basis).

(c)   It is not clear that a conceptual framework makes the task of preparing and then implementing standards any easier than without a framework.

2 The IASB Framework

In July 1989 the IASB (then IASC) produced a document, *Framework for the preparation and presentation of financial statements* ('*Framework*'). The Framework is, in effect, the **conceptual** framework upon which all IASs are based and hence which determines how financial statements are prepared and the information they contain.

The *Framework* consists of a number of sections or chapters, following on after a preface and introduction. These chapters are as follows.

*   The objective of financial statements.
*   Underlying assumptions
*   Qualitative characteristics of financial statements
*   The elements of financial statements
*   Recognition of the elements of financial statements
*   Measurement of the elements of financial statements
*   Concepts of capital and capital maintenance

Preface

The preface to the *Framework* points out the **fundamental reason** why financial statements are **produced worldwide**, ie to **satisfy the requirements of external users**, but that practice varies due to the individual pressures in each country. These pressures may be social, political, economic or legal, but they result in variations in practice from country to country, including the form of statements, the definition of their component parts (assets, liabilities etc), the criteria for recognition of items and both the scope and disclosure of financial statements.

It is these differences which the IASB wishes to narrow by **harmonising** all aspects of financial statements, including the regulations governing their accounting standards and their preparation and presentation.

The preface emphasises the way **financial statements are used to make economic decisions** and thus financial statements should be prepared to this end. The types of economic decisions for which financial statements are likely to be used include the following.

*   Decisions to buy, hold or sell equity investments
*   Assessment of management stewardship and accountability
*   Assessment of the entity's ability to pay employees
*   Assessment of the security of amounts lent to the entity
*   Determination of taxation policies

*   Determination of distributable profits and dividends
*   Inclusion in national income statistics
*   Regulations of the activities of entities

Any additional requirements imposed by national governments for their own purposes should not affect financial statements produced for the benefit of other users.

The *Framework* recognises that financial statements can be prepared using a **variety of models**. Although the most common is based on historical cost and a nominal unit of currency (ie pound sterling, US dollar etc), the *Framework* can be applied to financial statements prepared under a range of models.

The introduction gives a list of the purposes of the *Framework*.

(a) Assist the Board of the IASB in the **development of future IASs** and in its review of existing IASs.

(b) Assist the Board of the IASB in **promoting harmonisation** of regulations, accounting standards and procedures relating to the presentation of financial statements by providing a basis for reducing the number of alternative accounting treatments permitted by IASs.

(c) Assist **national standard-setting bodies** in developing national standards.

(d) Assist **preparers of financial statements** in applying IASs and in dealing with topics that have yet to form the subject of an IAS.

(e) Assist **auditors** in forming an opinion as to whether financial statements conform with IASs.

(f) Assist **users of financial statements** in interpreting the information contained in financial statements prepared in conformity with IASs.

(g) Provide those who are interested in the work of IASB with **information** about its approach to the formulation of IASs (now IFRSs).

The *Framework* is not an IFRS and so does not overrule any individual IAS/IFRS. In the (rare) cases of conflict between an IAS/IFRS and the *Framework*, the **IAS will prevail**. These cases will diminish over time as the *Framework* will be used as a guide in the production of future IASs. The *Framework* itself will be revised occasionally depending on the experience of the IASB in using it.

The *Framework* deals with:

(a) The **objective** of financial statements

(b) The **qualitative characteristics** that determine the usefulness of information in financial statements

(c) The **definition, recognition and measurement** of the elements from which financial statements are constructed

(d) Concepts of **capital and capital maintenance**

The *Framework* is concerned with **'general purpose' financial statements** (ie a normal set of annual statements), but it can be applied to other types of accounts. A complete set of financial statements includes:

(a) A statement of financial position (previously called a balance sheet)

(b) A statement of comprehensive income

(c) A statement of changes in equity

(d) A statement of changes in financial position (eg a statement of cash flows)

(e) Notes, other statements and explanatory material

Supplementary information may be included, but some items are not included, namely commentaries and reports by the directors, the chairman, management etc.

All types of financial reporting entities are included (commercial, industrial, business; public or private sector).

> A **reporting entity** is an entity for which there are users who rely on the financial statements as their major source of financial information about the entity
>
> *(Framework)*

Users and their information needs

Users of accounting information consist of investors, employees, lenders, suppliers and other trade creditors, customers, government and their agencies and the public. Their needs are as follows.

(a) **Investors** are the providers of risk capital
  (i) Information is required to help make a decision about buying or selling shares, taking up a rights issue and voting.
  (ii) Investors must have information about the level of dividend, past, present and future and any changes in share price.
  (iii) Investors will also need to know whether the management has been running the company efficiently.
  (iv) As well as the position indicated by the financial statements and earnings per share (EPS), investors will want to know about the liquidity position of the company, the company's future prospects, and how the company's shares compare with those of its competitors.

(b) **Employees** need information about the security of employment and future prospects for jobs in the company, and to help with collective pay bargaining.

(c) **Lenders** need information to help them decide whether to lend to a company. They will also need to check that the value of any security remains adequate, that the interest repayments are secure, that the cash is available for redemption at the appropriate time and that any financial restrictions (such as maximum debt/equity ratios) have not been breached.

(d) **Suppliers** need to know whether the company will be a good customer and pay its debts.

(e) **Customers** need to know whether the company will be able to continue producing and supplying goods.

(f) **Government's** interest in a company may be one of creditor or customer, as well as being specifically concerned with compliance with tax and company law, ability to pay tax and the general contribution of the company to the economy.

(g) The **public** at large would wish to have information for all the reasons mentioned above, but it could be suggested that it would be impossible to provide general purpose accounting information which was specifically designed for the needs of the public.

Financial statements cannot meet all these users' needs, but financial statements which meet the **needs of investors** (providers of risk capital) will meet most of the needs of other users.

The *Framework* emphasises that the preparation and presentation of financial statements is primarily the **responsibility of an entity's management**. Management also has an interest in the information appearing in financial statements.

3 The objective of financial statements

The *Framework* states that:

> 'The objective of financial statements is to provide information about the financial position performance and changes in financial position of an entity that is useful to a wide range of users in making economic decisions.'

The statements also show the results of **management's stewardship**.

Financial position, performance and changes in financial position

It is important for users to assess the ability of an entity to produce **cash and cash equivalents** to pay employees, lenders etc.

Financial position information is affected by the following and information about each one can aid the user.

(a) **Economic resources controlled**: to predict the ability to generate cash
(b) **Financial structure**: to predict borrowing needs, the distribution of future profits/cash and likely success in raising new finance
(c) **Liquidity and solvency**: to predict whether financial commitments will be met as they fall due (liquidity relates to short-term commitments, solvency is longer-term)

Liquidity. The availability of sufficient funds to meet deposit withdrawals and other financial commitments as they fall due.

Solvency. The availability of cash over the longer term to meet financial commitments as they fall due. *(Framework)*

In all these areas, the capacity to adapt to changes in the environment in which the entity operates is very important.

Financial performance (statement of comprehensive income) information, particularly profitability, is used to assess potential changes in the economic resources the entity is likely to control in future. Information about performance variability is therefore important.

Changes in financial position (statement of cash flows) information is used to assess the entity's investing, financing and operating activities. They show the entity's ability to produce cash and the needs which utilise those cash flows.

All parts of the financial statements are **interrelated**, reflecting different aspects of the same transactions or events. Each statement provides different information; none can provide all the information required by users.

4 Underlying assumptions

Accruals basis

> **Accruals basis**. The effects of transactions and other events are recognised when they occur (and not as cash or its equivalent is received or paid) and they are recorded in the accounting records and reported in the financial statements of the periods to which they relate. *(Framework)*

Financial statements prepared under the accruals basis show users past transactions involving cash and also obligations to pay cash in the future and resources which represent cash to be received in the future.

Going concern

> **Going concern**. The entity is normally viewed as a going concern, that is, as continuing in operation for the foreseeable future. It is assumed that the entity has neither the intention nor the necessity of liquidation or of curtailing materially the scale of its operations. *(Framework)*

It is assumed that the entity has no intention to liquidate or curtail major operations. If it did, then the financial statements would be prepared on a **different (disclosed) basis**.

5 Qualitative characteristics of financial statements

The *Framework* states that qualitative characteristics are the attributes that make the information provided in financial statements useful to users. The four principal qualitative characteristics are **understandability, relevance, reliability and comparability**.

Understandability

Users must be able to understand financial statements. They are assumed to have some business, economic and accounting knowledge and to be able to apply themselves to study the information properly. **Complex matters should not be left out** of financial statements simply due to its difficulty if it is relevant information.

Relevance

The **predictive and confirmatory roles** of information are interrelated.

> **Relevance**. Information has the quality of relevance when it influences the economic decisions of users by helping them evaluate past, present or future events or confirming, or correcting, their past evaluations. *(Framework)*

Information on financial position and performance is often used to predict future position and performance and other things of interest to the user, eg likely dividend, wage rises. The manner of **showing information** will enhance the ability to make predictions, eg by highlighting unusual items.

Materiality

The relevance of information is affected by its **nature and materiality**.

> **Materiality.** Information is material if its omission or misstatement could influence the economic decisions of users taken on the basis of the financial statements.
>
> *(Framework)*

Information may be judged relevant simply because of its nature (eg remuneration of management). In other cases, both the nature and materiality of the information are important. Materiality is not a primary qualitative characteristic itself (like reliability or relevance), because it is merely a threshold or cut-off point.

Reliability

Information must also be reliable to be useful. The user must be able to depend on it being a **faithful representation**.

> **Reliability.** Information has the quality of reliability when it is free from material error and bias and can be depended upon by users to represent faithfully that which it either purports to represent or could reasonably be expected to represent.
>
> *(Framework)*

Even if information is relevant, if it is very unreliable it may be **misleading to recognise it**, eg a disputed claim for damages in a legal action.

Faithful representation

Information must represent faithfully the transactions it purports to represent in order to be reliable. There is a risk that this may not be the case, not due to bias, but due to **inherent difficulties in identifying the transactions** or finding an **appropriate method of measurement or presentation**. Where measurement of the financial effects of an item is so uncertain, entities should not recognise such an item, eg internally generated goodwill.

Substance over form

Faithful representation of a transaction is only possible if it is accounted for according to its **substance and economic reality**, not with its legal form.

> **Substance over form**. The principle that transactions and other events are accounted for and presented in accordance with their substance and economic reality and not merely their legal form *(Framework)*

Neutrality

Information must be **free from bias** to be reliable. Neutrality is lost if the financial statements are prepared so as to influence the user to make a judgement or decision in order to achieve a predetermined outcome.

Prudence

Uncertainties exist in the preparation of financial information, eg the collectability of doubtful receivables. These uncertainties are recognised through disclosure and through the application of prudence. Prudence does not, however, allow the creation of hidden reserves or excessive provisions, understatement of assets or income or overstatement of liabilities or expenses.

Completeness

Financial information must be complete, within the **restrictions of materiality and cost**, to be reliable. Omission may cause information to be misleading.

Comparability

Users must be able to compare an entity's financial statements:

(a) **Through time** to identify trends
(b) **With other entity's statements**, to evaluate their relative financial position, performance and changes in financial position

The consistency of treatment is therefore important across like items over time, within the entity and across all entities.

The **disclosure of accounting policies** is particularly important here. Users must be able to distinguish between different accounting policies in order to be able to make a valid comparison of similar items in the accounts of different entities.

Comparability is **not the same as uniformity.** Entities should change accounting policies if they become inappropriate.

Corresponding information for **preceding periods** should be shown to enable comparison over time.

Constraints on relevant and reliable information

Timeliness

Information may become irrelevant if there is a delay in reporting it. There is a **balance between timeliness and the provision of reliable information**. Information may be reported on a timely basis when not all aspects of the transaction are known, thus compromising reliability.

If every detail of a transaction is known, it may be too late to publish the information because it has become irrelevant. The overriding consideration is how best to satisfy the economic decision-making needs of the users.

Balance between benefits and cost

This is a pervasive constraint, not a qualitative characteristic. When information is provided, its benefits must exceed the costs of obtaining and presenting it. This is a **subjective area** and there are other difficulties: others than the intended users may gain a benefit; also the cost may be paid by someone other than the users. It is therefore difficult to apply a cost-benefit analysis, but preparers and users should be aware of the constraint.

Balance between qualitative characteristics

A **trade off between qualitative characteristics** of often necessary, the aim being to achieve an appropriate balance to meet the objective of financial statements. It is a matter for professional judgement as to the relative importance of these characteristics in each case.

True and fair view/fair presentation

The Framework does not attempt to define these concepts directly. It does state, however, that the application of the **principal 'qualitative' characteristics** and of **appropriate accounting standards** will usually result in financial statements which show a true and fair view, or present fairly.

6 The elements of financial statements

Transactions and other events are grouped together in broad classes and in this way their financial effects are shown in the financial statements. These broad classes are the elements of financial statements. The *Framework* lays out these elements as follows.

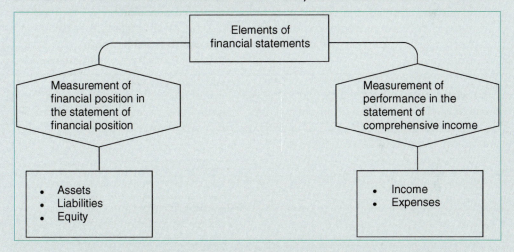

A process of **sub-classification** then takes place for presentation in the financial statements, eg assets are classified by their nature or function in the business to show information in the best way for users to take economic decisions.

Financial position

We need to define the three terms listed under this heading above.

- **Asset**. A resource controlled by an entity as a result of past events and from which future economic benefits are expected to flow to the entity.
- **Liability**. A present obligation of the entity arising from past events, the settlement of which is expected to result in an outflow from the entity of resources embodying economic benefits.
- **Equity**. The residual interest in the assets of the entity after deducting all its liabilities. *(Framework)*

These definitions are important, but they do not cover the **criteria for recognition** of any of these items. This means that the definitions may include items which would not actually be recognised in the financial statements because they fail to satisfy recognition criteria particularly, as we will see below, the **probable flow of any economic benefit** to or from the business.

Whether an item satisfies any of the definitions above will depend on the **substance and economic reality** of the transaction, not merely its legal form.

Performance

Profit is used as a **measure of performance**, or as a basis for other measures (eg EPS). It depends directly on the measurement of income and expenses, which in turn depend (in part) on the concepts of capital and capital maintenance adopted.

The elements of income and expense are therefore defined.

> • **Income**. Increases in economic benefits during the accounting period in the form of inflows or enhancements of assets or decreases of liabilities that result in increases in equity, other than those relating to contributions from equity participants.

> • **Expenses**. Decreases in economic benefits during the accounting period in the form of outflows or depletions of assets or incurrences of liabilities that result in decreases in equity, other than those relating to distributions to equity participants. *(Framework)*

Both **revenue** and **gains** are included in the definition of income. **Revenue** arises in the course of ordinary activities of an entity. Gains include those arising on the disposal of non-current assets. The definition of income also includes **unrealised gains**, eg on revaluation of marketable securities.

7 Recognition of the elements of financial statements

Items which meet the definition of assets or liabilities may still not be recognised in financial statements because they must also meet certain **recognition criteria**.

> **Recognition**. The process of incorporating in the financial statements an item that meets the definition of an element and satisfies the following criteria for recognition:
>
> (a) it is probable that any future economic benefit associated with the item will flow to or from the entity; and
> (b) the item has a cost or value that can be measured with reliability. *(Framework)*

Regard must be given to **materiality**.

Probability of future economic benefits

Probability here means the **degree of uncertainty** that the future economic benefits associated with an item will flow to or from the entity. This must be judged on the basis of the **characteristics of the entity's environment** and the **evidence available** when the financial statements are prepared.

Reliability of measurement

The cost or value of an item, in many cases, **must be estimated**. The Framework states, however, that the use of reasonable estimates is an essential part of the preparation of financial statements and does not undermine their reliability. Where no reasonable estimate can be made, the item should not be recognised, although its existence should be disclosed in the notes, or other explanatory material.

Items may still qualify for recognition **at a later date** due to changes in circumstances or subsequent events.

Recognition of items

We can summarise the recognition criteria for assets, liabilities, income and expenses, based on the definition of recognition given above.

Item	Recognised in	When
Asset	The statement of financial position	It is probable that the future economic benefits will flow to the entity and the asset has a cost or value that can be measured reliably.
Liability	The statement of financial position	It is probable that an outflow of resources embodying economic benefits will result from the settlement of a present obligation and the amount at which the settlement will take place can be measured reliably.
Income	The statement of comprehensive income	An increase in future economic benefits related to an increase in an asset or a decrease of a liability has arisen that can be measured reliably.
Expenses	The statement of comprehensive income	A decrease in future economic benefits related to a decrease in an asset or an increase of a liability has arisen that can be measured reliably.

8 Measurement of the elements of financial statements

> **Measurement**. The process of determining the monetary amounts at which the elements of the financial statements are to be recognised and carried in the statement of financial position and statement of comprehensive income.
>
> *(Framework)*

This involves the selection of a particular **basis of measurement**. A number of these are used to different degrees and in varying combinations in financial statements. They include the following.

- **Historical cost**. Assets are recorded at the amount of cash or cash equivalents paid or the fair value of the consideration given to acquire them at the time of their acquisition. Liabilities are recorded at the amount of proceeds received in exchange for the obligation, or in some circumstances (for example, income taxes), at the amounts of cash or cash equivalents expected to be paid to satisfy the liability in the normal course of business.

- • **Current cost.** The amount of cash or cash equivalents that would have to be paid if the same or an equivalent asset was acquired currently.

  The undisclosed amount of cash or cash equivalents that would be required to settle an obligation currently.
- • **Realisable (settlement) value.**
  - – **Realisable value.** The amount of cash or cash equivalents that could currently be obtained by selling an asset in an orderly disposal.
  - – **Settlement value.** The undiscounted amounts of cash or cash equivalents expected to be paid to satisfy the liabilities in the normal course of business.
- • **Present value.** A current estimate of the present discounted value of the future net cash flows in the normal course of business. *(Framework)*

Historical cost is the most commonly adopted measurement basis, but this is usually combined with other bases, eg inventory is carried at the lower of cost and net realisable value.

1 IAS 1 (revised): Presentation of financial statements

The main objective of IAS 1 is:

'to prescribe the basis for presentation of general purpose financial statements, in order to ensure comparability both with the entity's own financial statements of previous periods and with the financial statements of other entities.'

IAS 1 applies to all **general purpose financial statements** prepared in accordance with IASs, ie those intended to meet the needs of users who are not in a position to demand reports tailored to their specific needs.

The **objective of financial statements** is to provide information about the financial position, performance and cash flows of an entity that is useful to a wide range of users in making economic decisions. They also show the result of **management stewardship** of the resources of the entity.

In order to fulfil this objective, financial statements must provide information about the following aspects of an entity's results.

- Assets
- Liabilities
- Equity
- Income and expenses (including gains and losses)
- Contributions by and distributions to owners in their capacity as owners
- Cash flows

This information, along with other information in the notes, assists users in predicting the entity's **future cash flows** and, in particular, their timing and certainty.

Responsibility for the preparation and presentation of an entity's financial statements rests with the **board of directors** (or equivalent).

Components of financial statements

A complete set of financial statements includes the following components.

- A statement of financial position as at the end of the reporting period
- A statement of comprehensive income for the reporting period
- A statement of changes in equity for the reporting period
- A statement of cash flows for the reporting period
- Notes, comprising a summary of significant accounting policies and other explanatory information
- A statement of financial position as at the beginning of the earliest comparative period when an entity applies an accounting policy retrospectively or makes a retrospective restatement of items in its financial statements, or when it reclassifies items in its financial statements

In addition, IAS 1 encourages, but does not require, a **financial review** by management (which is not part of the financial statements), explaining the main features of the entity's performance and position, and the principal uncertainties it faces. The report may include a review of the following.

(a) **Factors/influences determining performance**: changes in the environment in which the entity operates, the entity's response to those changes and their effect, and the entity's policy for investment to maintain and enhance performance, including its dividend policy

(b) Entity's **sources of funding**, the policy on **gearing** and its **risk management policies**

(c) **Strengths and resources** of the entity whose value is not reflected in the statement of financial position under IASs

Entities are encouraged to produce any other reports and statements which may aid users.

Fair presentation and compliance with IFRS

Most importantly, financial statements should present fairly the financial position, financial performance and cash flows of an entity. **Compliance with IFRS** is presumed to result in financial statements that achieve a fair presentation.

The following points made by IAS 1 expand on this principle.

(a) **Compliance with IFRS** should be disclosed

(b) **All relevant IFRS** must be followed if compliance with IFRS is disclosed

(c) Use of an **inappropriate accounting treatment** cannot be rectified either by disclosure of accounting policies or notes/explanatory material

IAS 1 states what is required for a fair presentation.

> **Step 1**
> Selection and application of **accounting policies**

> **Step 2**
> **Presentation of information** in a manner which provides relevant, reliable, comparable and understandable information

> **Step 3**
> **Additional disclosures** where required

The IAS then goes on to consider certain important assumptions which underpin the preparation and presentation of financial statements, which we might call fundamental assumptions.

Going concern

> The entity is normally viewed as a **going concern**, that is, as continuing in operation for the foreseeable future. Financial statements are prepared on a going concern basis unless management intends to liquidate the entity or to cease trading.

This assumption is based on the notion that, when preparing a normal set of accounts, it is always expected that the business will **continue to operate** in approximately the same manner for the foreseeable future (at least the next 12 months should be considered). In particular, the entity will not go into liquidation or scale down its operations in a material way. The main significance of the going concern assumption is that the assets of the business **should not be valued at their 'break up' value**, which is the amount that they would sell for if they were sold off piecemeal and the business were thus broken up.

If the going concern assumption is not followed, that fact must be disclosed, together with:

- The **basis** on which the financial statements have been prepared
- The **reasons** why the entity is not considered to be a going concern

Accrual basis of accounting

Accrual basis of accounting. Items are recognised as assets liabilities, equity, income and expenses when they satisfy the definition and recognition criteria for those elements in the Framework. *(IAS 1)*

Entities should prepare their financial statements on the basis that transactions are recorded in them, not as the cash is paid or received, but as the revenues or expenses are **earned or incurred** in the accounting period to which they relate.

According to the accrual assumption, then, in computing profit revenue earned must be matched against the expenditure incurred in earning it.

Consistency of presentation

To maintain consistency, the presentation and classification of items in the financial statements should **stay the same from one period to the next. There are two exceptions**.

(a) There is a significant change in the **nature of the operations** or a review of the financial statements presentation indicates a **more appropriate presentation**.
(b) A change in presentation is **required by an IFRS**.

Materiality and aggregation

All material items should be **disclosed** in the financial statements.

Amounts which are **immaterial** can be aggregated with amounts of a similar nature or function and need not be presented separately.

Materiality. Omissions or misstatement of items are material if they could, individually or collectively, influence the economic decisions of users taken on the basis of the financial statements. Materiality depends on the size and nature of the omission or misstatement judged in the surrounding circumstances. The size or nature of the item, or a combination of both, could be the determining factor. *(IAS 1)*

An error which is too trivial to affect anyone's understanding of the accounts is referred to as **immaterial**. In preparing accounts it is important to assess what is material and what is not, so that time and money are not wasted in the pursuit of excessive detail.

Determining whether or not an item is material is a very **subjective exercise**. There is no absolute measure of materiality. It is common to apply a convenient rule of thumb (for example to define material items as those with a value greater than 5% of the net profit disclosed by the accounts). But some items disclosed in accounts are regarded as particularly sensitive and even a very small misstatement of such an item would be regarded as a material error. An example in the accounts of a limited liability company might be the amount of remuneration paid to directors of the company.

The assessment of an item as material or immaterial may **affect its treatment in the accounts**. For example, the income statement of a business will show the expenses incurred by the business grouped under suitable captions (heating and lighting expenses, rent and local taxes etc); but in the case of very small expenses it may be appropriate to lump them together under a caption such as 'sundry expenses', because a more detailed breakdown would be inappropriate for such immaterial amounts.

In assessing whether or not an item is material, it is not only the amount of the item which needs to be considered. The **context** is also important.

(a) If a statement of financial position shows non-current assets of $2 million and inventories of $30,000 an error of $20,000 in the depreciation calculations might not be regarded as material, whereas an error of $20,000 in the inventory valuation probably would be. In other words, the total of which the erroneous item forms part must be considered.

(b) If a business has a bank loan of $50,000 and a $55,000 balance on bank deposit account, it might well be regarded as a material misstatement if these two amounts were displayed on the statement of financial position as 'cash at bank $5,000'. In other words, incorrect presentation may amount to material misstatement even if there is no monetary error.

Users are assumed to have a personal knowledge of business and economic activities and accounting and a willingness to study the information with reasonable diligence.

Offsetting

IAS 1 does not allow **assets and liabilities to be offset** against each other unless such a treatment is required or permitted by another IFRS.

Income and expenses can be offset only when:

(a) an IAS requires/permits it; or
(b) gains, losses and related expenses arising from the same/similar transactions are not material (aggregate).

Comparative information

IAS 1 requires comparative information to be disclosed for the previous period for all **numerical information**, unless another IAS permits/requires otherwise. Comparatives should also be given in narrative information where helpful.

Comparatives should be **reclassified** when the presentation or classification of items in the financial statements is amended (see IAS 8: Chapter 16).

Disclosure of accounting policies

There should be a specific section for accounting policies in the notes to the financial statements and the following should be disclosed there.

(a) **Measurement bases** used in preparing the financial statements
(b) Each **specific accounting policy** necessary for a proper understanding of the financial statements

To be clear and understandable it is essential that financial statements should disclose the accounting policies used in their preparation. This is because **policies may vary**, not only from entity to entity, but also from country to country. As an aid to users, all the major accounting policies used should be disclosed in the same place.

2 Structure and content of financial statements

IAS 1 *Presentation of financial statements* gives substantial guidance on the form and content of published financial statements. It was revised in September 2007. The standard looks at the statement of financial position and statement of comprehensive income (the statement of cash flows is covered by IAS 7). First of all, some general points are made about financial statements.

Profit or loss for the period

The statement of comprehensive income is the most significant indicator of a company's financial performance. So it is important to ensure that it is not misleading.

IAS 1 stipulates that all items of income and expense recognised in a period shall be included in profit or loss unless a **Standard** or an **Interpretation** requires otherwise.

Circumstances where items may be excluded from profit or loss for the current year include the correction of errors and the effect of changes in accounting policies. These are covered in IAS 8.

How items are disclosed

IAS 1 specifies disclosures of certain items in certain ways.

*   Some items must appear on the face of the statement of financial position or statement of comprehensive income
*   Other items can appear in a **note to the financial statements** instead
*   **Recommended formats** are given which entities may or may not follow, depending on their circumstances

Obviously, disclosures specified by **other standards** must also be made, and we will mention the necessary disclosures when we cover each statement in turn. Disclosures in both IAS 1 and other standards must be made either on the face of the statement or in the notes unless otherwise stated, ie disclosures cannot be made in an accompanying commentary or report.

Identification of financial statements

As a result of the above point, it is most important that entities **distinguish the financial statements** very clearly from any other information published with them. This is because all IASs/IFRSs apply only to the financial statements (ie the main statements and related notes), so readers of the annual report must be able to differentiate between the parts of the report which are prepared under IFRSs, and other parts which are not.

The entity should **identify each** financial statement and the notes very clearly. IAS 1 also requires disclosure of the following information in a prominent position. If necessary it should be repeated wherever it is felt to be of use to the reader in his understanding of the information presented.

*   **Name** of the reporting entity (or other means of identification)
*   Whether the accounts cover the **single entity** only or a group of entities

- The **date of the end of the reporting period** or the period covered by the financial statements (as appropriate)
- The **presentation currency**
- The **level of rounding** used in presenting amounts in the financial statements

Judgement must be used to determine the best method of presenting this information. In particular, the standard suggests that the approach to this will be very different when the financial statements are communicated electronically.

The **level of rounding** is important, as presenting figures in thousands or millions of units makes the figures more understandable. The level of rounding must be disclosed, however, and it should not obscure necessary details or make the information less relevant.

Reporting period

It is normal for entities to present financial statements **annually** and IAS 1 states that they should be prepared at least as often as this. If (unusually) the end of an entity's reporting period is changed, for whatever reason, the period for which the statements are presented will be less or more than one year. In such cases the entity should also disclose:

(a)   the **reason(s) why** a period other than one year is used; and
(b)   the fact that the comparative figures given **are not in fact comparable**.

For practical purposes, some entities prefer to use a period which **approximates to a year**, eg 52 weeks, and the IAS allows this approach as it will produce statements not materially different from those produced on an annual basis.

Timeliness

If the publication of financial statements is delayed too long after the reporting period, their usefulness will be severely diminished. The standard states that entities should be able to produce their financial statements **within six months** of the end of the reporting period. An entity with consistently complex operations cannot use this as a reason for its failure to report on a timely basis. Local legislation and market regulation imposes specific deadlines on certain entities.

3 Statement of financial position

IAS 1 discusses the distinction between current and non-current items in some detail, as we shall see in the next section. First of all we can look at the **suggested format** of the statement of financial position (given in an appendix to the standard) and then look at further disclosures required.

Statement of financial position example

The example given by IAS 1 revised is as follows.

XYZ GROUP – STATEMENT OF FINANCIAL POSITION AT 31 DECEMBER

	20X9 $'000	20X8 $'000
Assets		
Non-current assets		
Property, plant and equipment	350,700	360,020
Goodwill	80,800	91,200
Other intangible assets	227,470	227,470
Investments in associates	100,150	110,770
Available-for-sale financial assets	142,500	156,000
	901,620	945,460
Current assets		
Inventories	135,230	132,500
Trade receivables	91,600	110,800
Other current assets	25,650	12,540
Cash and cash equivalents	312,400	322,900
	564,880	578,740
Total assets	1,466,500	1,524,200
Equity and liabilities		
Equity attributable to owners of the parent		
Share capital	650,000	600,000
Retained earnings	243,500	161,700
Other components of equity	10,200	21,200
	903,700	782,900
Non-controlling interest	70,050	48,600
Total equity	973,750	831,500
Non-current liabilities		
Long-term borrowings	120,000	160,000
Deferred tax	28,800	26,040
Long-term provisions	28,850	52,240
Total non-current liabilities	117,650	238,280
Current liabilities		
Trade and other payables	115,100	187,620
Short-term borrowings	150,000	200,000
Current portion of long-term borrowings	10,000	20,000
Current tax payable	35,000	42,000
Short-term provisions	5,000	4,800
Total current liabilities	315,100	454,420
Total liabilities	492,750	692,700
Total equity and liabilities	1,466,500	1,524,200

IAS 1 (revised) specifies various items which must appear on the face of the statement of financial position as a minimum disclosure.

(a)   Property, plant and equipment

(b)   Investment property
(c)   Intangible assets
(d)   Financial assets (excluding amounts shown under (e), (h) and (i))
(e)   Investments accounted for using the equity method
(f)   Biological assets
(g)   Inventories
(h)   Trade and other receivables
(i)   Cash and cash equivalents
(j)   Assets classified as held for sale under IFRS 5
(k)   Trade and other payables
(l)   Provisions
(m)   Financial liabilities (other than (j) and (k))
(n)   Current tax liabilities and assets as in IAS 12
(o)   Deferred tax liabilities and assets
(p)   Liabilities included in disposal groups under IFRS 5
(q)   Non-controlling interests
(r)   Issued capital and reserves

Any **other line items,** headings or sub-totals should be shown on the face of the statement of financial position when it is necessary for an understanding of the entity's financial position.

The example shown above is for illustration only (although we will follow the format in this book). The IAS, however, does not prescribe the order or format in which the items listed should be presented. It simply states that they **must be presented separately** because they are so different in nature or function from each other.

Whether additional items are presented separately depends on judgements based on the assessment of the following factors.

(a)   **Nature and liquidity of assets and their materiality.** Thus goodwill and assets arising from development expenditure will be presented separately, as will monetary/non-monetary assets and current/non-current assets.
(b)   **Function within the entity.** Operating and financial assets, inventories, receivables and cash and cash equivalents are therefore shown separately.
(c)   **Amounts, nature and timing of liabilities.** Interest-bearing and non-interest-bearing liabilities and provisions will be shown separately, classified as current or non-current as appropriate.

The standard also requires separate presentation where **different measurement bases** are used for assets and liabilities which differ in nature or function. According to IAS 16, for example, it is permitted to carry certain items of property, plant and equipment at cost or at a revalued amount.

Information presented either on the face of the statement of financial position or by note

Further **sub-classification** of the line items listed above should be disclosed either on the face of the statement of financial position or in the notes. The classification will depend upon the nature of the entity's operations. As well as each item being sub-classified by its nature, any amounts payable to or receivable from any **group company or other related party** should also be disclosed separately.

The sub-classification details will in part depend on the requirements of IFRSs. The size, nature and function of the amounts involved will also be important and the factors listed above should be considered. **Disclosures** will vary from item to item and IAS 1 gives the following examples.

(a) **Property, plant and equipment** are classified by class as described in IAS 16, *Property, plant and equipment*

(b) **Receivables** are analysed between amounts receivable from trade customers, other members of the group, receivables from related parties, prepayments and other amounts

(c) **Inventories** are sub-classified, in accordance with IAS 2 *Inventories*, into classifications such as merchandise, production supplies, materials, work in progress and finished goods

(d) **Provisions** are analysed showing separately provisions for employee benefit costs and any other items classified in a manner appropriate to the entity's operations

(e) **Equity capital and reserves** are analysed showing separately the various classes of paid in capital, share premium and reserves

The standard then lists some **specific disclosures** which must be made, either on the face of the statement of financial position or in the related notes.

(a) **Share capital disclosures** (for each class of share capital)
  (i) Number of shares authorised
  (ii) Number of shares issued and fully paid, and issued but not fully paid
  (iii) Par value per share, or that the shares have no par value
  (iv) Reconciliation of the number of shares outstanding at the beginning and at the end of the year
  (v) Rights, preferences and restrictions attaching to that class including restrictions on the distribution of dividends and the repayment of capital
  (vi) Shares in the entity held by the entity itself or by related group companies
  (vii) Shares reserved for issuance under options and sales contracts, including the terms and amounts

(b) Description of the nature and purpose of **each reserve** within owners' equity

Some types of entity have no share capital, eg partnerships. Such entities should disclose information which is **equivalent** to that listed above. This means disclosing the movement during the period in each category of equity interest and any rights, preferences or restrictions attached to each category of equity interest.

4 The current/non-current distinction

An entity must present **current** and **non-current** assets as separate classifications on the face of the statement of financial position. A presentation based on liquidity should only be used where it provides more relevant and reliable information, in which case all assets and liabilities must be presented broadly **in order of liquidity**.

In either case, the entity should disclose any portion of an asset or liability which is expected to be recovered or settled **after more than twelve months**. For example, for an amount receivable which is due in instalments over 18 months, the portion due after more than twelve months must be disclosed.

The IAS emphasises how helpful information on the **operating cycle** is to users of financial statements. Where there is a clearly defined operating cycle within which the entity supplies goods or services, then information disclosing those net assets that are continuously circulating as **working capital** is useful.

This distinguishes them from those net assets used in the long-term operations of the entity. Assets that are expected to be realised and liabilities that are due for settlement within the operating cycle are therefore highlighted.

The liquidity and solvency of an entity is also indicated by information about the **maturity dates** of assets and liabilities. IFRS 7 *Financial instruments: disclosures* requires disclosure of maturity dates of both financial assets and financial liabilities. (Financial assets include trade and other receivables; financial liabilities include trade and other payables.) In the case of non-monetary assets, eg inventories, such information is also useful.

Current assets

An asset should be classified as a **current asset** when it:

- Is expected to be realised in, or is held for sale or consumption in, the normal course of the entity's operating cycle; or
- Is held primarily for trading purposes or for the short-term and expected to be realised within twelve months of the end of the reporting period; or
- Is cash or a cash equivalent asset which is not restricted in its use.

All other assets should be classified as non-current assets. *(IAS 1)*

Non-current assets includes tangible, intangible, operating and financial assets of a long-term nature. Other terms with the same meaning can be used (eg 'fixed', 'long-term').

The term 'operating cycle' has been used several times above and the standard defines it as follows.

The **operating cycle** of an entity is the time between the acquisition of assets for processing and their realisation in cash or cash equivalents. *(IAS 1)*

Current assets therefore include inventories and trade receivables that are sold, consumed and realised as part of the normal operating cycle. **This is the case even where they are not expected to be realised within twelve months.**

Current assets will also include **marketable securities** if they are expected to be realised within twelve months after the reporting period. If expected to be realised later, they should be included in non-current assets.

Current liabilities

A liability should be classified as a **current liability** when it:

- Is expected to be settled in the normal course of the entity's operating cycle; or
- Is held primarily for the purpose of trading; or
- Is due to be settled within twelve months after the reporting period; or
- The entity does not have an unconditional right to defer settlement of the liability for at least twelve months after the reporting period.

All other liabilities should be classified as non-current liabilities. *(IAS 1)*

The categorisation of current liabilities is very similar to that of current assets. Thus, some current liabilities are part of the **working capital** used in the normal operating cycle of the business (ie trade payables and accruals for employee and other operating costs). Such items will be classed as current liabilities **even where they are due to be settled more than twelve months after the end of the reporting period**.

There are also current liabilities which are not settled as part of the normal operating cycle, but which are due to be settled within twelve months of the end of the reporting period. These include bank overdrafts, income taxes, other non-trade payables and the current portion of interest-bearing liabilities. Any interest-bearing liabilities that are used to finance working capital on a long-term basis, and that are not due for settlement within twelve months, should be classed as **non-current liabilities**.

A **non-current financial liability** due to be **settled within twelve months** of the end of the reporting period should be classified as a **current liability**, even if an agreement to refinance, or to reschedule payments, on a long-term basis is completed after the end of the reporting period and before the financial statements are authorised for issue.

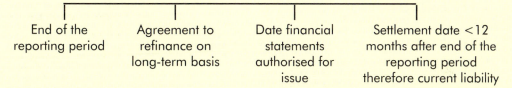

| End of the reporting period | Agreement to refinance on long-term basis | Date financial statements authorised for issue | Settlement date <12 months after end of the reporting period therefore current liability |

A **non-current financial liability** that is payable on **demand** because the entity **breached** a **condition** of its loan agreement should be classified as **current** at the end of the reporting period even if the **lender** has agreed **after the end of the reporting period**, and **before** the financial statements are **authorised for issue, not** to **demand payment** as a consequence of the breach.

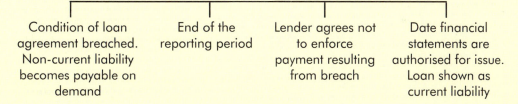

| Condition of loan agreement breached. Non-current liability becomes payable on demand | End of the reporting period | Lender agrees not to enforce payment resulting from breach | Date financial statements are authorised for issue. Loan shown as current liability |

However, if the **lender** has **agreed** by the **end of the reporting period** to provide a **period of grace** ending **at least twelve months after the end of the reporting period** within which the entity can rectify the breach and during that time the lender cannot demand immediate repayment, the liability is classified as **non-current**.

5 Statement of comprehensive income

IAS 1 (revised) allows income and expense items to be presented either:

(a)   in a single statement of comprehensive income; or
(b)   in two statements: a separate income statement and statement of other comprehensive income.

The format for a single statement of comprehensive income is shown as follows in the standard. The section down to 'profit for the year' can be shown as a separate 'income statement' with an additional 'statement of other comprehensive income'.

XYZ GROUP – STATEMENT OF COMPREHENSIVE INCOME FOR THE YEAR ENDED 31 DECEMBER

	20X9	20X8
	$'000	$'000
Revenue	390,000	355,000
Cost of sales	(245,000)	(230,000)
Gross profit	145,000	125,000
Other income	20,667	11,300
Distribution costs	(9,000)	(8,700)
Administrative expenses	(20,000)	(21,000)
Other expenses	(2,100)	(1,200)
Finance costs	(8,000)	(7,500)
Share of profit of associates	35,100	30,100
Profit before tax	161,667	128,000
Income tax expense	(40,417)	(32,000)
Profit for the year from continuing operations	121,250	96,000
Loss for the year from discontinued operations	–	(30,500)
Profit for the year	121,250	65,500
Other comprehensive income:		
Exchange differences on translating foreign operations	5,334	10,667
Available-for-sale financial assets	(24,000)	26,667
Cash flow hedges	(667)	(4,000)
Gains on property revaluation	993	3,367
Actuarial gains (losses) on defined benefit pension plans	(667)	1,333
Share of other comprehensive income of associates	400	(700)
Income tax relating to components of other comprehensive income	4,667	(9,334)
Other comprehensive income for the year, net of tax	(14,000)	28,000
Total comprehensive income for the year	107,250	93,500
Profit attributable to:		
Owners of the parent	97,000	52,400
Non-controlling interest	24,250	13,100
	121,250	65,500
Total comprehensive income attributable to		
Owners of the parent	85,800	74,800
Non-controlling interest	21,450	18,700
	107,250	93,500
Earnings per share	0.46	0.30

Companies are given the option of presenting this information in two statements as follows:

XYZ GROUP – INCOME STATEMENT FOR THE YEAR ENDED 31 DECEMBER

	20X9	20X8
	$'000	$'000
Revenue	390,000	355,000
Cost of sales	(245,000)	(230,000)
Gross profit	145,000	125,000
Other income	20,667	11,300
Distribution costs	(9,000)	(8,700)
Administrative expenses	(20,000)	(21,000)
Other expenses	(2,100)	(1,200)
Finance costs	(8,000)	(7,500)
Share of profit of associates	35,100	30,100
Profit before tax	161,667	128,000
Income tax expense	(40,417)	(32,000)
Profit for the year from continuing operations	121,250	96,000
Loss for the year from discontinued operations	–	(30,500)
Profit for the year	121,250	65,500
Profit attributable to:		
Owners of the parent	97,000	52,400
Non-controlling interest	24,250	13,100
	121,250	65,500

XYZ GROUP – STATEMENT OF COMPREHENSIVE INCOME FOR THE YEAR ENDED 31 DECEMBER

	20X9	20X8
	$'000	$'000
Profit for the year	121,250	65,500
Other comprehensive income:		
Exchange differences on translating foreign operations	5,334	10,667
Available-for-sale financial assets	(24,000)	26,667
Cash flow hedges	(667)	(4,000)
Gains on property revaluation	993	3,367
Actuarial gains (losses) on defined benefit pension plans	(667)	1,333
Share of other comprehensive income of associates	400	(700)
Income tax relating to components of other comprehensive income	4,667	(9,334)
Other comprehensive income for the year, net of tax	(14,000)	28,000
Total comprehensive income for the year	107,250	93,500
Total comprehensive income attributable to		
Owners of the parent	85,800	74,800
Non-controlling interest	21,450	18,700
	107,250	93,500

6 Income statement

There are two methods of presenting information in the income statement.

Nature of expense method

Expenses are not reallocated amongst various functions within the entity, but are aggregated in the income statement **according to their nature** (eg purchase of materials, depreciation, wages and salaries, transport costs). This is by far the easiest method, especially for smaller entities.

Function of expense/cost of sales method

This method is more widely used. Expenses are classified according to their function as part of cost of sales, distribution or administrative activities. This method often gives **more relevant** information for users, but the allocation of expenses by function requires the use of judgement and can be arbitrary. Consequently, perhaps, when this method is used, entities should disclose **additional** information on the nature of expenses, including staff costs, and depreciation and amortisation expense.

Which of the above methods is chosen by an entity will depend on historical and industry factors, and also the **nature of the organisation**. Under each method, there should be given an indication of costs which are likely to vary (directly or indirectly) with the level of sales or production. The choice of method should fairly reflect the main elements of the entity's performance.

Examples of separate income statements

XYZ GROUP
INCOME STATEMENT FOR THE YEAR ENDED 31 DECEMBER 20X8

Illustrating the classification of expenses by function

	20X8	20X7
	$'000	$'000
Revenue	X	X
Cost of sales	(X)	(X)
Gross profit	X	X
Other income	X	X
Distribution costs	(X)	(X)
Administrative expenses	(X)	(X)
Other expenses	(X)	(X)
Finance costs	(X)	(X)
Share of profit of associates	X	X
Profit before tax	X	X
Income tax expense	(X)	(X)
Profit for the year	X	X
Profit attributable to:		
Owners of the parent	X	X
Non-controlling interest	X	X
	X	X

Illustrating the classification of expenses by nature

	20X8 $'000	20X7 $'000
Revenue	X	X
Other operating income	X	X
Changes in inventories of finished goods and work in progress	(X)	X
Work performed by the entity and capitalised	X	X
Raw material and consumables used	(X)	(X)
Employee benefits expense	(X)	(X)
Depreciation and amortisation expense	(X)	(X)
Impairment of property, plant and equipment	(X)	(X)
Other expenses	(X)	(X)
Finance costs	(X)	(X)
Share of profit of associates	X	X
Profit before tax	X	X
Income tax expense	(X)	(X)
Profit for the year	X	X
Profit attributable to:		
Owners of the parent	X	X
Non-controlling interest	X	X
	X	X

Information presented in the statement of comprehensive income or separate income statement

The standard lists the following as the minimum to be disclosed on the face of the income statement.

(a) Revenue
(b) Finance costs
(c) Share of profits and losses of associates and joint ventures accounted for using the equity method
(d) Tax expense
(e) A single amount comprising the post-tax profit or loss of discontinued operations and the post-tax gain or loss recognised on measurement to fair value less costs to sell or on disposal of the assets of the discontinued operation.
(f) Profit or loss

The following items must be disclosed in the income statement as allocations of profit or loss for the period.

(a) Profit or loss attributable to non-controlling interest
(b) Profit or loss attributable to owners of the parent

Income and expense items can only be offset when, and only when:

(a) It is permitted or required by an IFRS, or
(b) Gains, losses and related expenses arising from the same or similar transactions and events are immaterial, in which case they can be aggregated.

Information presented either in the statement or in the notes

An analysis of expenses must be shown either in the income statement section (as above, which is encouraged by the standard) or by note, using a classification based on either the nature of the expenses or their function. This **sub-classification of expenses** indicates a range of components of financial performance; these may differ in terms of stability, potential for gain or loss and predictability.

Dividends

IAS 1 also requires disclosure of the amount of **dividends per share** for the period covered by the financial statements. This shown on the face of the income statement.

Further points

(a) All requirements previously set out in other Standards for the presentation of particular line items in the statement of financial position and income statement are now dealt with in IAS 1. These line items are: biological assets; liabilities and assets for current tax and deferred tax; and pre-tax gain or loss recognised on the disposal of assets or settlement of liabilities attributable to discontinued operations.

(b) An entity must disclose, in the summary of significant accounting policies and/or other notes, the **judgements** made by management in **applying** the **accounting policies** that have the **most** significant effect on the amounts of items recognised in the financial statements.

(c) An entity must disclose in the notes information regarding **key assumptions** about the **future**, and other sources of **measurement uncertainty**, that have a significant **risk of** causing a **material adjustment** to the carrying amounts of assets and liabilities within the **next financial year**.

7 Changes in equity

This is the format of the statement of changes in equity

XYZ GROUP – STATEMENT OF CHANGES IN EQUITY FOR THE YEAR ENDED 31 DECEMBER 20X9

	Share capital	Retained earnings	Available for-sale financial assets	Revaluation surplus	Total	Non-controlling interest	Total equity
	$'000	$'000	$'000	$'000	$'000	$'000	$'000
Balance at 1 January 20X8	600,000	118,100	1,600	–	719,700	29,800	749,500
Changes in accounting policy	–	400	–	–	400	100	500
Restated balance	600,000	118,500	1,600	–	720,100	29,900	750,000
Changes in equity							
Dividends	–	(10,000)	–	–	(10,000)	–	(10,000)
Total comprehensive income for the year	–	53,200	16,000	1,600	70,800	18,700	89,500
Balance at 31 December 20X8	600,000	161,700	17,600	1,600	780,900	48,600	829,500
Changes in equity for 20X9							
Issue of share capital	50,000	–	–	–	50,000	–	50,000
Dividends	–	(15,000)	–	–	(15,000)	–	(15,000)
Total comprehensive income for the year	–	96,600	(14,400)	800	83,000	21,450	104,450
Transfer to retained earnings	–	200	–	(200)	–	–	–
Balance at 31 December 20X9	650,000	243,500	3,200	2,200	898,900	70,050	968,950

Note that where there has been a change of accounting policy necessitating a retrospective restatement, the adjustment is disclosed for each period. So, rather than just showing an adjustment to the balance b/f on 1.1.X9, the balances for 20X8 are restated.

Gains and losses on cash flow hedges or on the translation of foreign operations would be shown in additional columns.

8 Notes to the financial statements

The notes to the financial statements will **amplify** the information given in the statement of financial position, statement of comprehensive income, statement of cash flows and statement of changes in equity. We have already noted above the information which the IAS allows to be shown by note rather than in the statements. To some extent, then, the contents of the notes will be determined by the level of detail shown on the **face of the statements**.

The notes to the financial statements should perform the following functions.

(a) Provide information about the **basis on which the financial statements were prepared** and which specific accounting policies were chosen and applied to significant transactions/events

(b)   Disclose any information, not shown elsewhere in the financial statements, which is required by **IFRSs**

(c)   Show any additional information that is relevant to understanding which is not shown elsewhere in the financial statements

The way the notes are presented is important. They should be given in a **systematic manner** and **cross referenced** back to the related figure(s) in the statement of financial position, statement of comprehensive income, statement of cash flows or statement of changes in equity.

Notes to the financial statements will amplify the information shown therein by giving the following.

(a)   More **detailed analysis** or breakdowns of figures in the statements

(b)   **Narrative information** explaining figures in the statements

(c)   **Additional information**, eg contingent liabilities and commitments

IAS 1 suggests a **certain order** for notes to the financial statements. This will assist users when comparing the statements of different entities.

(a)   Statement of **compliance** with IFRSs

(b)   Statement of the **measurement basis** (bases) and accounting policies applied

(c)   **Supporting information** for items presented in each financial statement in the same order as each line item and each financial statement is presented

(d)   Other disclosures, eg:

    (i)   Contingent liabilities, commitments and other financial disclosures

    (ii)   Non-financial disclosures

The order of specific items may have to be varied occasionally, but a systematic structure is still required.

Presentation of accounting policies

The accounting policies section should describe the following.

(a)   The **measurement basis** (or bases) used in preparing the financial statements

(b)   The **other accounting policies** used, as required for a proper understanding of the financial statements

This information may be shown in the notes or sometimes as a **separate component** of the financial statements.

The information on measurement bases used is obviously fundamental to an understanding of the financial statements. Where **more than one basis is used**, it should be stated to which assets or liabilities each basis has been applied.

Other disclosures

An entity must disclose in the notes:

(a)   The amount of dividends proposed or declared before the financial statements were authorised for issue but not recognised as a distribution to owners during the period, and the amount per share

(b)   The amount of any cumulative preference dividends not recognised

IAS 1 ends by listing some **specific disclosures** which will always be required if they are not shown elsewhere in the financial statements.

(a)   The domicile and legal form of the entity, its country of incorporation and the address of the registered office (or, if different, principal place of business)

(b)   A description of the nature of the entity's operations and its principal activities

(c)   The name of the parent entity and the ultimate parent entity of the group

9   Small and medium-sized entities (SMEs)

It could be argued that company financial statements should be of two types:

(a)   'Simple' ones for small companies with fewer regulations and disclosure requirements

(b)   'Complicated' ones for larger companies with extensive and detailed requirements

This is sometimes called the **big GAAP/little GAAP** divide.

This has been an area of discussion in IFRS accounting for many years. Many jurisdictions have their own standard for small and medium sized entities which reduce the reporting requirements for these entities. There has been no guidance on this area from the IASB until recently.

IFRS for SMEs

In July 2009 the IASB published its *International Financial Reporting Standard for SMEs*. This was the result of a project going back to 2003 in which an Exposure Draft had been field tested with the participation of 116 small companies in 20 countries.

The final IFRS for SMEs is a stand-alone document – users do not need to refer back to the full IFRSs. It applies to unquoted entities. Many of the principles in full IFRS for recognising and measuring the elements of financial statements have been simplified and topics not relevant to SMEs have been omitted. Substantially fewer disclosures are required. To further reduce the reporting burden, revisions to the IFRS for SMEs will be limited to once every three years.

Omitted topics

*   Earnings per share
*   Interim financial reporting
*   Segment reporting
*   Special accounting for assets held for sale

There are some options available under full IFRS which are not included in the IFRS for SMEs. Some of these are:

*   financial instrument options, including available-for-sale, held-to-maturity and fair value options
*   the revaluation model for PPE and intangible assets
*   proportionate consolidation for joint ventures
*   the accounting policy choice between cost and fair value models for investment property
*   the various options for treatment of government grants

Recognition and measurement

These are the main simplifications to the recognition and measurement principles in full IFRS:

*   **Financial instruments** meeting specified criteria are measured at cost or amortised cost. All others are measured at fair value through profit or loss. This replaces the four categories in full IFRS.

- **Goodwill** is amortised over its useful life or ten years, rather than being subjected to impairment reviews.
- **Investments in associates and joint ventures** can be measured at cost unless there is a published price quotation.
- **Research and development costs** must both be recognised as expenses.
- **Borrowing costs** must be recognised as expenses.
- **PPE and intangible assets** do not need an annual review as per IAS 16/IAS 38. A review is only required if indications suggest that useful life etc. have changed.
- A number of changes to **defined benefit plans**:
  - All past service cost to be recognised immediately in profit or loss
  - All actuarial gains and losses to be recognised immediately either in profit or loss or other comprehensive income
  - The projected unit credit method to be used only if it can be done without undue cost or effort
- For **income tax**, SMEs will use a simplified replacement for IAS 12 *Income taxes* as set out in the ED *Income Tax*, published in March 2009.
- No separate **held-for-sale** classification as per IFRS 5. Instead, holding assets for sale will be treated as an impairment indicator.
- **Biological assets** are to be held at fair value through profit or loss only when fair value can be determined without undue cost or effort. Otherwise the cost-depreciation-impairment model is used.
- **Share-based payment** expense is measured at the directors' best estimate of fair value if market prices are not available.

[These issues are all covered according to full IFRS in the relevant chapters of this text.]

10 IAS 34: Interim financial reporting

Governments, stock exchanges and regulators may require entities whose shares or loan notes are publicly traded to publish interim financial reports.

The following definitions are used in IAS 34.

> - **Interim period** is a financial reporting period shorter than a full financial year.
> - **Interim financial report** means a financial report containing either a complete set of financial statements (as described in IAS 1) or a set of condensed financial statements (as described in this standard) for an interim period.   (*IAS 34*)

The standard does not make the preparation of interim financial reports **mandatory**, taking the view that this is a matter for governments, securities regulators, stock exchanges or professional accountancy bodies to decide within each country. The IASB does, however, strongly recommend to governments, etc, that interim financial reporting should be a requirement for companies whose equity or debt securities are **publicly traded**. The specific recommendations are that:

(a) An interim financial report should be produced by such companies for **at least the first six months of their financial year** (ie a half year financial report).

(b) The report should be **available no later than 60 days** after the end of the interim period.

Thus, a company with a year ending 31 December would be required as a minimum to prepare an interim report for the half year to 30 June and this report should be available before the end of August.

Minimum components

The proposed standard specifies the minimum component elements of an interim financial report.

- Condensed statement of financial position
- Condensed statement of comprehensive income
- Condensed statement of changes in equity
- Condensed statement of cash flows
- Selected note disclosures

The rationale for requiring only condensed statements and selected note disclosures is that entities need not duplicate information in their interim report that is contained in their report for the previous financial year. Interim statements should focus more on new events, activities and circumstances.

Form and content

Where **full financial statements** are given as interim financial statements, IAS 1 should be used as a guide, otherwise IAS 34 specifies minimum contents.

The **condensed statement of financial position** should include, as a minimum, each of the major components of assets, liabilities and equity as were in the statement of financial position at the end of the previous financial year, thus providing a summary of the economic resources of the entity and its financial structure.

The **condensed statement of comprehensive income** should include, as a minimum, each of the component items of income and expense as are shown in profit or loss for the previous financial year, together with the earnings per share and diluted earnings per share.

The **condensed statement of cash flows** should show, as a minimum, the three major sub-totals of cash flow as required in statements of cash flows by IAS 7, namely: cash flows from operating activities, cash flows from investing activities and cash flows from financing activities.

The **condensed statement of changes in equity** should include, as a minimum, each of the major components of equity as were contained in the statement of changes in equity for the previous financial year of the entity.

Selected explanatory notes

IAS 34 states that **relatively minor changes** from the most recent annual financial statements need not be included in an interim report. However, the notes to interim report should include the following (unless the information is contained elsewhere in the report).

- A statement that the **same accounting policies and methods of computation** have been used for the interim statements as were used for the most recent annual financial statements. If not, the nature of the differences and their effect should be described. (The accounting policies for preparing the interim report should only differ from those used for the previous annual accounts in a situation where there has been a change in accounting policy since the end of the previous financial year, and the new policy will be applied for the annual accounts of the current financial period.)
- Explanatory comments on the **seasonality or 'cyclicality'** of operations in the interim period. For example, if a company earns most of its annual profits in the

first half of the year, because sales are much higher in the first six months, the interim report for the first half of the year should explain this fact

- The **nature and amount** of items during the interim period affecting assets, liabilities, capital, net income or cash flows, that are unusual, due to their nature, incidence or size
- The **issue or repurchase** of equity or debt securities
- Nature and amount of any **changes in estimates** of amounts reported in an earlier interim report during the financial year, or in prior financial years if these affect the current interim period
- **Dividends paid** on ordinary shares and the dividends paid on other shares
- **Segmental results** for the business segments or geographical segments of the entity (see IFRS 8)
- Any **significant events since the end of the interim period**
- Effect of the acquisition or disposal of subsidiaries during the interim period
- Any significant change in a **contingent liability or a contingent asset** since the date of the last annual statement of financial position

The entity should also disclose the fact that the interim report has been produced in compliance with IAS 34 on interim financial reporting.

The following are examples of the types of disclosures required:

(a) Write-down of inventories to net realisable value and the reversal of such a write-down
(b) Recognition of a loss from the impairment of property, plant and equipment, intangible assets, or other assets, and the reversal of such an impairment loss
(c) Reversal of any provisions for the costs of restructuring
(d) Acquisitions and disposals of items of property, plant and equipment
(e) Commitments for the purchase of property, plant and equipment
(f) Litigation settlements
(g) Corrections of fundamental errors in previously reported financial data
(h) Any debt default or any breach of a debt covenant that has not been corrected subsequently
(i) Related party transactions

Periods covered

The standard requires that interim financial reports should provide financial information for the following periods or as at the following dates.

- **Statement of financial position data** as at the end of the current interim period, and comparative data as at the end of the most recent financial year
- **Statement of comprehensive income data** for the current interim period and cumulative data for the current year to date, together with comparative data for the corresponding interim period and cumulative figures for the previous financial year
- **Statement of cash flows data** should be cumulative for the current year to date, with comparative cumulative data for the corresponding interim period in the previous financial year
- **Data for the statement of changes in equity** should be for both the current interim period and for the year to date, together with comparative data for the corresponding interim period, and cumulative figures, for the previous financial year

Materiality

Materiality should be assessed in relation to the interim period financial data. It should be recognised that interim measurements **rely to a greater extent on estimates** than annual financial data.

Recognition and measurement principles

A large part of IAS 34 deals with recognition and measurement principles, and guidelines as to their practical application. The **guiding principle** is that an entity should use the **same recognition and measurement principles in its interim statements as it does in its annual financial statements**.

This means, for example, that a cost that would not be capitalised in the year-end statement of financial position should not be capitalised in the statement of financial position for an interim period. Similarly, an accrual for an item of income or expense for a transaction that has not yet occurred (or a deferral of an item of income or expense for a transaction that has already occurred) is inappropriate for interim reporting, just as it is for year-end reporting.

Applying this principle of recognition and measurement may result, in a subsequent interim period or at the year-end, in a remeasurement of amounts that were reported in a financial statement for a previous interim period. The nature and amount of any significant remeasurements should be disclosed.

Revenues received occasionally, seasonally or cyclically

Revenue that is received as an occasional item, or within a seasonal or cyclical pattern, should not be anticipated or deferred in interim financial statements, if it would be inappropriate to anticipate or defer the revenue for the annual financial statements. In other words, the principles of revenue recognition should be applied consistently to the interim reports and year-end reports.

Costs incurred unevenly during the financial year

These should only be anticipated or deferred (ie treated as accruals or prepayments) if it would be appropriate to anticipate or defer the expense in the annual financial statements. For example, it would be appropriate to anticipate a cost for property rental where the rental is paid in arrears, but it would be inappropriate to anticipate part of the cost of a major advertising campaign later in the year, for which no expenses have yet been incurred.

The standard goes on, in an appendix, to deal with **specific applications** of the recognition and measurement principle. Some of these examples are explained below, by way of explanation and illustration.

Payroll taxes or insurance contributions paid by employers

In some countries these are assessed on an annual basis, but paid at an uneven rate during the course of the year, with a large proportion of the taxes being paid in the early part of the year, and a much smaller proportion paid later on in the year. In this situation, it would be appropriate to use an estimated average annual tax rate for the year in an interim statement, not the actual tax paid. This treatment is appropriate because it reflects the fact that the taxes are assessed on an annual basis, even though the payment pattern is uneven.

Cost of a planned major periodic maintenance or overhaul

The cost of such an event later in the year must not be anticipated in an interim financial statement unless there is a legal or constructive obligation to carry out this work. The fact that a maintenance or overhaul is planned and is carried out annually is not of itself sufficient to justify anticipating the cost in an interim financial report.

Other planned but irregularly-occurring costs

Similarly, these costs such as charitable donations or employee training costs, should not be accrued in an interim report. These costs, even if they occur regularly and are planned, are nevertheless discretionary.

A year-end bonus should not be provided for in an interim financial statement unless there is a constructive obligation to pay a year-end bonus (eg a contractual obligation, or a regular past practice) and the size of the bonus can be reliably measured.

The same principle applies to holiday pay. If holiday pay is an enforceable obligation on the employer, then any unpaid accumulated holiday pay may be accrued in the interim financial report.

Non-mandatory intangible assets

The entity might incur expenses during an interim period on items that might or will generate non-monetary intangible assets. IAS 38 *Intangible assets* requires that costs to generate non-monetary intangible assets (eg development expenses) should be recognised as an expense when incurred unless the costs form part of an identifiable intangible asset. Costs that were initially recognised as an expense cannot subsequently be treated instead as part of the cost of an intangible asset. IAS 34 states that interim financial statements should adopt the same approach. This means that it would be inappropriate in an interim financial statement to 'defer' a cost in the expectation that it will eventually be part of a non-monetary intangible asset that has not yet been recognised: such costs should be treated as an expense in the interim statement.

Depreciation

Depreciation should only be charged in an interim statement on non-current assets that have been acquired, not on non-current assets that will be acquired later in the financial year.

Tax on income

An entity will include an expense for income tax (tax on profits) in its interim statements. The tax rate to use should be the estimated average annual tax rate for the year. For example, suppose that in a particular jurisdiction, the rate of tax on company profits is 30% on the first $200,000 of profit and 40% on profits above $200,000. Now suppose that a company makes a profit of $200,000 in its first half year, and expects to make $200,000 in the second half year. The rate of tax to be applied in the interim financial report should be 35%, not 30%, ie the expected average rate of tax for the year as a whole. This approach is appropriate because income tax on company profits is charged on an annual basis, and an effective annual rate should therefore be applied to each interim period.

As another illustration, suppose a company earns pre-tax income in the first quarter of the year of $30,000, but expects to make a loss of $10,000 in each of the next three quarters, so that net income before tax for the year is zero. Suppose also that the rate of tax is 30%. In this case, it would be inappropriate to anticipate the losses, and the tax charge should be $9,000 for the first quarter of the year (30% of $30,000) and a negative tax charge of $3,000 for each of the next three quarters, if actual losses are the same as anticipated.

Where the tax year for a company does not coincide with its financial year, a separate estimated weighted average tax rate should be applied for each tax year, to the interim periods that fall within that tax year.

Some countries give entities tax credits against the tax payable, based on amounts of capital expenditure or research and development, etc. Under most tax regimes, these credits are calculated and granted on an annual basis; therefore it is appropriate to include anticipated tax credits within the calculation of the estimated average tax rate for the year, and apply this rate to calculate the tax on income for interim periods. However, if a tax benefit relates to a specific one-time event, it should be recognised within the tax expense for the interim period in which the event occurs.

Inventory valuations

Within interim reports, inventories should be valued in the same way as for year-end accounts. It is recognised, however, that it will be necessary to rely more heavily on estimates for interim reporting than for year-end reporting.

In addition, it will normally be the case that the net realisable value of inventories should be estimated from selling prices and related costs to complete and dispose at interim dates.

Use of estimates

Although accounting information must be reliable and free from material error, it may be necessary to sacrifice some accuracy and reliability for the sake of timeliness and cost-benefits. This is particularly the case with interim financial reporting, where there will be much less time to produce reports than at the financial year end. The proposed standard therefore recognises that estimates will have to be used to a greater extent in interim reporting, to assess values or even some costs, than in year-end reporting.

An appendix to IAS 34 gives some examples of the use of estimates.

(a) **Inventories**. An entity might not need to carry out a full inventory count at the end of each interim period. Instead, it may be sufficient to estimate inventory values using sales margins.
(b) **Provisions**. An entity might employ outside experts or consultants to advise on the appropriate amount of a provision, as at the year end. It will probably be inappropriate to employ an expert to make a similar assessment at each interim date. Similarly, an entity might employ a professional valuer to revalue fixed assets at the year end, whereas at the interim date(s) the entity will not rely on such experts.
(c) **Income taxes**. The rate of income tax (tax on profits) will be calculated at the year end by applying the tax rate in each country/jurisdiction to the profits earned there. At the interim stage, it may be sufficient to estimate the rate of income tax by applying the same 'blended' estimated weighted average tax rate to the income earned in all countries/jurisdictions.

The principle of **materiality** applies to interim financial reporting, as it does to year-end reporting. In assessing materiality, it needs to be recognised that interim financial reports will rely more heavily on estimates than year-end reports. Materiality should be assessed in relation to the interim financial statements themselves, and should be independent of 'annual materiality' considerations.

Part
B

Single entity financial statements

Accounting for tangible non-current assets

4

1 IAS 16: Property, plant and equipment

IAS 16 was first issued in 1993. It was revised in 1998 and again in 2003.

IAS 16 should be followed when accounting for property, plant and equipment unless another international accounting standard requires a **different treatment**.

IAS 16 **does not apply** to the following.

(a) Biological assets related to agricultural activity
(b) Mineral rights and mineral reserves, such as oil, gas and other non-regenerative resources

However, it does apply to property, plant and equipment used to develop these assets.

Definitions

The standard gives a large number of definitions.

> * **Property, plant and equipment** are tangible assets that:
>   - are held for use in the production or supply of goods or services, for rental to others, or for administrative purposes; and
>   - are expected to be used during more than one period.
> * **Cost** is the amount of cash or cash equivalents paid or the fair value of the other consideration given to acquire an asset at the time of its acquisition or construction.
> * **Residual value** is the net amount which the entity expects to obtain for an asset at the end of its useful life after deducting the expected costs of disposal.
> * **Entity specific value** is the present value of the cash flows an entity expects to arise from the continuing use of an asset and from its disposal at the end of its useful life, or expects to incur when settling a liability.
> * **Fair value** is the amount for which an asset could be exchanged between knowledgeable, willing parties in an arm's length transaction.
> * **Carrying amount** is the amount at which an asset is recognised in the statement of financial position after deducting any accumulated depreciation and accumulated impairment losses.
> * An **impairment loss** is the amount by which the carrying amount of an asset exceeds its recoverable amount.
> * **Depreciation** is the result of systematic allocation of the depreciable amount of an asset over its estimated useful life. Depreciation for the accounting period is charged to net profit or loss for the period either directly or indirectly.

> • **Useful life** is one of two things.
>   – The period over which a depreciable asset is expected to be used by the entity, or
>   – The number of production or similar units expected to be obtained from the asset by the entity.   (IAS 16)

Recognition

In this context, recognition simply means incorporation of the item in the entity's accounts, in this case as a non-current asset. The recognition of property, plant and equipment depends on two criteria.

(a)   It is probable that **future economic benefits** associated with the asset will flow to the entity

(b)   The cost of the asset to the entity can be **measured reliably**

These recognition criteria apply to **subsequent expenditure** as well as costs incurred initially. There are no longer any separate criteria for recognising subsequent expenditure.

Major components or spare parts, should also be recognised as property, plant and equipment.

For very **large and specialised items**, an apparently single asset should be broken down into its composite parts. This occurs where the different parts have different useful lives and different depreciation rates are applied to each part, eg an aircraft, where the body and engines are separated as they have different useful lives.

Once an item of property, plant and equipment qualifies for recognition as an asset, it will initially be **measured at cost**.

Components of cost

The standard lists the components of the cost of an item of property, plant and equipment.

*   **Purchase price**, less any trade discount or rebate
*   **Import duties** and non-refundable purchase taxes
*   **Directly attributable costs** of bringing the asset to working condition for its intended use, eg:
    –   The cost of site preparation
    –   Initial delivery and handling costs
    –   Installation costs
    –   Testing
    –   Professional fees (architects, engineers)
*   Initial estimate of the unavoidable cost of dismantling and removing the asset and restoring the site on which it is located

The revised IAS 16 provides **additional guidance on directly attributable** costs included in the cost of an item of property, plant and equipment.

(a)   These costs bring the asset to the location and working conditions necessary for it to be capable of operating in the manner intended by management, including those costs to test whether the asset is functioning properly.

(b)   They are determined after deducting the net proceeds from selling any items produced when bringing the asset to its location and condition.

The revised standard also states that income and related expenses of operations that are incidental to the construction or development of an item of property, plant and equipment should be recognised in the income statement.

The following costs **will not be part of the cost** of property, plant or equipment unless they can be attributed directly to the asset's acquisition, or bringing it into its working condition.

- Administration and other general overhead costs
- Start-up and similar pre-production costs
- Initial operating losses before the asset reaches planned performance

All of these will be recognised as an **expense** rather than an asset.

In the case of **self-constructed assets**, the same principles are applied as for acquired assets. If the entity makes similar assets during the normal course of business for sale externally, then the cost of the asset will be the cost of its production under IAS 2 *Inventories*. This also means that abnormal costs (wasted material, labour or other resources) are excluded from the cost of the asset. An example of a self-constructed asset is when a building company builds its own head office.

Expenditure incurred in replacing or renewing a component of an item of property, plant and equipment must be **recognised in the carrying amount of the item**. The carrying amount of the replaced or renewed component must be derecognised. A similar approach is also applied when a separate component of an item of property, plant and equipment is identified in respect of a major inspection to enable the continued use of the item.

Measurement subsequent to initial recognition

The standard offers two possible treatments here, essentially a choice between keeping an asset recorded at **cost** or revaluing it to **fair value**.

Cost model	Revaluation model
Carry the asset at its cost less any accumulated depreciation and any accumulated impairment loss.	• Carry the asset at a revalued amount, being its fair value at the date of the revaluation less any subsequent accumulated impairment losses. • Revaluations shall be made regularly enough so that the carrying amount approximates to fair value at the reporting date.

The revised IAS 16 specifies that the revaluation model is available only if the fair value of the asset can be measured reliably.

Revaluation model

The **market value** of land and buildings usually represents fair value, assuming existing use and line of business. Such valuations are usually carried out by professionally qualified valuers.

In the case of **plant and equipment**, fair value can also be taken as **market value**. Where a market value is not available, however, depreciated replacement cost should be used. There may be no market value where types of plant and equipment are sold only rarely or because of their specialised nature (ie they would normally only be sold as part of an ongoing business).

The frequency of valuation depends on the **volatility of the fair values** of individual items of property, plant and equipment. The more volatile the fair value, the more frequently revaluations should be carried out. Where the current fair value is very different from the carrying value then a revaluation should be carried out.

Most importantly, when an item of property, plant and equipment is revalued, **the whole class of assets to which it belongs should be revalued**.

All the items within a class should be **revalued at the same time**, to prevent selective revaluation of certain assets and to avoid disclosing a mixture of costs and values from different dates in the financial statements. A rolling basis of revaluation is allowed if the revaluations are kept up to date and the revaluation of the whole class is completed in a short period of time.

How should any **increase in value** be treated when a revaluation takes place? The debit will be the increase in value in the statement of financial position, but what about the credit? IAS 16 requires the increase to be credited to a **revaluation surplus** (ie part of owners' equity), unless the increase is reversing a previous decrease which was recognised as an expense. To the extent that this offset is made, the increase is recognised as income; any excess is then taken to the revaluation surplus.

Example: revaluation gain

B Co has an item of land carried in its books at $13,000. Two years ago a slump in land values led the company to reduce the carrying value from $15,000. This was taken as an expense in profit or loss. There has been a surge in land prices in the current year, however, and the land is now worth $20,000.

How do we account for the revaluation in the current year?

The double entry is:

DEBIT	Asset value (statement of financial position)	$7,000	
CREDIT	Profit or loss		$2,000
	Revaluation surplus		$5,000

The case is similar for a **decrease in value** on revaluation. Any decrease should be recognised as an expense, except where it offsets a previous increase taken as a revaluation surplus in owners' equity. Any decrease greater than the previous upwards increase in value must be taken as an expense in profit or loss.

Example: revaluation and depreciation

A company bought an asset for $10,000 at the beginning of 20X6. It had a useful life of five years. On 1 January 20X8 the asset was revalued to $15,000. The expected useful life has remained unchanged (ie three years remain). How is this accounted for?

On 1 January 20X8 the carrying value of the asset is $10,000 – (2 × ($10,000 ÷ 5)) = $6,000. For the revaluation:

DEBIT	Asset value	$9,000	
CREDIT	Revaluation surplus		$9,000

The depreciation for the next three years will be $15,000 ÷ 3 = $5,000, compared to depreciation on cost of $10,000 ÷ 5 = $2,000. So each year, the extra $3,000 can be treated as part of the surplus which has become realised:

DEBIT	Revaluation surplus	$3,000	
CREDIT	Retained earnings		$3,000

This is a movement on owners' equity, not an item in the income statement.

Cost model: Depreciation

The standard states that:

- The **depreciable amount** of an item of property, plant and equipment should be allocated on a systematic basis over its useful life.
- The **depreciation method** used should reflect the pattern in which the asset's economic benefits are consumed by the entity.
- The **depreciation charge** for each period should be recognised as an expense unless it is included in the carrying amount of another asset.

Land and buildings are dealt with separately even when they are acquired together because land normally has an unlimited life and is therefore not depreciated. In contrast buildings do have a limited life and must be depreciated. Any increase in the value of land on which a building is standing will have no impact on the determination of the building's useful life.

Depreciation is usually treated as an **expense**, but not where it is absorbed by the entity in the process of producing other assets. For example, depreciation of plant and machinery can be incurred in the production of goods for sale (inventory items). In such circumstances, the depreciation is included in the cost of the new assets produced.

Review of useful life

The following factors should be considered when **estimating the useful life** of a depreciable asset.

- Expected physical **wear and tear**
- **Obsolescence**
- Legal or other **limits on the use** of the assets

Once decided, the useful life should be **reviewed at least every financial year** end and depreciation rates adjusted for the current and future periods if expectations vary significantly from the original estimates.

The effect of the change should be disclosed in the accounting period in which the change takes place.

The assessment of useful life requires **judgement** based on previous experience with similar assets or classes of asset. When a completely new type of asset is acquired (ie through technological advancement or through use in producing a brand new product or service) it is still necessary to estimate useful life, even though the exercise will be much more difficult.

The standard also points out that the physical life of the asset might be longer than its useful life to the entity in question. One of the main factors to be taken into consideration is the **physical wear and tear** the asset is likely to endure. This will depend on various circumstances, including the number of shifts for which the asset will be used, the entity's repair and maintenance programme and so on. Other factors to be considered include obsolescence (due to technological advances in production or due to a reduction in demand for the product the asset produces) and legal restrictions, eg length of a related lease.

Review of depreciation method

The **depreciation method** should also be reviewed at least at each financial year end and, if there has been a significant change in the expected pattern of economic benefits from those assets, the method should be changed to suit this changed pattern. When such a change in depreciation method takes place the change should be accounted for as a change in accounting estimate and the depreciation charge for the current and future periods should be adjusted.

Impairment of asset values

An **impairment loss** should be treated in the same way as a **revaluation decrease** ie the decrease should be **recognised as an expense**. However, a revaluation decrease (or impairment loss) should be charged directly against any related revaluation surplus to the extent that the decrease does not exceed the amount held in the revaluation surplus in respect of that same asset.

A **reversal of an impairment** loss should be treated in the same way as a **revaluation increase**, ie a revaluation increase should be recognised as income to the extent that it reverses a revaluation decrease or an impairment loss of the same asset previously recognised as an expense.

Retirements and disposals

When an asset is permanently **withdrawn from use, or sold or scrapped**, and no future economic benefits are expected from its disposal, it should be withdrawn from the statement of financial position.

Gains or losses are the difference between the estimated net disposal proceeds and the carrying amount of the asset. They should be recognised as income or expense in the profit or loss.

An entity is required to **derecognise the carrying amount** of an item of property, plant or equipment that it disposes of on the date the **criteria for the sale of goods** in IAS 18 *Revenue* would be met. This also applies to parts of an asset.

An entity cannot classify as revenue (ie in the top line of the income statement) a gain it realises on the disposal of an item of property, plant and equipment.

Disclosure

The standard has a long list of disclosure requirements, for each class of property, plant and equipment.

(a)   **Measurement bases** for determining the gross carrying amount (if more than one, the gross carrying amount for that basis in each category)

(b)   **Depreciation methods** used

(c)   **Useful lives** or depreciation rates used

(d)   **Gross carrying amount** and accumulated depreciation (aggregated with accumulated impairment losses) at the beginning and end of the period

(e) **Reconciliation** of the carrying amount at the beginning and end of the period showing:

    (i)   Additions

    (ii)   Disposals

    (iii) Acquisitions through business combinations (see Chapter 17)

    (iv) Increases/decreases during the period from revaluations and from impairment losses

    (v)   Impairment losses recognised in profit or loss

    (vi) Impairment losses reversed in profit or loss

    (vii) Depreciation

    (viii) Net exchange differences (from translation of statements of foreign entity)

    (ix) Any other movements.

2 IAS 20: Accounting for government grants and disclosure of government assistance

It is common for entities to receive government grants for various purposes (grants may be called subsidies, premiums, etc). They may also receive other types of assistance which may be in many forms. The treatment of government grants is covered by IAS 20 *Accounting for government grants and disclosure of government assistance.*

Prior to the issue of IAS 20, government grants provided companies with an easy way to ramp up profits. In some cases grants would be credited to revenue in full, as soon as they were received. IAS 20 was issued to remedy this abuse.

IAS 20 does **not** cover the following situations.

- Accounting for government grants in financial statements reflecting the effects of **changing prices**
- Government assistance given in the form of **'tax breaks'**
- Government acting as **part-owner** of the entity

These definitions are given by the standard.

- **Government**. Government, government agencies and similar bodies whether local, national or international.
- **Government assistance**. Action by government designed to provide an economic benefit specific to an entity or range of entities qualifying under certain criteria.
- **Government grants**. Assistance by government in the form of transfers of resources to an entity in return for past or future compliance with certain conditions relating to the operating activities of the entity. They exclude those forms of government assistance which cannot reasonably have a value placed upon them and transactions with government which cannot be distinguished from the normal trading transactions of the entity.
- **Grants related to assets**. Government grants whose primary condition is that an entity qualifying for them should purchase, construct or otherwise acquire non-current assets. Subsidiary conditions may also be attached restricting the type or location of the assets or the periods during which they are to be acquired or held.
- **Grants related to income**. Government grants other than those related to assets.
- **Forgivable loans**. Loans which the lender undertakes to waive repayment of under certain prescribed conditions.

> • **Fair value**. The amount for which an asset could be exchanged, or a liability settled, between knowledgeable, willing parties in an arm's length transaction.
>
> *(IAS 20)*

There are many **different forms** of government assistance: both the type of assistance and the conditions attached to it will vary. Government assistance may have encouraged an entity to undertake something it would not otherwise have done.

How will the receipt of government assistance affect the financial statements?

(a) An appropriate method must be found to account for any **resources transferred**.
(b) The extent to which an entity has **benefited** from such assistance during the reporting period should be shown.

An entity should not recognise government grants (including non-monetary grants at fair value) until it has **reasonable assurance** that:

• The entity will comply with any **conditions** attached to the grant
• The entity will **actually receive** the grant

Even if the grant has been received, this does not prove that the conditions attached to it have been or will be fulfilled.

It makes no difference in the treatment of the grant whether it is received in cash or given as a reduction in a liability to government, ie the **manner of receipt is irrelevant**.

Any related **contingency** should be recognised under *IAS 37 Provisions, contingent liabilities and contingent assets*, once the grant has been recognised.

In the case of a **forgivable loan** (as defined in the key terms above) from government, it should be treated in the same way as a government grant when it is reasonably assured that the entity will meet the relevant terms for forgiveness.

Accounting treatment of government grants

There are two methods which could be used to account for government grants, and the arguments for each are given in IAS 20.

Capital approach	Income approach
Credit the grant directly to shareholders' interests.	The grant is credited to the income statement over one or more periods.

The standard gives the following arguments in support of each method.

Capital approach

(a) The grants are a **financing device**, so should go through the statement of financial position. In the income statement they would simply offset the expenses which they are financing. No repayment is expected by the Government, so the grants should be credited directly to shareholders' interests.
(b) Grants are **not earned**, they are incentives without related costs, so it would be wrong to take them to the income statement.

Income approach

(a) The grants are **not received from shareholders** so should not be credited directly to shareholders' interests.

(b)   Grants are **not given or received for nothing**. They are earned by compliance with conditions and by meeting obligations. There are therefore associated costs with which the grant can be matched in the income statement as these costs are being compensated by the grant.

(c)   Grants are an extension of **fiscal policies** and so as income taxes and other taxes are charged against income, so grants should be credited to income.

IAS 20 requires grants to be recognised under the income approach, ie grants are recognised as income over the relevant periods to match them with related costs which they have been received to compensate. This should be done on a systematic basis. **Grants should not, therefore, be credited directly to shareholders' interests**.

It would be against the accruals assumption to credit grants to income on a receipts basis, so a **systematic basis of matching** must be used. A receipts basis would only be acceptable if no other basis was available.

It will usually be easy to identify the **costs related to a government grant**, and thereby the period(s) in which the grant should be recognised as income, ie when the costs are incurred. Where grants are received in relation to a depreciating asset, the grant will be recognised over the periods in which the asset is depreciated and in the same proportions.

In the case of **grants for non-depreciable assets**, certain obligations may need to be fulfilled, in which case the grant should be recognised as income over the periods in which the cost of meeting the obligation is incurred. For example, if a piece of land is granted on condition that a building is erected on it, then the grant should be recognised as income over the building's life.

There may be a **series of conditions** attached to a grant, in the nature of a package of financial aid. An entity must take care to identify precisely those conditions which give rise to costs which in turn determine the periods over which the grant will be earned. When appropriate, the grant may be split and the parts allocated on different bases.

An entity may receive a grant as compensation for expenses or losses which it has **already incurred**. Alternatively, a grant may be given to an entity simply to provide immediate financial support where no future related costs are expected. In cases such as these, the grant received should be recognised as income of the period in which it becomes receivable.

Presentation of grants related to assets

There are two choices here for how government grants related to assets (including non-monetary grants at fair value) should be shown in the statement of financial position.

(a)   Set up the grant as **deferred income**.

(b)   **Deduct the grant** in arriving at the carrying amount of the asset.

Whichever of these methods is used, the **cash flows** in relation to the purchase of the asset and the receipt of the grant are often disclosed separately because of the significance of the movements in cash flow.

Example

On 1 January 20X8, X Co purchased a non-current asset for cash of $100,000 and received a grant of $20,000 towards the cost of the asset. X Co's accounting policy is to treat the grant as deferred income. The asset has a useful life of 5 years.

What will be the accounting entries to record the asset and the grant in the year ended 31 December 20X8?

Acquisition of the asset and receipt of the grant on 1 January 20X8:

DR Non-current assets	$100,000
CR Cash	$100,000

– to record the asset at its cost

DR Cash	$20,000
CR Deferred income	$20,000

– to record the receipt of the grant

In the year ended 31 December 20X8 the asset is depreciated and a portion of the grant is released to the income statement:

DR Depreciation expense ($100,000 / 5 years)	$20,000
CR Accumulated depreciation	$20,000
DR Deferred income ($20,000 / 5 years)	$4,000
CR Operating expenses	$4,000

The release of the deferred income is matched to the depreciation expense, so the net effect is an expense of **$16,000** relating to the asset.

If X Co had deducted the grant from the carrying amount of the asset, the net expense would have been:

	$	
Cost of asset	100,000	
Less grant received	(20,000)	
Carrying amount	80,000	
Depreciation (80,000 / 5 years)	**16,000**	Same result

Presentation of grants related to income

These grants are a credit to profit or loss, but there is a choice in the method of disclosure.

Method (a)	Method (b) Income approach
Present as a separate credit or under a general heading, eg 'other income'	Deduct from the related expense.

Some would argue that offsetting income and expenses in the in profit or loss for the year is not good practice. Others would say that the expenses would not have been incurred had the grant not been available, so offsetting the two is acceptable. Although both methods are acceptable, disclosure of the grant may be necessary for a **proper understanding** of the financial statements, particularly the effect on any item of income or expense which is required to be separately disclosed.

Repayment of government grants

If a grant must be repaid it should be accounted for as a revision of an accounting estimate (see IAS 8 Chapter 6).

Repayment of a grant related to income	Repayment of a grant related to an asset
• Apply first against any unamortised deferred income set up in respect of the grant. • Any excess should be recognised immediately as an expense.	• Increase the carrying amount of the asset or reduce the deferred income balance by the amount repayable. • The cumulative additional depreciation that would have been recognised to date in the absence of the grant should be immediately recognised as an expense.

It is possible that the circumstances surrounding repayment may require a review of the **asset value** and an impairment of the new carrying amount of the asset.

Disclosure is required of the following.

- **Accounting policy** adopted, including method of presentation
- **Nature and extent** of government grants recognised and other forms of assistance received
- **Unfulfilled conditions and other contingencies** attached to recognised government assistance

The IASB is intending to amend IAS 20 but the project is currently deferred. It is unhappy with the following aspects:

- Grants being treated as a deferred credit when there is no liability. This is not consistent with the Framework.
- IAS 20 allows alternative treatments, which does not enhance comparability
- The option to deduct the grant from the carrying amount of the asset results in understatement of assets.

SIC 10 Government assistance – no specific relation to operating activities

In some countries government assistance to entities may be aimed at encouragement or long-term support of business activities either in certain regions or industry sectors. Conditions to receive such assistance may not be specifically related to the operating activities of the entity. Examples of such assistance are transfers of resources by governments to entities which:

(a) Operate in a particular industry
(b) Continue operating in recently privatised industries
(c) Start or continue to run their business in underdeveloped areas

The issue is whether such government assistance is a 'government grant' within the scope of IAS 20 and, therefore, should be accounted for in accordance with this standard.

Government assistance to entities meets the definition of government grants in IAS 20, even if there are no conditions specifically relating to the operating activities of the entity other than the requirement to operate in certain regions or industry sectors. Such grants should therefore not be credited directly to equity.

3 IAS 40: Investment property

Consider the following definitions.

Investment property is property (land or a building – or part of a building – or both) held (by the owner or by the lessee under a finance lease) to earn rentals or for capital appreciation or both, rather than for:

(a) Use in the production or supply of goods or services or for administrative purposes, or

(b) Sale in the ordinary course of business

Owner-occupied property is property held by the owner (or by the lessee under a finance lease) for use in the production or supply of goods or services or for administrative purposes.

Fair value is the amount for which an asset could be exchanged between knowledgeable, willing parties in an arm's length transaction.

Cost is the amount of cash or cash equivalents paid or the fair value of other consideration given to acquire an asset at the time of its acquisition or construction.

Carrying amount is the amount at which an asset is recognised in the statement of financial position.

A property interest that is held by a lessee under an **operating lease** may be classified and accounted for as an **investment property**, if and only if the property would otherwise meet the definition of an investment property and the lessee uses the IAS 40 **fair value model**. This classification is available on a property-by-property basis.

Examples of investment property include:

(a) **Land held for long-term capital appreciation** rather than for short-term sale in the ordinary course of business

(b) A **building** owned by the reporting entity (or held by the entity under a finance lease) and **leased out under an operating lease**

A company owns a piece of land. The directors have not yet decided whether to build a factory on it for use in its business or to keep it and sell it when its value has risen.

Would this be classified as an investment property under IAS 40?

Yes under IAS 40 para 8. If an entity has not determined that it will use the land either as an owner-occupied property or for short-term sale in the ordinary course of business, the land is considered as being held for capital appreciation.

IAS 40 was published in March 2000 and has recently been revised. Its objective is to prescribe the accounting treatment for investment property and related disclosure requirements.

Below are examples of things that are **not investment property** under IAS 40.

Type of non-investment property	Applicable IAS
Property intended for sale in the ordinary course of business	IAS 2 *Inventories*
Property being constructed or developed on behalf of third parties	IAS 11 *Construction contracts*
Owner-occupied property	IAS 16 *Property, plant and equipment*
Property leased to another entity under a finance lease	IAS 11 *Leases*

Investment property should be recognised as an asset when two conditions are met.

(a)   It is probable that the future economic benefits that are associated with the investment property will flow to the entity
(b)   The cost of the investment property can be measured reliably

Initial measurement

An investment property should be measured initially at its **cost**, including transaction costs.

A property interest held under a lease and classified as an investment property shall be accounted for **as if it were a finance lease**. The asset is recognised at the lower of the fair value of the property and the present value of the minimum lease payments. An equivalent amount is recognised as a liability.

Measurement subsequent to initial recognition

IAS 40 requires an entity to **choose between two models**.
*   **The fair value model**
*   **The cost model**

Whatever policy it chooses should be applied to **all of its investment property**.

Where an entity chooses to classify a property held under an **operating lease** as an investment property, there is **no choice**. The **fair value model must be used** for **all the entity's investment property**, regardless of whether it is owned or leased.

Fair value model

(a)   After initial recognition, an entity that chooses the **fair value model** should measure all of its investment property at fair value, except in the extremely rare cases where this cannot be measured reliably. In such cases it should apply the IAS 16 cost model.
(b)   A gain or loss arising from a change in the fair value of an investment property should be recognised in net profit or loss for the period in which it arises.
(c)   The fair value of investment property should reflect market conditions at the reporting date.

This was the first time that the IASB has allowed a fair value model for non-financial assets. This is not the same as a revaluation, where increases in carrying amount above a cost-based measure are recognised as revaluation surplus. Under the fair-value model all changes in fair value are recognised in profit or loss.

The standard elaborates on **issues relating to fair value**.

(a)   Fair value assumes that an arm's length transaction has taken place between **'knowledgeable, willing parties'**, ie both buyer and seller are reasonably informed about the nature and characteristics of the investment property.

(b)   A willing buyer is **motivated but not compelled** to buy. A willing seller is neither an over-eager nor a forced seller, nor one prepared to sell at any price or to hold out for a price not considered reasonable in the current market.

(c)   **Fair value is not the same as 'value in use'** as defined in IAS 36 *Impairment of assets*. Value in use reflects factors and knowledge specific to the entity, while fair value reflects factors and knowledge relevant to the market.

(d)   In determining fair value an entity **should not double count assets**. For example, elevators or air conditioning are often an integral part of a building and should be included in the investment property, rather than recognised separately.

(e)   In those rare cases where the **entity cannot determine the fair value of an investment property reliably**, the cost model in **IAS 16** must be applied until the investment property is disposed of. The **residual value must be assumed to be zero**.

The cost model is the **cost model in IAS 16**. Investment property should be measured at **depreciated cost, less any accumulated impairment losses**. An entity that chooses the cost model should **disclose the fair value of its investment property**.

Once the entity has chosen the fair value or cost model, it should apply it to all of its investment property. It **should not change from one model to the other unless the change will result in a more appropriate presentation**. IAS 40 states that it is highly unlikely that a change from the fair value model to the cost model will result in a more appropriate presentation.

Transfers

Transfers to or from investment property should **only** be made **when there is a change in use**. For example, owner occupation commences so the investment property will be treated under IAS 16 as an owner-occupied property.

When there is a transfer from investment property carried at fair value to owner-occupied property or inventories, the property's cost for subsequent accounting under IAS 16 or IAS 2 should be its fair value at the date of change of use.

Conversely, an owner-occupied property may become an investment property and need to be carried at fair value. An entity should apply IAS 16 up to the date of change of use. It should treat any difference at that date between the carrying amount of the property under IAS 16 and its fair value as a revaluation under IAS 16.

An investment property should be derecognised on disposal or when it is permanently withdrawn from use and no future economic benefits are expected from its disposal.

Any **gain or loss** on disposal is the difference between the net disposal proceeds and the carrying amount of the asset. It should generally be **recognised as income or expense in profit or loss**.

Disclosure requirements

These relate to:

- Choice of fair value model or cost model
- Whether property interests held as operating leases are included in investment property
- Criteria for classification as investment property
- Assumptions in determining fair value
- Use of independent professional valuer (encouraged but not required)
- Rental income and expenses
- Any restrictions or obligations

An entity that adopts the fair value model must also disclose a reconciliation of the carrying amount of the investment property at the beginning and end of the period.

4 IAS 36: Impairment of assets

There is an established principle that assets should not be carried at more than their recoverable amount. An entity should write down the carrying value of an asset to its recoverable amount if the carrying value of an asset is not recoverable in full. IAS 36 puts in place a detailed methodology for carrying out impairment reviews and related accounting treatments and disclosures.

IAS 36 applies to all tangible, intangible and financial assets **except** inventories, assets arising from construction contracts, deferred tax assets, assets arising under IAS 19 *Employee benefits* and financial assets within the scope of IAS 32 *Financial instruments: Presentation*. This is because those IASs already have rules for recognising and measuring impairment. Note also that IAS 36 does not apply to non-current assets held for sale, which are dealt with under IFRS 5 *Non-current assets held for sale and discontinued operations*.

- **Impairment**: a fall in the value of an asset, so that its 'recoverable amount' is now less than its carrying amount in the statement of financial position.
- **Carrying amount**: is the net value at which the asset is included in the statement of financial position (ie after deducting accumulated depreciation and any impairment losses). (IAS 36)

The basic principle underlying IAS 36 is relatively straightforward. If an asset's value in the accounts is higher than its realistic value, measured as its 'recoverable amount', the asset is judged to have suffered an impairment loss. It should therefore be reduced in value, by the amount of the impairment loss. The amount of the **impairment loss** should be **written off against profit** immediately.

The main accounting issues to consider are therefore as follows.

- (a) How is it possible to **identify when** an impairment loss may have occurred?
- (b) How should the **recoverable amount** of the asset be measured?
- (c) How should an 'impairment loss' be **reported in the accounts**?

Identifying a potentially impaired asset

An entity should assess at each year end whether there are any indications of impairment to any assets. The concept of **materiality** applies, and only material impairment needs to be identified.

If there are indications of possible impairment, the entity is required to make a formal estimate of the **recoverable amount** of the assets concerned.

IAS 36 suggests how **indications of a possible impairment** of assets might be recognised. The suggestions are based largely on common sense.

(a) **External sources of information**
  (i) A fall in the asset's market value that is more significant than would normally be expected from passage of time over normal use.
  (ii) A significant change in the technological, market, legal or economic environment of the business in which the assets are employed.
  (iii) An increase in market interest rates or market rates of return on investments likely to affect the discount rate used in calculating value in use.
  (iv) The carrying amount of the entity's net assets being more than its market capitalisation.

(b) **Internal sources of information**: evidence of obsolescence or physical damage, adverse changes in the use to which the asset is put, or the asset's economic performance

Even if there are no indications of impairment, the following assets must **always** be tested for impairment annually.

(a) An intangible asset with an **indefinite useful life**
(b) **Goodwill** acquired in a business combination

Measuring the recoverable amount of the asset

What is an asset's recoverable amount?

> The **recoverable amount of an asset** should be measured as the higher value of:
>
> (a) The asset's fair value less costs to sell; and
> (b) Its value in use. (IAS 36)

An asset's fair value less costs to sell is the amount net of selling costs that could be obtained from the sale of the asset. Selling costs include sales transaction costs, such as legal expenses.

(a) If there is **an active market** in the asset, the net selling price should be based on the **market value**, or on the price of recent transactions in similar assets.
(b) If there is **no active market** in the assets it might be possible to **estimate** a net selling price using best estimates of what 'knowledgeable, willing parties' might pay in an arm's length transaction.

Net selling price **cannot** be reduced, however, by including within selling costs any **restructuring or reorganisation expenses**, or any costs that have already been recognised in the accounts as liabilities.

The concept of 'value in use' is very important.

> The **value in use** of an asset is measured as the present value of estimated future cash flows (inflows minus outflows) generated by the asset, including its estimated net disposal value (if any) at the end of its expected useful life.   *(IAS 36)*

The cash flows used in the calculation should be **pre-tax cash flows** and a **pre-tax discount rate** should be applied to calculate the present value.

The calculation of **value in use** must reflect the following.

(a)   An estimate of the **future cash flows** the entity expects to derive from the asset
(b)   Expectations about **possible variations** in the amount and timing of future cash flows
(c)   The **time value of money**
(d)   The price for bearing the **uncertainty** inherent in the asset, and
(e)   **Other factors** that would be reflected in pricing future cash flows from the asset

Calculating a value in use therefore calls for estimates of future cash flows, and the possibility exists that an entity might come up with over-optimistic estimates of cash flows. The IAS therefore states the following.

(a)   Cash flow projections should be based on **'reasonable and supportable'** **assumptions**.
(b)   Projections of cash flows, normally up to a maximum period of five years, should be based on the most **recent budgets or financial forecasts**.
(c)   Cash flow projections beyond this period should be obtained by extrapolating short-term projections, using either a **steady or declining growth rate** for each subsequent year (unless a rising growth rate can be justified). The long term growth rate applied should not exceed the average long term growth rate for the product, market, industry or country, unless a higher growth rate can be justified.

Composition of estimates of future cash flows

These should include the following.

(a)   Projections of **cash inflows** from **continuing use** of the asset
(b)   Projections of **cash outflows** necessarily incurred to **generate the cash inflows** from continuing use of the asset
(c)   **Net cash flows** received/paid on **disposal** of the asset at the end of its useful life

There is an underlying principle that future cash flows should be estimated for the asset in its current condition. Future cash flows relating to restructurings to which the entity is not yet committed, or to future costs to add to, replace part of, or service the asset are excluded.

Estimates of future cash flows should exclude the following.

(a)   Cash inflows/outflows from financing activities
(b)   Income tax receipts/payments

The amount of net cash inflow/outflow on **disposal** of an asset should assume an arm's length transaction.

Foreign currency future cash flows should be forecast in the currency in which they will arise and will be discounted using a rate appropriate for that currency. The resulting figure should then be translated into the reporting currency at the spot rate at the end of the reporting period.

The **discount rate** should be a current pre-tax rate (or rates) that reflects the current assessment of the time value of money and the risks specific to the asset. The discount rate should not include a risk weighting if the underlying cash flows have already been adjusted for risk.

Recognition and measurement of an impairment loss

The rule for assets at historical cost is:

> If the recoverable amount of an asset is lower than the carrying amount, the carrying amount should be reduced by the difference (ie the impairment loss) which should be charged as an expense in the income statement.

The rule for assets held at a revalued amount (such as property revalued under IAS 16) is:

> The impairment loss is to be treated as a revaluation decrease under the relevant IAS.

In practice this means:

*   To the extent that there is a revaluation surplus held in respect of the asset, the impairment loss should be charged to revaluation surplus.
*   Any excess should be charged to the income statement.

If it is not possible to calculate the recoverable amount for an individual asset, the recoverable amount of the asset's cash generating unit should be measured instead.

> A **cash generating unit** is the smallest identifiable group of assets for which independent cash flows can be identified and measured.

How would a cash generating unit be identified?

Here are two possibilities.

(a)   A mining company owns a private railway that it uses to transport output from one of its mines. The railway now has no market value other than as scrap, and it is impossible to identify any separate cash inflows with the use of the railway itself. Consequently, if the mining company suspects an impairment in the value of the railway, it should treat the mine as a whole as a cash generating unit, and measure the recoverable amount of the mine as a whole.

(b)   A bus company has an arrangement with a town's authorities to run a bus service on four routes in the town. Separately identifiable assets are allocated to each of the bus routes, and cash inflows and outflows can be attributed to each individual route. Three routes are running at a profit and one is running at a loss. The bus company suspects that there is an impairment of assets on the loss-making route. However, the company will be unable to close the loss-making route, because it is under an obligation to operate all four routes, as part of its contract with the local authority. Consequently, the company should treat all four bus routes together as a cash generating unit, and calculate the recoverable amount for the unit as a whole.

If an active market exists for the output produced by the asset or a group of assets, this asset or group should be identified as a cash generating unit, even if some or all of the output is used internally.

Cash generating units should be identified consistently from period to period for the same type of asset unless a change is justified.

The group of net assets less liabilities that are considered for impairment should be the same as those considered in the calculation of the recoverable amount.

Goodwill and the impairment of assets

Goodwill acquired in a business combination does not generate cash flows independently of other assets. It must be **allocated** to each of the acquirer's **cash-generating units** (or groups of cash-generating units) that are expected to benefit from the synergies of the combination. Each unit to which the goodwill is so allocated should:

(a)   Represent the **lowest level** within the entity at which the goodwill is monitored for internal management purposes

(b)   Not be **larger than a reporting segment** determined in accordance with IFRS 8 *Operating Segments* (Chapter 18)

It may be impractical to complete the allocation of goodwill before the first reporting date after a business combination, particularly if the acquirer is accounting for the combination for the first time using provisional values. The initial allocation of goodwill must be completed before the end of the first reporting period after the acquisition date.

There are two situations to consider.

(a)   Where goodwill has been allocated to a cash-generating unit

(b)   Where it has not been possible to allocate goodwill to a specific cash-generating unit, but only to a group of units

A cash-generating unit to which goodwill has been allocated is tested for impairment annually. The **carrying amount** of the unit, including goodwill, is compared **with the recoverable amount**. If the carrying amount of the unit exceeds the recoverable amount, the entity must recognise an impairment loss.

Where goodwill relates to a cash-generating unit but has not been allocated to that unit, the unit is tested for impairment by **comparing its carrying amount** (excluding goodwill) **with its recoverable amount**. The entity must recognise an impairment loss if the carrying amount exceeds the recoverable amount.

The annual impairment test may be performed at any time during an accounting period, but must be performed at the **same time every year**.

Corporate assets

Corporate assets are group or divisional assets such as a head office building, computer equipment or a research centre. Essentially, corporate assets are assets that do not generate cash inflows independently from other assets, hence their carrying amount cannot be fully attributed to a cash-generating unit under review.

In testing a cash generating unit for impairment, an entity should identify all the corporate assets that relate to the cash-generating unit.

(a)   If a portion of the carrying amount of a corporate asset **can be allocated** to the unit on a reasonable and consistent basis, the entity compares the carrying amount of the unit (including the portion of the asset) with its recoverable amount.

(b)   If a portion of the carrying amount of a corporate asset **cannot be allocated** to the unit on a reasonable and consistent basis, the entity:

(i) Compares the carrying amount of the unit (excluding the asset) with its recoverable amount and recognises any impairment loss

(ii) Identifies the smallest group of cash-generating units that includes the cash-generating unit to which the asset belongs and to which a portion of the carrying amount of the asset can be allocated on a reasonable and consistent basis

(iii) Compares the carrying amount of that group of cash-generating units (including the portion of the asset allocated to the group of units) with the recoverable amount of the group of units and recognises any impairment loss

Accounting treatment of an impairment loss

If, and only if, the recoverable amount of an asset is less than its carrying amount in the statement of financial position, an impairment loss has occurred. This loss should be **recognised immediately**.

(a) The asset's **carrying amount** should be reduced to its recoverable amount in the statement of financial position.

(b) The **impairment loss** should be recognised immediately in the income statement (unless the asset has been revalued in which case the loss is treated as a revaluation decrease).

After reducing an asset to its recoverable amount, the **depreciation charge** on the asset should then be based on its new carrying amount, its estimated residual value (if any) and its estimated remaining useful life.

An impairment loss should be recognised for a **cash generating unit** if (and only if) the recoverable amount for the cash generating unit is less than the carrying amount in the statement of financial position for all the assets in the unit. When an impairment loss is recognised for a cash generating unit, the loss should be allocated between the assets in the unit in the following order.

(a) First, to the goodwill allocated to the cash generating unit

(b) Then to all other assets in the cash-generating unit, on a pro rata basis

In allocating an impairment loss, the carrying amount of an asset should not be reduced below the highest of:

(a) Its fair value less costs to sell

(b) Its value in use (if determinable)

(c) Zero

Any remaining amount of an impairment loss should be recognised as a liability if required by other IASs.

Example 1: impairment loss

A company that extracts natural gas and oil has a drilling platform in the Caspian Sea. It is required by legislation of the country concerned to remove and dismantle the platform at the end of its useful life. Accordingly, the company has included an amount in its accounts for removal and dismantling costs, and is depreciating this amount over the platform's expected life.

The company is carrying out an exercise to establish whether there has been an impairment of the platform.

(a) Its carrying amount in the statement of financial position is $3m.
(b) The company has received an offer of $2.8m for the platform from another oil company. The bidder would take over the responsibility (and costs) for dismantling and removing the platform at the end of its life.
(c) The present value of the estimated cash flows from the platform's continued use is $3.3m.
(d) The carrying amount in the statement of financial position for the provision for dismantling and removal is currently $0.6m.

What should be the value of the drilling platform in the statement of financial position, and what, if anything, is the impairment loss?

Fair value less costs to sell	=	$2.8m
Value in use	=	PV of cash flows from use less the carrying amount of the provision/liability
	=	$3.3m –$0.6m
	=	$2.7m
Recoverable amount	=	Higher of these two amounts, ie $2.8m
Carrying value	=	$3m
Impairment loss	=	$0.2m

The carrying value should be reduced to $2.8m

Example 2: impairment loss

A company has acquired another business for $4.5m: tangible assets are valued at $4.0m and goodwill at $0.5m.

An asset with a carrying value of $1m is destroyed in a terrorist attack. The asset was not insured. The loss of the asset, without insurance, has prompted the company to assess whether there has been an impairment of assets in the acquired business and what the amount of any such loss is.

The recoverable amount of the business (a single cash generating unit) is measured as $3.1m.

There has been an impairment loss of $1.4m ($4.5m – $3.1m).

The impairment loss will be recognised in profit or loss. The loss will be allocated between the assets in the cash generating unit as follows.

(a) A loss of $1m can be attributed directly to the uninsured asset that has been destroyed.
(b) The remaining loss of $0.4m should be allocated to goodwill.

The carrying value of the assets will now be $3m for tangible assets and $0.1m for goodwill.

Reversal of an impairment loss

The annual assessment to determine whether there may have been some impairment should be **applied to all assets**, including assets that have already been impaired in the past.

In some cases, the recoverable amount of an asset that has previously been impaired might turn out to be **higher** than the asset's current carrying value. In other words, there might have been a reversal of some of the previous impairment loss.

(a) The reversal of the impairment loss should be **recognised immediately** as income in the profit or loss.

(b) The carrying amount of the asset should be increased to its **new recoverable amount**.

> An impairment loss recognised for an asset in prior years should be reversed if, and only if, there has been a change in the estimates used to determine the asset's recoverable amount since the last impairment loss was recognised.   *(IAS 36)*

The asset cannot be revalued to a carrying amount that is higher than its value would have been if the asset had not been impaired originally, ie its **depreciated carrying value** had the impairment not taken place. Depreciation of the asset should now be based on its new revalued amount, its estimated residual value (if any) and its estimated remaining useful life.

An exception to this rule is for **goodwill**. An impairment loss for goodwill should not be reversed in a subsequent period.

Disclosure

IAS 36 calls for substantial disclosure about impairment of assets. The information to be disclosed includes the following.

(a) For each class of assets, the amount of **impairment losses recognised** and the amount of any **impairment losses recovered** (ie reversals of impairment losses)

(b) For each individual asset or cash generating unit that has suffered a **significant impairment loss**, details of the nature of the asset, the amount of the loss, the events that led to recognition of the loss, whether the recoverable amount is fair value less costs to sell or value in use, and if the recoverable amount is value in use, the basis on which this value was estimated (eg the discount rate applied)

An entity may receive monetary or non-monetary compensation from third parties for the impairment or loss of items of property, plant and equipment. The compensation may be used to restore the asset. Examples include:

*   Reimbursement by insurance companies after an impairment of items of plant and equipment
*   Physical replacement of an impaired or lost asset

The accounting treatment is as follows.

(a) Impairments of items of property, plant and equipment should be recognised under IAS 36, disposals should be recognised under IAS 16.

(b) Monetary or non-monetary compensation from third parties for items of property etc that were impaired, lost or given up, should be included in the profit or loss.

(c) The cost of assets restored, purchased, constructed as a replacement or received as compensation should be determined and presented under IAS 16.

5 IAS 23: Borrowing costs

IAS 23 *Borrowing costs* was revised in March 2007. Previously it gave a choice of methods in dealing with borrowing costs: capitalisation or expense. The revised standard requires capitalisation.

Only two definitions are given by the standard.

> • **Borrowing costs**. Interest and other costs incurred by an entity in connection with the borrowing of funds.
> • **Qualifying asset**. An asset that necessarily takes a substantial period of time to get ready for its intended use or sale. *(IAS 23)*

The standard lists what may be **included in borrowing costs**.

- Interest expense calculated using the effective interest rate method as per IAS 39
- Finance charges in respect of finance leases recognised in accordance with IAS 17
- Exchange differences arising from foreign currency borrowings to the extent that they are regarded as an adjustment to interest costs

Depending on the circumstances, any of the following may be qualifying assets.

- Inventories
- Manufacturing plants
- Power generation facilities
- Intangible assets
- Investment properties

Financial assets and inventories that are manufactured or otherwise produced over a short period of time are **not qualifying assets**. Assets that are ready for their intended use or sale when purchased are not qualifying assets.

Recognition

Borrowing costs should be capitalised if they are directly attributable to the acquisition, construction or production of a qualifying asset as part of its cost. Other borrowing costs are expensed as incurred.

Those borrowing costs directly attributable to the acquisition, construction or production of a qualifying asset are costs that **would have been avoided** had the expenditure on the qualifying asset not been made. This is obviously straightforward where funds have been borrowed for the financing of one particular asset.

Difficulties arise, however, where the entity uses a **range of debt instruments** to finance a wide range of assets, so that there is no direct relationship between particular borrowings and a specific asset. For example, all borrowings may be made centrally and then lent to different parts of the group or entity. Judgement is therefore required, particularly where further complications can arise (eg foreign currency loans).

Once the relevant borrowings are identified, which relate to a specific asset, then the **amount of borrowing costs eligible for capitalisation** will be the actual borrowing costs incurred on those borrowings during the period, *less* any investment income on the temporary investment of those borrowings. It would not be unusual for some or all of the funds to be invested before they are actually used on the qualifying asset.

Example

On 1 January 20X9 a company borrowed $1.5m to finance the production of two assets, both of which were expected to take a year to build. Production started during 20X9. The loan facility was drawn down on 1 January 20X9, and was utilised as follows, with the remaining funds invested temporarily.

	Asset A $'000	Asset B $'000
1 January 20X9	250	500
1 July 20X9	250	500

The loan rate was 9% and the company can invest surplus funds at 7%.

Ignoring compound interest, what are the borrowing costs which may be capitalised for each of the assets and consequently the cost of each asset as at 31 December 20X9?

		Asset A $	Asset B $
Borrowing costs			
To 31 December 20X9	$500,000/$1,000,000 × 9%	45,000	90,000
Less investment income			
To 30 June 20X9	$250,000/$500,000 × 7% × 6/12	(8,750)	(17,500)
		36,250	72,500
Cost of assets			
Expenditure incurred		500,000	1,000,000
Borrowing costs		36,250	72,500
		536,250	1,072,500

In a situation where **borrowings are obtained generally**, but are applied in part to obtaining a qualifying asset, then the amount of borrowing costs eligible for capitalisation is found by applying the 'capitalisation rate' to the expenditure on the asset.

The **capitalisation rate** is the weighted average of the borrowing costs applicable to the entity's borrowings that are outstanding during the period, excluding borrowings made specifically to obtain a qualifying asset. However, there is a cap on the amount of borrowing costs calculated in this way: it must not exceed actual borrowing costs incurred.

Sometimes one overall weighted average can be calculated for a group or entity, but in some situations it may be more appropriate to use a weighted average for borrowing costs for **individual parts of the group or entity**.

Example

A company had the following loans in place at the beginning and end of 20X6.

	1 January 20X6	31 December 20X6
	$	$
10% Bank loan repayable 20X8	120	120
9.5% Bank loan repayable 20X9	80	80
8.9% debenture repayable 20X7	–	150

The 8.9% debenture was issued to fund the construction of a qualifying asset (a piece of mining equipment), construction of which began on 1 July 20X6.

On 1 January 20X6, the company began construction of a qualifying asset, a piece of machinery for a hydro-electric plant, using existing borrowings. Expenditure drawn down for the construction was: $30m on 1 January 20X6, $20m on 1 October 20X6.

What are the borrowing costs to be capitalised for the hydro-electric plant machine?

Capitalisation rate = weighted average rate

$$= (10\% \times \frac{120}{120 + 80}) + (9.5\% \times \frac{80}{120 + 80})$$

$$= 9.8\%$$

Borrowing costs $= (\$30m \times 9.8\%) + (\$20m \times 9.8\% \times 3/12)$

$$= \$3.43m$$

Commencement of capitalisation

An entity can start to capitalise borrowing costs on the **commencement date**. This is the date when the following conditions are met:

(a) Expenditure on the asset is being incurred
(b) Borrowing costs are being incurred
(c) Activities are undertaken that are necessary to prepare the asset for its intended use or sale

Expenditure must result in the payment of cash, transfer of other assets or assumption of interest-bearing liabilities. **Deductions from expenditure** will be made for any progress payments or grants received in connection with the asset. IAS 23 allows the **average carrying amount** of the asset during a period (including borrowing costs previously capitalised) to be used as a reasonable approximation of the expenditure to which the capitalisation rate is applied in the period. Presumably more exact calculations can be used.

Activities necessary to prepare the asset for its intended sale or use extend further than physical construction work. They encompass technical and administrative work prior to construction, eg obtaining permits. They do not include holding an asset when no production or development that changes the asset's condition is taking place, eg where land is held without any associated development activity.

Cessation of capitalisation

Once substantially all the activities necessary to prepare the qualifying asset for its intended use or sale are complete, then capitalisation of borrowing costs should cease. This will normally be when **physical construction of the asset is completed**, although minor modifications may still be outstanding.

The asset may be completed in **parts or stages**, where each part can be used while construction is still taking place on the other parts. Capitalisation of borrowing costs should cease for each part as it is completed. The example given by the standard is a business park consisting of several buildings.

Disclosures

The following should be disclosed in the financial statements in relation to borrowing costs.

(a)   Amount of borrowing costs **capitalised during the period**
(b)   **Capitalisation rate** used to determine the amount of borrowing costs eligible for capitalisation

1 IAS 38: Intangible assets

IAS 38 *Intangible assets* was originally published in September 1998. It has recently been revised to reflect changes introduced by the revision of IFRS 3 *Business combinations*. The objectives of the standard are:

(a)   To establish the criteria for when an intangible asset may or should be **recognised**
(b)   To specify how intangible assets should be **measured**
(c)   To specify the **disclosure requirements** for intangible assets

IAS 38 applies to all intangible assets with certain **exceptions**: deferred tax assets (IAS 12), leases that fall within the scope of IAS 17, financial assets, insurance contracts, assets arising from employee benefits (IAS 19), non-current assets held for sale, and mineral rights and exploration and extraction costs for minerals (although *some* of this material *is covered* by IAS 38). It does *not* apply to goodwill acquired in a business combination, which is dealt with under IFRS 3 *Business combinations*.

Definition

The definition of an intangible asset is a key aspect of the standard, because the rules for deciding whether or not an intangible asset may be **recognised** in the accounts of an entity are based on the definition of what an intangible asset is.

> An **intangible asset** is an identifiable non-monetary asset without physical substance The asset must be:
>
> (a)   controlled by the entity as a result of events in the past, and
>
> (b)   something from which the entity expects future economic benefits to flow.
>
> *(IAS 38)*

Examples of items that might be considered as intangible assets include computer software, patents, copyrights, motion picture films, customer lists, franchises and fishing rights. An item should not be recognised as an intangible asset, however, unless it **fully meets the definition** in the standard. The guidelines go into great detail on this matter.

An intangible asset must be identifiable in order to distinguish it from goodwill. With non-physical items, there may be a problem with 'identifiability'.

(a)   If an intangible asset is **acquired separately through purchase**, there may be a transfer of a legal right that would help to make an asset identifiable.
(b)   An intangible asset may be identifiable if it is **separable**, ie if it could be rented or sold separately. However, 'separability' is not an essential feature of an intangible asset.

Another element of the definition of an intangible asset is that it must be under the control of the entity as a result of a past event. The entity must therefore be able to enjoy the future economic benefits from the asset, and prevent the access of others to those benefits. A **legally enforceable right** is evidence of such control, but is not always a necessary condition.

(a)   Control over **technical knowledge or know-how** only exists if it is protected by a **legal right**.

(b)   The skill of employees, arising out of the benefits of **training costs**, are most unlikely to be recognisable as an intangible asset, because an entity does not control the future actions of its staff.

(c)   Similarly, **market share and customer loyalty** cannot normally be intangible assets, since an entity cannot control the actions of its customers.

Expected future economic benefits

An item can only be recognised as an intangible asset if economic benefits are expected to flow in the future from ownership of the asset. Economic benefits may come from the **sale** of products or services, or from a reduction in expenditures (cost savings).

An intangible asset, when recognised initially, must be measured at **cost**. It should be recognised if, and only if **both** the following occur.

(a)   It is probable that the **future economic benefits** that are attributable to the asset will **flow to the entity**.

(b)   The **cost can be measured reliably**.

Management has to exercise its judgement in assessing the degree of certainty attached to the flow of economic benefits to the entity. External evidence is best.

(a)   If an intangible asset is **acquired separately**, its cost can usually be measured reliably as its purchase price (including incidental costs of purchase such as legal fees, and any costs incurred in getting the asset ready for use).

(b)   When an intangible asset is acquired as **part of a business combination** (ie an acquisition or takeover), the cost of the intangible asset is its fair value at the date of the acquisition.

IFRS 3 explains that the fair value of intangible assets acquired in business combinations can normally be measured with sufficient reliability to be **recognised separately** from goodwill.

Quoted market prices in an active market provide the most reliable estimate of the fair value of an intangible asset. If no active market exists for an intangible asset, its fair value is the amount that the entity would have paid for the asset, at the acquisition date, in an arm's length transaction between knowledgeable and willing parties, on the basis of the best information available. In determining this amount, an entity should consider the outcome of recent transactions for similar assets. There are techniques for estimating the fair values of unique intangible assets (such as brand names) and these may be used to measure an intangible asset acquired in a business combination.

In accordance with IAS 20, intangible assets acquired by way of government grant and the grant itself may be recorded initially either at cost (which may be zero) or fair value.

Internally generated goodwill

The standard deliberately precludes recognition of internally generated goodwill because it requires that, for initial recognition, the cost of the asset rather than its fair value should be capable of being measured reliably and that it should be identifiable and controlled. Thus you do not recognise an asset which is subjective and cannot be measured reliably.

Research and development costs

Research activities by definition do not meet the criteria for recognition under IAS 38. This is because, at the research stage of a project, it cannot be certain that future economic benefits will probably flow to the entity from the project. There is too much uncertainty about the likely success or otherwise of the project. **Research costs should therefore be written off as an expense as they are incurred**.

Examples of research costs

(a)   Activities aimed at obtaining new knowledge
(b)   The search for, evaluation and final selection of, applications of research findings or other knowledge
(c)   The search for alternatives for materials, devices, products, processes, systems or services
(d)   The formulation, design evaluation and final selection of possible alternatives for new or improved materials, devices, products, systems or services

Development

Development costs **may qualify** for recognition as intangible assets provided that the following **strict criteria** can be demonstrated.

(a)   The technical feasibility of completing the intangible asset so that it will be available for use or sale.
(b)   Its intention to complete the intangible asset and use or sell it.
(c)   Its ability to use or sell the intangible asset.
(d)   How the intangible asset will generate probable future economic benefits. Among other things, the entity should demonstrate the existence of a market for the output of the intangible asset or the intangible asset itself or, if it is to be used internally, the usefulness of the intangible asset.
(e)   Its ability to measure the expenditure attributable to the intangible asset during its development reliably.

In contrast with research costs development costs are incurred at a later stage in a project, and the probability of success should be more apparent. Examples of development costs include the following.

(a)   The design, construction and testing of pre-production or pre-use prototypes and models
(b)   The design of tools, jigs, moulds and dies involving new technology
(c)   The design, construction and operation of a pilot plant that is not of a scale economically feasible for commercial production
(d)   The design, construction and testing of a chosen alternative for new or improved materials, devices, products, processes, systems or services

The standard **prohibits** the recognition of **internally generated brands, mastheads, publishing titles and customer lists** and similar items as intangible assets. These all fail to meet one or more (in some cases all) the definition and recognition criteria and in some cases are probably indistinguishable from internally generated goodwill.

Cost of an internally generated intangible asset

The costs allocated to an internally generated intangible asset should be only costs that can be **directly attributed** or allocated on a reasonable and consistent basis to creating, producing or preparing the asset for its intended use. The principles underlying the costs which may or may not be included are similar to those for other non-current assets and inventory.

The cost of an internally generated intangible asset is the sum of the **expenditure incurred from the date when** the intangible asset first **meets the recognition criteria**. If, as often happens, considerable costs have already been recognised as expenses before management could demonstrate that the criteria have been met, this earlier expenditure should not be retrospectively recognised at a later date as part of the cost of an intangible asset.

Example

A company is developing a new production process. During 20X9, expenditure incurred was $100,000, of which $90,000 was incurred before 1 December 20X9 and $10,000 between 1 December 20X9 and 31 December 20X9. The company can demonstrate that, at 1 December 20X9, the production process met the criteria for recognition as an intangible asset. The recoverable amount of the know-how embodied in the process is estimated to be $50,000.

How should the expenditure be treated?

At the end of 20X9, the production process is recognised as an intangible asset at a cost of $10,000. This is the expenditure incurred since the date when the recognition criteria were met, that is 1 December 20X9. The $90,000 expenditure incurred before 1 December 20X9 is expensed, because the recognition criteria were not met. It will never form part of the cost of the production process recognised in the statement of financial position.

All expenditure related to an intangible which does not meet the criteria for recognition either as an identifiable intangible asset or as goodwill arising on an acquisition should be **expensed as incurred**. The IAS gives examples of such expenditure.

*   Start up costs
*   Training costs
*   Advertising costs
*   Business relocation costs

Prepaid costs for services, for example advertising or marketing costs for campaigns that have been prepared but not launched, can still be recognised as a **prepayment**.

Measurement subsequent to initial recognition

The standard allows two methods of valuation for intangible assets after they have been first recognised.

Applying the **cost model**, an intangible asset should be **carried at its cost**, less any accumulated amortisation and less any accumulated impairment losses.

The **revaluation model** allows an intangible asset to be carried at a revalued amount, which is its **fair value** at the date of revaluation, less any subsequent accumulated amortisation and any subsequent accumulated impairment losses.

(a) The fair value must be able to be measured reliably with reference to an **active market** in that type of asset.
(b) The **entire class** of intangible assets of that type must be revalued at the same time (to prevent selective revaluations).
(c) If an intangible asset in a class of revalued intangible assets cannot be revalued because there is **no active market** for this asset, the asset should be carried at its **cost less any accumulated amortisation and impairment losses**.
(d) Revaluations should be made with such **regularity** that the carrying amount does not differ from that which would be determined using fair value at the reporting date.

The guidelines state that there **will not usually be an active market** in an intangible asset; therefore the revaluation model will usually not be available. For example, although copyrights, publishing rights and film rights can be sold, each has a unique sale value. In such cases, revaluation to fair value would be inappropriate. A fair value might be obtainable however for assets such as fishing rights or quotas or taxi cab licences.

Where an intangible asset is revalued upwards to a fair value, the amount of the revaluation should be credited directly to equity under the heading of a **revaluation surplus**.

However, if a revaluation surplus is a **reversal of a revaluation decrease** that was previously charged against income, the increase can be recognised as income.

Where the carrying amount of an intangible asset is revalued downwards, the amount of the **downward revaluation** should be charged as an expense against income, unless the asset has previously been revalued upwards. A revaluation decrease should be first charged against any previous revaluation surplus in respect of that asset.

Example

An intangible asset is measured by a company at fair value. The asset was revalued upwards by $400 in 20X8, and there is a revaluation surplus of $400 in the statement of financial position. At the end of 20X9, the asset is valued again, and a downward valuation of $500 is required.

How is the downward revaluation accounted for?

In this example, the downward valuation of $500 can first be set against the revaluation surplus of $400. The revaluation surplus will be reduced to 0 and a charge of $100 made as an expense in 20X9.

When the revaluation model is used, and an intangible asset is revalued upwards, the cumulative revaluation **surplus may be transferred to retained earnings** when the surplus is eventually realised. The surplus would be realised when the asset is disposed of. However, the surplus may also be realised over time as the **asset is used** by the entity. The amount of the surplus realised each year is the difference between the amortisation charge for the asset based on the revalued amount of the asset, and the amortisation that would be charged on the basis of the asset's historical cost. The realised surplus in such case should be transferred from revaluation surplus directly to retained earnings, and should not be taken through the income statement.

Useful life

An entity should **assess** the useful life of an intangible asset, which may be **finite or indefinite**. An intangible asset has an indefinite useful life when there is **no foreseeable limit** to the period over which the asset is expected to generate net cash inflows for the entity.

Many factors are considered in determining the useful life of an intangible asset, including: expected usage; typical product life cycles; technical, technological, commercial or other types of obsolescence; the stability of the industry; expected actions by competitors; the level of maintenance expenditure required; and legal or similar limits on the use of the asset, such as the expiry dates of related leases. Computer software and many other intangible assets normally have short lives because they are susceptible to technological obsolescence. However, uncertainty does not justify choosing a life that is unrealistically short.

The useful life of an intangible asset that arises from **contractual or other legal rights** should not exceed the period of the rights, but may be shorter depending on the period over which the entity expects to use the asset.

Amortisation

An intangible asset with a finite useful life should be amortised over its **expected useful life**.

(a)   Amortisation should start when the asset is **available for use**.

(b)   Amortisation should cease at the earlier of the date that the asset is classified **as held for sale** in accordance with IFRS 5 *Non-current assets held for sale and discontinued operations* and the date that the asset is **derecognised**.

(c)   The amortisation method used should reflect the pattern in which the asset's future economic benefits are consumed. If such a pattern cannot be predicted reliably, the straight-line method should be used.

(d)   The amortisation charge for each period should normally be recognised **in profit or loss**.

The **residual value** of an intangible asset with a finite useful life is **assumed to be zero** unless a third party is committed to buying the intangible asset at the end of its useful life or unless there is an active market for that type of asset (so that its expected residual value can be measured) and it is probable that there will be a market for the asset at the end of its useful life.

The amortisation period and the amortisation method used for an intangible asset with a finite useful life should be **reviewed at each financial year-end**.

Indefinite useful lives

An intangible asset with an indefinite useful life **should not be amortised**. (IAS 36 requires that such an asset is tested for impairment at least annually.)

The useful life of an intangible asset that is not being amortised should be **reviewed each year** to determine whether it is still appropriate to assess its useful life as indefinite. Reassessing the useful life of an intangible asset as finite rather than indefinite is an indicator that the asset may be impaired and therefore it should be tested for impairment.

Disposals/retirements of intangible assets

An intangible asset should be eliminated from the statement of financial position when it is disposed of or when there is no further expected economic benefit from its future use. On disposal the gain or loss arising from the **difference between the net disposal proceeds and the carrying amount** of the asset should be taken to profit or loss as a gain or loss on disposal (ie treated as income or expense).

Disclosure requirements

The standard has fairly extensive disclosure requirements for intangible assets. The financial statements should disclose the **accounting policies** for intangible assets that have been adopted.

For **each class of intangible assets**, disclosure is required of the following.

- Whether the useful life is indefinite or finite
- The **method of amortisation** used
- The **useful life** of the assets or the amortisation rate used
- The **gross carrying amount**, the **accumulated amortisation** and the **accumulated impairment losses** as at the beginning and the end of the period
- The line in the statement of comprehensive income in which any amortisation of intangible assets is included
- A **reconciliation of the carrying amount** as at the beginning and at the end of the period (additions, retirements/disposals, revaluations, impairment losses, impairment losses reversed, amortisation charge for the period, net exchange differences, other movements)
- The carrying amount of **internally-generated intangible assets**

The financial statements should also disclose the amount of research and development expenditure that have been charged as expenses of the period.

2 Goodwill (IFRS 3)

'Inherent' goodwill may exist in a business but it is not recognised as an asset because no value can be assigned to it. This is not the case for purchased goodwill which is dealt with by IFRS 3.

IFRS 3: Business combinations

IFRS 3 covers the accounting treatment of goodwill acquired in a business combination.

> **Goodwill.** Future economic benefits arising from assets that are not capable of being individually identified and separately recognised. *(IFRS 3)*

Goodwill acquired in a business combination is **recognised as an asset** and is initially measured at **cost**. Cost of goodwill is the excess of the cost of the combination over the acquirer's interest in the net fair value of the acquiree's identifiable assets, liabilities and contingent liabilities.

After initial recognition goodwill acquired in a business combination is measured **at cost less any accumulated impairment losses**. It is **not amortised**. Instead it is tested for impairment at least annually, in accordance with IAS 36 *Impairment of assets*.

Negative goodwill arises when the acquirer's interest in the net fair value of the acquiree's identifiable assets, liabilities and contingent liabilities exceeds the cost of the business combination. IFRS 3 refers to negative goodwill as the 'excess of acquirer's interest in the net fair value of acquiree's identifiable assets, liabilities and contingent liabilities over cost'.

Negative goodwill can arise as the result of **errors** in measuring the fair value of either the cost of the combination or the acquiree's identifiable net assets. It can also arise as the result of a **bargain purchase**.

Where there is negative goodwill, an entity should first **reassess** the amounts at which it has measured both the cost of the combination and the acquiree's identifiable net assets. This exercise should identify any errors.

Any negative goodwill remaining should be **recognised immediately in profit or loss** (that is, in the income statement).

IFRS 3 requires extensive **disclosures**. These include a **reconciliation** of the carrying amount of goodwill at the beginning and end of the period, showing separately:

(a)   The gross amount and accumulated impairment losses at the beginning of the period
(b)   Additional goodwill recognised during the period
(c)   Impairment losses recognised during the period
(d)   Net exchange differences arising during the period, and
(e)   The gross amount and accumulated impairment losses at the end of the period

What are the main characteristics of goodwill which distinguish it from other intangible non-current assets?

Goodwill may be distinguished from other intangible non-current assets by reference to the following characteristics.

(a)   It is incapable of realisation separately from the business as a whole.
(b)   Its value has no reliable or predictable relationship to any costs which may have been incurred.
(c)   Its value arises from various intangible factors such as skilled employees, effective advertising or a strategic location. These indirect factors cannot be valued.
(d)   The value of goodwill may fluctuate widely according to internal and external circumstances over relatively short periods of time.
(e)   The assessment of the value of goodwill is highly subjective.

It could be argued that, because goodwill is so different from other intangible non-current assets it does not make sense to account for it in the same way. Thus the capitalisation and amortisation treatment would not be acceptable. Furthermore, because goodwill is so difficult to value, any valuation may be misleading, and it is best eliminated from the statement of financial position altogether. However, there are strong arguments for treating it like any other intangible non-current asset. This issue remains controversial.

1 IAS 10: (revised) Events after the reporting period

The financial statements are significant indicators of a company's success or failure. It is important, therefore, that they include all the information necessary for an understanding of the company's position.

IAS 10 (*Revised*) *Events after the reporting period* requires the provision of additional information in order to facilitate such an understanding. IAS 10 deals with events **after** the reporting date which may affect the position **at** the reporting date.

The standard gives the following definition.

> Events after the reporting period are those events, both favourable and unfavourable, that occur between the reporting date and the date on which the financial statements are authorised for issue. Two types of events can be identified:
>
> • Those that provide evidence of conditions that existed at the end of the reporting period; and
> • Those that are indicative of conditions that arose subsequent to the reporting period. *(IAS 10)*

Between the end of the reporting period and the date on which the financial statements are authorised (ie for issue outside the organisation), events may occur which show that assets and liabilities at the end of the reporting period should be adjusted, or that disclosure of such events should be given.

Events requiring adjustment

The standard requires adjustment of assets and liabilities in certain circumstances.

An **example** of additional evidence which becomes available after the reporting period is where a **customer goes bankrupt, thus confirming that the trade account receivable balance at the year end is uncollectable.**

In relation to going concern, the standard states that, where operating results and the financial position have deteriorated after the reporting period, it may be necessary to reconsider whether the going concern assumption is appropriate in the preparation of the financial statements.

For instance, a warehouse fire destroying inventory after the year end would be non-adjusting, because the inventory did exist at the year end. **But** if the loss of inventory means the entity can no longer continue to trade, then the going concern assumption is no longer valid and the basis of preparing the financial statements must change.

Events not requiring adjustment

The standard then looks at events which do **not** require adjustment.

One **example** of such an event is where the **value of an investment falls between the end of reporting period and and the date the financial statements are authorised** for issue. The fall in value represents circumstances during the current period, not conditions existing at the end of the previous reporting period, so it is not appropriate to adjust the value of the investment in the financial statements. Disclosure is an aid to users, however, indicating 'unusual changes' in the state of assets and liabilities after the reporting date.

The rule for **disclosure** of events occurring after the reporting period which relate to conditions that arose after that date, is that disclosure should be made if non-disclosure would hinder the user's ability to made **proper evaluations** and decision based on the financial statements. An example might be the acquisition of another business.

The distinction between an **adjusting event** and a **non-adjusting event** can be shown by the following diagram.

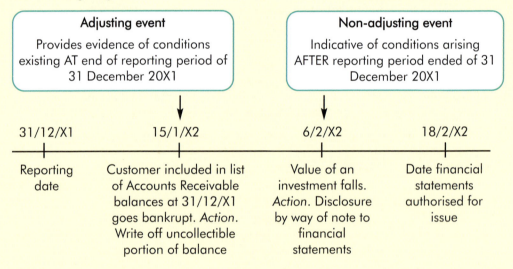

Dividends

Dividends declared by the entity after the reporting period are a special case. Even if they are stated to be in respect of the period covered by the financial statements, they should **not** be **provided for**. They should simply be disclosed in the notes.

Disclosures

The following **disclosure requirements** are given **for events** which occur after the reporting period which do *not* require adjustment. If disclosure of events occurring after the reporting period is required by this standard, the following information should be provided:

(a)   The nature of the event
(b)   An estimate of the financial effect, or a statement that such an estimate cannot be made

2 IAS 8: Accounting policies, changes in accounting estimates and errors

IAS 8 deals with the treatment of changes in accounting estimates, changes in accounting policies and errors, as defined below. The standard was extensively revised in December 2003.

Definitions

- **Accounting policies** are the specific principles, bases, conventions, rules and practices adopted by an entity in preparing and presenting financial statements.
- A **change in accounting estimate** is an adjustment of the carrying amount of an asset or a liability or the amount of the periodic consumption of an asset, that results from the assessment of the present status of, and expected future benefits and obligations associated with, assets and liabilities. Changes in accounting estimates result from new information or new developments and, accordingly, are not corrections of errors.
- **Material**: as defined in IAS 1
- **Prior period errors** are omissions from, and misstatements in, the entity's financial statements for one or more prior periods arising from a failure to use, or misuse of, reliable information that:
  - (a) Was available when financial statements for those periods were authorised for issue, and
  - (b) Could reasonably be expected to have been obtained and taken into account in the preparation and presentation of those financial statements.

  Such errors include the effects of mathematical mistakes, mistakes in applying accounting policies, oversights or misinterpretations of facts, and fraud.
- **Retrospective application** is applying a new accounting policy to transactions, other events and conditions as if that policy had always been applied.
- **Retrospective restatement** is correcting the recognition, measurement and disclosure of amounts of elements of financial statements as if a prior period error had never occurred.
- **Prospective application** of a change in accounting policy and of recognising the effect of a change in an accounting estimate, respectively, are:
  - (a) Applying the new accounting policy to transactions, other events and conditions occurring after the date as at which the policy is changes; and
  - (b) Recognising the effect of the change in the accounting estimate in the current and future periods affected by the change.
- **Impracticable** Applying a requirement is impracticable when the entity cannot apply it after making every reasonable effort to do so. It is impracticable to apply a change in an accounting policy retrospectively or to make a retrospective restatement to correct an error if one of the following apply.
  - (a) The effects or the retrospective application or retrospective restatement are not determinable.
  - (b) The retrospective application or retrospective restatement requires assumptions about what management's intent would have been in that period.
  - (c) The retrospective application or retrospective restatement requires significant estimates of amounts and it is impossible to distinguish objectively information about those estimates that: provides evidence of circumstances that existed on the date(s) at which those amounts are to be recognised, measured or disclosed; and would have been available when the financial statements for that prior period were authorised for issue from other information.   *(IAS 8)*

3 Accounting policies

Accounting policies are determined by **applying the relevant IFRS or IAS** and considering any relevant Implementation Guidance issued by the IASB for that IFRS/IAS.

Where there is no applicable IFRS management should use its **judgement** in developing and applying an accounting policy that results in information that is **relevant** and **reliable**. Management should refer to:

(a) The requirements and guidance in IFRSs dealing with **similar** and **related issues**
(b) The definitions, recognition criteria and measurement concepts for assets, liabilities and expenses in the **Framework**

Management may also consider the most recent pronouncements of **other standard setting bodies** that use a similar conceptual framework to develop standards, other accounting literature and accepted industry practices if these do not conflict with the sources above.

An entity must select and apply its accounting policies for a period **consistently** for similar transactions, other events and conditions, unless an IFRS specifically requires or permits categorisation of items for which different policies may be appropriate. If an IFRS requires or permits categorisation of items, an appropriate accounting policy must be selected and applied consistently to each category.

4 Changes in accounting policies

The same accounting policies are usually adopted from period to period, to allow users to analyse trends over time in profit, cash flows and financial position. **Changes in accounting policy will therefore be rare** and should be made only if required by one of three things.

(a) By **statute**
(b) By an **accounting standard setting body**
(c) If the change will result in a **more appropriate presentation** of events or transactions in the financial statements of the entity

The standard highlights two types of event **which do not constitute changes in accounting policy**.

(a) Adopting an accounting policy for a **new type of transaction** or event not dealt with previously by the entity.
(b) Adopting a **new accounting policy** for a transaction or event which has not occurred in the past or which was not material.

In the case of tangible non-current assets, if a policy of revaluation is adopted for the first time then this is treated, not as a change of accounting policy under IAS 8, but as a revaluation under IAS 16 *Property, plant and equipment*. The following paragraphs do not therefore apply to a changes in policy to adopt revaluations.

A change in accounting policy **must be applied retrospectively. Retrospective application** means that the new accounting policy is applied to transactions and events as if it had always been in use. In other words, at the earliest date such transactions or events occurred, the policy is applied from that date.

Prospective application is **no longer allowed** under the revised IAS 8 unless it is **impracticable** to determine the cumulative amount of change.

What would constitute a change in accounting policy? Examples are:

- A change from inventory valuation using FIFO to weighted average, or vice versa.
- A change in presentation, such as depreciation transferred from cost of sales to expenses.

Adoption of an IAS/IFRS

Where a new IAS or IFRS is adopted, IAS 8 requires any transitional provisions in the new IAS itself to be followed. If none are given in the IAS which is being adopted, then IAS 8 offers a benchmark and an allowed alternative treatment.

Other changes in accounting policy

IAS 8 requires **retrospective application**, *unless* it is **impracticable** to determine the cumulative amount of charge. Any resulting adjustment should be reported as an adjustment to the opening balance of retained earnings. Comparative information should be restated unless it is impracticable to do so.

This means that all comparative information must be restated **as if the new policy had always been in force**, with amounts relating to earlier periods reflected in an adjustment to opening reserves of the earliest period presented.

Prospective application is allowed only when it is impracticable to determine the cumulative effect of the change.

Certain **disclosures** are required when a change in accounting policy has a material effect on the current period or any prior period presented, or when it may have a material effect in subsequent periods.

(a)   Reasons for the change
(b)   Amount of the adjustment for the current period and for each period presented
(c)   Amount of the adjustment relating to periods prior to those included in the comparative information
(d)   The fact that comparative information has been restated or that it is impracticable to do so

An entity should also disclose information relevant to assessing the **impact of new IFRS** on the financial statements where these **have not yet come into force**.

5 Changes in accounting estimates

Estimates arise in relation to business activities because of the **uncertainties inherent within them**. Judgements are made based on the most up to date information and the use of such estimates is a necessary part of the preparation of financial statements. It does not undermine their reliability. Here are some examples of accounting estimates.

- A necessary **bad debt provision**
- **Useful lives** of depreciable assets
- Provision for **obsolescence of inventory**

The rule here is that the **effect of a change in an accounting estimate** should be included in the determination of net profit or loss in one of:

(a)   The period of the change, if the change affects that period only
(b)   The period of the change and future periods, if the change affects both

Changes may occur in the circumstances which were in force at the time the estimate was calculated, or perhaps additional information or subsequent developments have come to light.

An example of a change in accounting estimate which affects only the **current period** is the bad debt estimate. However, a revision in the life over which an asset is depreciated would affect both the **current and future periods**, in the amount of the depreciation expense.

The effect of a change in an accounting estimate should be included in the **same income statement classification** as was used previously for the estimate. This rule helps to ensure **consistency** between the financial statements of different periods. Similarly, where an accounting estimate was previously reported as an extraordinary item, so the change of estimate should be too.

The **materiality** of the change is also relevant. The nature and amount of a change in an accounting estimate that has a material effect in the current period (or which is expected to have a material effect in subsequent periods) should be disclosed. If it is not possible to quantify the amount, this impracticability should be disclosed.

6 Errors

Errors discovered during a current period may have arisen through mathematical mistakes, incorrect application of accounting policies, misinterpretation of facts, oversights or fraud.

A more formal definition was given above.

Most of the time these errors can be **corrected through net profit or loss for the current period**. Where they fulfil the definition of prior period errors (given earlier), however, this is not appropriate.

Accounting treatment

Prior period errors are corrected retrospectively.

This involves:

(a)   Either restating the comparative amounts for the prior period(s) in which the error occurred,
(b)   Or, when the error occurred before the earliest prior period presented, restating the opening balances of assets, liabilities and equity for that period so that the financial statements are presented **as if the error had never occurred**.

Only where it is **impracticable** to determine the cumulative effect of an error on prior periods can an entity correct an error **prospectively**.

Various **disclosures** are required.

(a)   Nature of the prior period error
(b)   For each prior period, to the extent practicable, the **amount** of the correction.
    (i)   For each financial statement line item affected
    (ii)   If IAS 33 applies, for basic and diluted earnings per share
(c)   The amount of the correction at the **beginning of the earliest prior** period presented
(d)   If **retrospective restatement is impracticable** for a particular prior period, the **circumstances** that led to the existence of that condition and a description of how and from when the error has been corrected. Subsequent periods need not repeat these disclosures.

Example

During 20X7 P Co discovered that certain items had been included in inventory at 31 December 20X6, valued at $4.2m, which had in fact been sold before the year end. The following figures for 20X6 (as reported) and 20X7 (draft) are available.

	20X6 $'000	20X7 (draft) $'000
Sales	47,400	67,200
Cost of goods sold	(34,570)	(55,800)
Profit before taxation	12,830	11,400
Income taxes	(3,880)	(3,400)
Net profit	8,950	8,000

Reserves at 1 January 20X6 were $13m. The cost of goods sold for 20X7 includes the $4.2m error in opening inventory. The income tax rate was 30% for 20X6 and 20X7.

How will this be shown in the income statement and retained earnings of P Co for 20X7?

P CO

INCOME STATEMENT

	20X6 $'000	20X7 $'000
Sales	47,400	67,200
Cost of goods sold	(38,770)	(51,600)
Profit before taxation	8,630	15,600
Income taxes	(2,620)	(4,660)
Net profit	6,010	10,940

RETAINED EARNINGS

	20X6	20X7
Opening retained earnings		
As previously reported	13,000	21,950
Correction of prior period error	–	(2,940)
As restated	13,000	19,010
Net profit for year	6,010	10,940
Closing retained earnings	19,010	29,950

Workings

1. Cost of goods sold	20X6 $'000	20X7 $'000
As stated in question	34,570	55,800
Inventory adjustment	4,200	(4,200)
	38,770	51,600

2.	Income tax	20X6	20X7
		$'000	$'000
	As stated in question	3,880	3,400
	Inventory adjustment (4,200 × 30%)	(1,260)	1,260
		2,620	4,660

7 IFRS 5: Non-current assets held for sale and discontinued operations

IFRS 5 is the result of a short-term convergence project with the US Financial Accounting Standards Board (FASB). It replaced IAS 35 *Discontinuing operations*.

IFRS 5 requires assets and groups of assets that are 'held for sale' to be **presented separately** on the face of the statement of financial position and the results of discontinued operations to be presented separately in the income statement. This is required so that users of financial statements will be better able to make **projections** about the financial position, profits and cash flows of the entity.

> **Disposal group**: a group of assets to be disposed of, by sale or otherwise, together as a group in a single transaction, and liabilities directly associated with those assets that will be transferred in the transaction. (In practice a disposal group could be a subsidiary, a cash-generating unit or a single operation within an entity.) *(IFRS 5)*

IFRS 5 does not apply to certain assets covered by other accounting standards:

(a) Deferred tax assets (IAS 12)
(b) Assets arising from employee benefits (IAS 19)
(c) Financial assets (IAS 39)
(d) Investment properties accounted for in accordance with the fair value model (IAS 40)
(e) Agricultural and biological assets that are measured at fair value less estimated point of sale costs (IAS 41)
(f) Insurance contracts (IFRS 4)

Classification of assets held for sale

A non-current asset (or disposal group) should be classified as **held for sale** if its carrying amount will be recovered **principally through a sale transaction** rather than **through continuing use**. A number of detailed criteria must be met:

(a) The asset must be **available for immediate sale** in its present condition.
(b) Its sale must be **highly probable** (ie, significantly more likely than not).

For the sale to be highly probable, the following must apply.

(a) Management must be **committed** to a plan to sell the asset.
(b) There must be an active programme to **locate a buyer**.
(c) The asset must be marketed for sale at a **price that is reasonable** in relation to its current fair value.
(d) The sale should be expected to take place **within one year** from the date of classification.

(e)   It is unlikely that significant changes to the plan will be made or that the plan will be withdrawn.

An asset (or disposal group) can still be classified as held for sale, even if the sale has not actually taken place within one year. However, the delay must have been **caused by events or circumstances beyond the entity's control** and there must be sufficient evidence that the entity is still committed to sell the asset or disposal group. Otherwise the entity must cease to classify the asset as held for sale.

If an entity acquires a disposal group (eg, a subsidiary) exclusively with a view to its subsequent disposal it can classify the asset as held for sale only if the sale is expected to take place within one year and it is highly probable that all the other criteria will be met within a short time (normally three months).

An asset that is to be **abandoned** should not be classified as held for sale. This is because its carrying amount will be recovered principally through continuing use. However, a disposal group to be abandoned may meet the definition of a discontinued operation and therefore separate disclosure may be required (see below).

Example

On 1 December 20X8, B Co became committed to a plan to sell a manufacturing facility and has already found a potential buyer. The company does not intend to discontinue the operations currently carried out in the facility. At 31 December 20X8 there is a backlog of uncompleted customer orders. The subsidiary will not be able to transfer the facility to the buyer until after it ceases to operate the facility and has eliminated the backlog of uncompleted customer orders. This is not expected to occur until spring 20X9.

Can the manufacturing facility be classified as 'held for sale' at 31 December 20X8?

The facility will not be transferred until the backlog of orders is completed; this demonstrates that the facility is not available for immediate sale in its present condition. The facility cannot be classified as 'held for sale' at 31 December 20X8. It must be treated in the same way as other items of property, plant and equipment: it should continue to be depreciated and should not be separately disclosed.

Measurement of assets held for sale

Fair value: the amount for which an asset could be exchanged, or a liability settled, between knowledgeable, willing parties in an arm's length transaction.

Costs to sell: the incremental costs directly attributable to the disposal of an asset (or disposal group), excluding finance costs and income tax expense.

Recoverable amount: the higher of an asset's fair value less costs to sell and its value in use.

Value in use: the present value of estimated future cash flows expected to arise from the continuing use of an asset and from its disposal at the end of its useful life.

(IFRS 5)

A non-current asset (or disposal group) that is held for sale should be measured at the **lower of** its **carrying amount** and **fair value less costs to sell**. Fair value less costs to sell is equivalent to net realisable value.

An impairment loss should be recognised where fair value less costs to sell is lower than carrying amount. Note that this is an exception to the normal rule. IAS 36 *Impairment of assets* requires an entity to recognise an impairment loss only where an asset's recoverable amount is lower than its carrying value. Recoverable amount is defined as the higher of net realisable value and value in use. IAS 36 does not apply to assets held for sale.

Non-current assets held for sale **should not be depreciated**, even if they are still being used by the entity.

A non-current asset (or disposal group) that is **no longer classified as held for sale** (for example, because the sale has not taken place within one year) is measured at the **lower of**:

(a)   Its **carrying amount** before it was classified as held for sale, adjusted for any depreciation that would have been charged had the asset not been held for sale
(b)   Its **recoverable amount** at the date of the decision not to sell

Presenting discontinued operations

> **Discontinued operation**: a component of an entity that has either been disposed of, or is classified as held for sale, and:
>
> * Represents a separate major line of business or geographical area of operations
> * Is part of a single co-ordinated plan to dispose of a separate major line of business or geographical area of operations, or
> * Is a subsidiary acquired exclusively with a view to resale.
>
> **Component of an entity**: operations and cash flows that can be clearly distinguished, operationally and for financial reporting purposes, from the rest of the entity.
>
> *(IFRS 5)*

An entity should **present and disclose information** that enables users of the financial statements to evaluate the financial effects of **discontinued operations** and disposals of non-current assets or disposal groups.

An entity should disclose a **single amount** on the **face of the income statement** comprising the total of:

(a)   The **post-tax profit or loss** of discontinued operations and
(b)   The post-tax gain or loss recognised on the **measurement to fair value less costs to sell** or on the disposal of the assets or disposal group(s) constituting the discontinued operation.

An entity should also disclose an **analysis** of the single amount into:

(a)   The revenue, expenses and pre-tax profit or loss of discontinued operations
(b)   The related income tax expense
(c)   The gain or loss recognised on the measurement to fair value less costs to sell or on the disposal of the assets or the discontinued operation
(d)   The related income tax expense

This may be presented either on the face of the income statement or in the notes. If it is presented on the face of the income statement it should be presented in a section identified as relating to discontinued operations, ie separately from continuing operations. This analysis is not required where the discontinued operation is a newly acquired subsidiary that has been classified as held for sale.

An entity should disclose the **net cash flows** attributable to the operating, investing and financing activities of discontinued operations. These disclosures may be presented either on the face of the cash flow statement or in the notes.

Gains and losses on the remeasurement of a disposal group that is not a discontinued operation but is held for sale should be included in profit or loss from continuing operations.

Illustration

The following illustration is taken from the implementation guidance to IFRS 5. Profit for the period from discontinued operations would be analysed in the notes.

XYZ GROUP

STATEMENT OF COMPREHENSIVE INCOME (INCOME STATEMENT)
FOR THE YEAR ENDED 31 DECEMBER 20X9

	20X9 $'000	20X8 $'000
Continuing operations		
Revenue	X	X
Cost of sales	(X)	(X)
Gross profit	X	X
Other income	X	X
Distribution costs	(X)	(X)
Administrative expenses	(X)	(X)
Other expenses	(X)	(X)
Finance costs	(X)	(X)
Share of profit of associates	X	X
Profit before tax	X	X
Income tax expense	(X)	(X)
Profit for the year from continuing operations	X	X
Discontinued operations		
Profit for the year from discontinued operations	X	X
Profit for the year	X	X
Profit attributable to		
Owners of the parent		
Profit for the year from continuing operations	X	X
Profit for the year from discontinued operations	X	X
Profit for the year attributable to owners of the parent	X	X
Non-controlling interests		
Profit for the year from continuing operations	X	X
Profit for the year from discontinued operations	X	X
Profit for the year attributable to non-controlling interests	X	X

An alternative to this presentation would be to analyse the profit from discontinued operations in a separate column on the face of the statement of comprehensive income.

Presentation of a non-current asset or disposal group classified as held for sale

Non-current assets and disposal groups classified as held for sale should be **presented separately** from other assets in the statement of financial position. The liabilities of a disposal group should be presented separately from other liabilities in the statement of financial position.

(a) Assets and liabilities held for sale **should not be offset**.
(b) The **major classes** of assets and liabilities held for sale should be **separately disclosed** either on the face of the statement of financial position or in the notes.

Additional disclosures

In the period in which a non-current asset (or disposal group) has been either classified as held for sale or sold the following should be disclosed.

(a) A description of the non-current asset (or disposal group)
(b) A description of the facts and circumstances of the disposal
(c) Any gain or loss recognised when the item was classified as held for sale
(d) If applicable, the segment in which the non-current asset (or disposal group) is presented in accordance with IFRS 8 *Operating Segments*

Where an asset previously classified as held for sale is **no longer held for sale**, the entity should disclose a description of the facts and circumstances leading to the decision and its effect on results.

1 Introduction

Accruals accounting is based on the **matching of costs with the revenue they generate**. It is crucially important under this convention that we can establish the point at which revenue may be recognised so that the correct treatment can be applied to the related costs. For example, the costs of producing an item of finished goods should be carried as an asset in the statement of financial position until such time as it is sold; they should then be written off as a charge to the trading account. Which of these two treatments should be applied cannot be decided until it is clear at what moment the sale of the item takes place.

The decision has a **direct impact on profit** since under the **prudence concept** it would be unacceptable to recognise the profit on sale until a sale had taken place in accordance with the **criteria of revenue recognition**.

Revenue is of course open to manipulation. The latest scandal is at Satyam Computer Services in India where the Chairman recently admitted that profits were massively inflated for years and that in the quarter to 30 September 2008 revenue was overstated by 78%. How this got past the auditors has yet to be explained, but it does illustrate why rules on revenue recognition are needed.

2 IAS 18: Revenue

IAS 18 governs the recognition of revenue in specific (common) types of transaction. Generally, recognition should be when it is probable that **future economic benefits** will flow to the entity and when these benefits can be **measured reliably**.

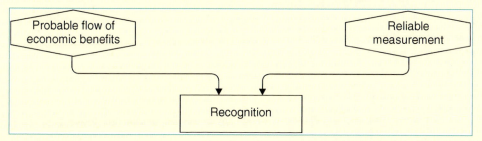

Income, as defined by the IASB's *Framework* document, includes both revenues and gains. Revenue is income arising in the ordinary course of an entity's activities and it may be called different names, such as sales, fees, interest, dividends or royalties.

Interest, royalties and dividends are included as income because they arise from the use of an entity's assets by other parties.

> **Interest** is the charge for the use of cash or cash equivalents or amounts due to the entity.
>
> **Royalties** are charges for the use of non-current assets of the entity, eg patents, computer software and trademarks.
>
> **Dividends** are distributions of profit to holders of equity investments, in proportion with their holdings, of each relevant class of capital.   (IAS 18)

The standard specifically **excludes** various types of revenue arising from leases, insurance contracts, changes in value of financial instruments or other current assets, natural increases in agricultural assets and mineral ore extraction.

The following definitions are given in the standard.

> **Revenue** is the gross inflow of economic benefits during the period arising in the course of the ordinary activities of an entity when those inflows result in increases in equity, other than increases relating to contributions from equity participants.
>
> **Fair value** is the amount for which an asset could be exchanged, or a liability settled, between knowledgeable, willing parties in an arm's length transaction.   (IAS 18)

Revenue **does not include** sales taxes, value added taxes or goods and service taxes which are only collected for third parties, because these do not represent an economic benefit flowing to the entity. The same is true for revenues collected by an agent on behalf of a principal. Revenue for the agent is only the commission received for acting as agent.

When a transaction takes place, the amount of revenue is usually decided by the **agreement of the buyer and seller**. The revenue is actually measured, however, as the **fair value of the consideration received**, which will take account of any trade discounts and volume rebates

Normally, each transaction can be looked at **as a whole**. Sometimes, however, transactions are more complicated, and it is necessary to break a transaction down into its **component parts**. For example, a sale may include the transfer of goods and the provision of future servicing, the revenue for which should be deferred over the period the service is performed.

At the other end of the scale, **seemingly separate transactions must be considered together** if apart they lose their commercial meaning. An example would be to sell an asset with an agreement to buy it back at a later date. The second transaction cancels the first and so both must be considered together.

Sale of goods

Revenue from the sale of goods should only be recognised when *all* these conditions are satisfied.

(a)   The entity has transferred the **significant risks and rewards** of ownership of the goods to the buyer

(b)   The entity has **no continuing managerial involvement** to the degree usually associated with ownership, and no longer has effective control over the goods sold

(c)   The amount of revenue can be **measured reliably**

(d)   It is probable that the **economic benefits** associated with the transaction will flow to the entity

(e)   The **costs incurred** in respect of the transaction can be measured reliably

The transfer of risks and rewards can only be decided by examining each transaction. Mainly, the transfer occurs at the same time as either the **transfer of legal title**, or the **passing of possession** to the buyer – this is what happens when you buy something in a shop.

If **significant risks and rewards remain with the seller**, then the transaction is not a sale and revenue cannot be recognised, for example if the receipt of the revenue from a particular sale depends on the buyer receiving revenue from his own sale of the goods.

It is possible for the seller to retain only an **'insignificant' risk of ownership** and for the sale and revenue to be recognised. The main example here is where the seller retains title only to ensure collection of what is owed on the goods. This is a common commercial situation, and when it arises the revenue should be recognised on the date of sale.

The probability of the entity receiving the revenue arising from a transaction must be assessed. It may only become probable that the economic benefits will be received when an uncertainty is removed, for example government permission for funds to be received from another country. Only when the uncertainty is removed should the revenue be recognised. This is in contrast with the situation where revenue has already been recognised but where the **collectability of the cash** is brought into doubt. Where recovery has ceased to be probable, the amount should be recognised as an expense, not an adjustment of the revenue previously recognised. These points also refer to services and interest, royalties and dividends below.

Matching should take place, ie the **revenue** and **expenses** relating to the **same transaction** should be recognised at the **same time**. It is usually easy to estimate expenses at the date of sale (eg warranty costs, shipment costs, etc). Where they cannot be estimated reliably, then revenue cannot be recognised; any consideration which has already been received is treated as a liability. Remember the definition of an asset and that revenue is recognised only when it is probably that the economic benefit associated with the transaction will flow to the entity.

Rendering of services

When the outcome of a transaction involving the rendering of services can be estimated reliably, the associated revenue should be recognised by reference to the stage of completion of the transaction at the reporting date. The outcome of a transaction can be estimated reliably when all these conditions are satisfied.

(a)   The amount of revenue can be **measured reliably**

(b)   It is probable that the **economic benefits** associated with the transaction will flow to the entity

(c)   The **stage of completion** of the transaction at the end of the reporting period can be measured reliably

(d)   The **costs incurred** for the transaction and the costs to complete the transaction can be measured reliably

The parties to the transaction will normally have to agree the following before an entity can make reliable estimates.

(a)   Each party's **enforceable rights** regarding the service to be provided and received by the parties

(b)   The **consideration** to be exchanged

(c)   The **manner and terms of settlement**

There are various methods of determining the **stage of completion** of a transaction, but for practical purposes, when services are performed by an indeterminate number of acts over a period of time, revenue should be recognised on a **straight line basis** over the period, unless there is evidence for the use of a more appropriate method. If one act is of more significance than the others, then the significant act should be carried out before revenue is recognised.

In uncertain situations, when the outcome of the transaction involving the rendering of services cannot be estimated reliably, the standard recommends a **no loss/no gain approach**. Revenue is recognised only to the extent of the expenses recognised that are recoverable.

This is particularly likely during the **early stages of a transaction**, but it is still probable that the entity will recover the costs incurred. So the revenue recognised in such a period will be equal to the expenses incurred, with no profit.

Obviously, if the **costs** are **not likely** to **be reimbursed**, then they must be recognised as an **expense immediately**. When the uncertainties cease to exist, revenue should be recognised as laid out above.

Reporting the substance of the transaction

In some cases, what initially appears to be a sale transaction may turn out to be something different and a sale should not be recognised. It is important that the substance of the transaction is reported and not just its legal form. In other words, you need to understand exactly what is happening with a single transaction or series of transactions.

Example:

For example, MacDougal Drinks sold 100 barrels of Brew No 1 to the Scots Bank, on 30 June 2009 for $100 per barrel. When Brew No 1 is mature in two years time it will be worth $500 per barrel. MacDougal retains custody of the barrels. The sale contract contains a clause requiring MacDougal to repurchase the barrels on 30 June 2011 for $150 per barrel.

How should this transaction be recognised?

Often, the substance of a transaction can only be determined by looking at all transactions relating to an item as a whole.

In this case, MacDougal sells his barrels to the Scots Bank which would appear to be a standard transaction. However, on maturity of the barrels, he repurchases them from the bank. It is important to note that he does not physically give the barrels to the bank, they are still kept at his premises.

Normally once an item is sold, the goods are transferred and the seller transfers the risks and rewards of ownership to the purchaser. This does not happen in this case. MacDougal still retains physical ownership and with the option of buying the barrels back at below their market price, retains the rewards of ownership.

In substance, this transactions is not a sale. Rather, it is a loan from Scots Bank to MacDougal, secured on the inventory.

The accounting for this transaction is to continue to recognise the barrels as inventory and record the cash received from the bank as the proceeds of a loan. The difference between the $100 'sales' price and the $150 repurchase price should be accounted for as loan interest over the two year period of the loan. No sale has taken place.

Realised profit

The realisation concept states that revenue and profits should not be anticipated, but should be recognised by inclusion in the income statement only when **realised** in the form either of **cash**, or of other assets the ultimate cash realisation of which can be assessed with reasonable certainty.

Unfortunately there is no standard definition of realised profits. It could be said that they are such profits or losses of a company as fall to be treated as realised in accordance with principles generally accepted at the time when the accounts are prepared.

The language of accounting has recently moved away from the concept of realisation to focus instead on whether the **conditions** have been **met** for an **item** to be **recognised** in the financial statements. In this regard we have progressed from an income statement approach to a **statement of financial position-driven approach** as fostered by the **IASB**. We review this in the section below.

This IASB approach acknowledges the concept of matching, but views **recognition** in terms of including items in the financial statements in the periods to which they **relate** rather than the period of payment or receipt.

IAS 1 specifically notes that the application of the matching concept does not allow the **recognition** of items in the statement of financial position which do not meet the **definition of assets and liabilities**.

Interest, royalties and dividends

When others use the entity's assets yielding interest, royalties and dividends, the revenue should be recognised on the bases set out below when:

(a)   it is probable that the **economic benefits** associated with the transaction will flow to the entity; and
(b)   the amount of the revenue can be **measured reliably**.

The revenue is recognised on the following bases.

(a)   **Interest** is recognised on a **time proportion** basis that takes into account the **effective yield** on the asset
(b)   **Royalties** are recognised on an **accruals** basis in accordance with the **substance** of the **relevant agreement**
(c)   **Dividends** are recognised when the **shareholder's right to receive payment** is established

Disclosure

The following items should be disclosed.

(a)   The **accounting policies** adopted for the recognition of revenue, including the methods used to determine the stage of completion of transactions involving the rendering of services

(b)   The amount of each **significant category of revenue** recognised during the period including revenue arising from:
(i)   The sale of goods
(ii)   The rendering of services
(iii)   Interest
(iv)   Royalties
(v)   Dividends

(c)   The amount of revenue arising from **exchanges of goods or services** included in each significant category of revenue

Any **contingent gains or losses**, such as those relating to warranty costs, claims or penalties should be treated according to IAS 10 *Events after the reporting period*.

IFRS improvements

Improvements in 2009 included an addition to IAS 18 giving guidance on the **agent vs principal** issue. An entity is acting as a principal when:

(a)   the entity has primary responsibility for providing goods or services to the customer

(b)   the entity has inventory risk before or after the customer order, during shipping or on return

(c)   the entity has latitude in establishing prices, either directly or indirectly

(d)   the entity bears the customers credit risk for the amount receivable from the customer

1 IAS 37: Provisions, contingent liabilities and contingent assets

Financial statements must include **all the information necessary for an understanding of the company's financial position**. Provisions, contingent liabilities and contingent assets are 'uncertainties' that must be accounted for consistently if we are to achieve this understanding.

IAS 37 *Provisions, contingent liabilities and contingent assets* aims to ensure that appropriate **recognition criteria** and **measurement bases** are applied to provisions, contingent liabilities and contingent assets and that **sufficient information** is disclosed in the **notes** to the financial statements to enable users to understand their nature, timing and amount.

Before IAS 37, there was no accounting standard dealing with provisions. Companies wanting to show their results in the most favourable light used to make large 'one off' provisions in years where a high level of underlying profits was generated. These provisions, often known as 'big bath' provisions, were then available to shield expenditure in future years when perhaps the underlying profits were not so good. In other words, provisions were used for profit smoothing.

Just as an example, Worldcom had set aside $3.3bn reserves in order to be able to dip into them to boost profits in the future. These were brought into current year earnings in 2002. The key aim of IAS 37 is to ensure that **provisions are made only** where there are valid grounds for them.

IAS 37 views a provision as a liability.

A **provision** is a **liability** of uncertain timing or amount.

A **liability** is an obligation of an entity to transfer economic benefits as a result of past transactions or events.   (IAS 37)

The IAS distinguishes provisions from other liabilities such as trade payables and accruals. This is on the basis that for a provision there is uncertainty about the timing or amount of the future expenditure. Whilst **uncertainty** is clearly present in the case of certain accruals the uncertainty is generally much less than for provisions.

IAS 37 states that a provision should be **recognised** as a liability in the financial statements when:

* An entity has a **present obligation** (legal or constructive) as a result of a past event
* It is probable that a **transfer of economic benefits** will be required to settle the obligation

- A **reliable estimate** can be made of the obligation

Meaning of obligation

It is fairly clear what a legal obligation is. However, there can also be a constructive obligation.

> IAS 37 defines a **constructive obligation** as
>
> 'An obligation that derives from an entity's actions where:
>
> - by an established pattern of past practice, published policies or a sufficiently specific current statement the entity has indicated to other parties that it will accept certain responsibilities; and
> - as a result, the entity has created a valid expectation on the part of those other parties that it will discharge those responsibilities.' *(IAS 37)*

In which circumstances might a provision be recognised?

(a) On 13 December 20X9 the board of an entity decided to close down a division. The accounting date of the company is 31 December. Before 31 December 20X9 the decision was not communicated to any of those affected and no other steps were taken to implement the decision.

No provision would be recognised as the decision has not been communicated and so could still be avoided.

(b) The board agreed a detailed closure plan on 20 December 20X9 and details were given to customers and employees.

A provision would be made in the 20X9 financial statements.

(c) A company is obliged to incur clean up costs for environmental damage (that has already been caused).

A provision for such costs is appropriate, because the obligation arises from a past event.

(d) A company intends to carry out future expenditure to operate in a particular way in the future.

No present obligation exists and under IAS 37 no provision would be appropriate. This is because the entity could avoid the future expenditure by its future actions, maybe by changing its method of operation.

Transfer of economic benefits

For the purpose of the IAS, a transfer of resources embodying economic benefits is regarded as '**probable**' if the event is **more likely than not** to occur. This appears to indicate a probability of more than 50%. However, the standard makes it clear that where there is a number of similar obligations the probability should be based on considering the population as a whole, rather than one single item.

If a company has entered into a warranty obligation then the probability of transfer of resources embodying economic benefits may well be extremely small in respect of one specific item. However, when considering the population as a whole the probability of some transfer of resources is quite likely to be much higher. If there is a **greater than 50% probability** of some transfer of economic benefits then a provision should be made for the **expected amount**.

Measurement of provisions

The amount recognised as a provision should be the best estimate of the expenditure required to settle the present obligation at the end of the reporting period.

The estimates will be determined by the **judgement** of the entity's management supplemented by the experience of similar transactions.

Allowance is made for **uncertainty**. Where the provision being measured involves a large population of items, the obligation is estimated by weighting all possible outcomes by their associated probabilities, ie expected value.

Example

A company sells goods with a warranty under which customers are covered for the cost of repairs of any manufacturing defect that becomes apparent within the first six months of purchase. The company's past experience and future expectations indicate the following pattern of likely repairs.

% of goods sold	Defects	Cost of repairs if all items suffered from these defects $m
75	None	–
20	Minor	1.0
5	Major	4.0

The cost is found using 'expected values' (75% × $nil) + (20% × $1.0m) + (5% × $4.0m) = $400,000.

Where the effect of the **time value of money** is material, the amount of a provision should be the **present value** of the expenditure required to settle the obligation. An appropriate **discount** rate should be used.

The discount rate should be a pre-tax rate that reflects current market assessments of the time value of money. The discount rate(s) should not reflect risks for which future cash flow estimates have been adjusted.

Example

A company knows that when it ceases a certain operation in 5 years time it will have to pay environmental cleanup costs of $5m.

The provision to be made now will be the present value of $5m in 5 years time.

The relevant discount rate in this case is 10%.

Therefore a provision will be made for:

	$
$5m × 0.62092*	3,104,600

* The discount rate for 5 years at 10%.

The following year the provision will be:

	$
$5m × 0.68301**	3,415,050
Increase	310,450

**The discount rate for 4 years at 10%

The increase in the liability in the second year of $310,450 will be charged to profit or loss. It is referred to as the **unwinding** of the discount. This is accounted for as a finance cost.

Future events which are reasonably expected to occur (eg new legislation, changes in technology) may affect the amount required to settle the entity's obligation and should be taken into account.

Gains from the expected disposal of assets should not be taken into account in measuring a provision.

Reimbursements

Some or all of the expenditure needed to settle a provision may be expected to be recovered from a third party. If so, **the reimbursement should be recognised only when it is virtually certain that reimbursement will be received if the entity settles the obligation**.

- The reimbursement should be treated as a separate asset, and the amount recognised should not be greater than the provision itself.
- The provision and the amount recognised for reimbursement may be netted off in profit or loss.

Changes in provisions

Provisions should be **reviewed at the end of each reporting period** and adjusted to reflect the current best estimate. If it is no longer probable that a transfer of resources will be required to settle the obligation, the provision should be reversed.

Use of provisions

A provision should be used only for expenditures for which the provision was originally recognised. Setting expenditures against a provision that was originally recognised for another purpose would conceal the impact of two different events.

Future operating losses

Provisions should not be recognised for future operating losses. They do not meet the definition of a liability and the general recognition criteria set out in the standard.

Onerous contracts

If an entity has a contract that is onerous, the present obligation under the contract **should be recognised and measured** as a provision. An example might be vacant leasehold property. The entity is under an obligation to maintain the property but is receiving no income from it.

An **onerous contract** is a contract entered into with another party under which the unavoidable costs of fulfilling the terms of the contract exceed any revenues expected to be received from the goods or services supplied or purchased directly or indirectly under the contract and where the entity would have to compensate the other party if it did not fulfil the terms of the contract. *(IAS 37)*

Examples of possible provisions

(a) **Warranties**. These are argued to be genuine provisions as on past experience it is probable, ie more likely than not, that some claims will emerge. The provision must be estimated, however, on the basis of the class as a whole and not on individual claims. There is a clear legal obligation in this case.

(b) **Major repairs**. In the past it has been quite popular for companies to provide for expenditure on a major overhaul to be accrued gradually over the intervening years between overhauls. Under IAS 37 this is no longer possible as IAS 37 would argue that this is a mere intention to carry out repairs, not an obligation. The entity can always sell the asset in the meantime. The only solution is to treat major assets such as aircraft, ships, furnaces etc as a series of smaller assets where each part is depreciated over shorter lives. Thus any major overhaul may be argued to be replacement and therefore capital rather than revenue expenditure.

(c) **Self insurance**. A number of companies have created a provision for self insurance based on the expected cost of making good fire damage etc instead of paying premiums to an insurance company. Under IAS 37 this provision is no longer justifiable as the entity has no obligation until a fire or accident occurs. No obligation exists until that time.

(d) **Environmental contamination**. If the company has an environmental policy such that other parties would expect the company to clean up any contamination or if the company has broken current environmental legislation then a provision for environmental damage must be made.

(e) **Decommissioning or abandonment costs**. When an oil company initially purchases an oilfield it is put under a legal obligation to decommission the site at the end of its life. Prior to IAS 37 most oil companies set up the provision gradually over the life of the field so that no one year would be unduly burdened with the cost.

IAS 37, however, insists that a legal obligation exists on the initial expenditure on the field and therefore a liability exists immediately. This would appear to result in a large charge to profit and loss in the first year of operation of the field. However, the IAS takes the view that the cost of purchasing the field in the first place is not only the cost of the field itself but also the costs of putting it right again. Thus all the costs of decommissioning may be capitalised.

(f) **Restructuring**. This is considered in detail below.

2 Provisions for restructuring

IAS 37 defines a **restructuring** as:

A programme that is planned and is controlled by management and materially changes one of two things.

- The scope of a business undertaken by an entity
- The manner in which that business is conducted   *(IAS 37)*

The IAS gives the following **examples** of events that may fall under the definition of restructuring.

- The **sale or termination** of a line of business

- The **closure of business locations** in a country or region or the **relocation** of business activities from one country region to another
- **Changes in management structure**, for example, the elimination of a layer of management
- **Fundamental reorganisations** that have a material effect on the **nature and focus** of the entity's operations

The question is whether or not an entity has an obligation – legal or constructive – at the end of the reporting period. For this to be the case:

- An entity must have a **detailed formal plan** for the restructuring
- It must have **raised a valid expectation** in those affected that it will carry out the restructuring by starting to implement that plan or announcing its main features to those affected by it

A mere management decision is not normally sufficient. Management decisions may sometimes trigger off recognition, but only if earlier events such as negotiations with employee representatives and other interested parties have been concluded subject only to management approval. *(IAS 37)*

Where the restructuring involves the **sale of an operation** then IAS 37 states that no obligation arises until the entity has entered into a **binding sale agreement**. This is because until this has occurred the entity will be able to change its mind and withdraw from the sale even if its intentions have been announced publicly.

Costs to be included within a restructuring provision

The IAS states that a restructuring provision should include only the direct expenditures arising from the restructuring, which are those that are both:

- **Necessarily entailed** by the restructuring; and
- Not associated with the **ongoing activities** of the entity.

The following costs should specifically **not** be included within a restructuring provision.

- **Retraining** or relocating continuing staff
- **Marketing**
- **Investment in new systems** and distribution networks

Disclosure

Disclosures for provisions fall into two parts.

- Disclosure of details of the **change in carrying value** of a provision from the beginning to the end of the year
- Disclosure of the **background** to the making of the provision and the uncertainties affecting its outcome

3 Contingent liabilities and contingent assets

IAS 37 defines a **contingent liability** as:

- A possible obligation that arises from past events and whose existence will be confirmed only by the occurrence or non-occurrence of one or more uncertain future events not wholly within the control of the entity; or

> - A present obligation that arises from past events but is not recognised because:
>   - It is not probable that an outflow of resources embodying economic benefits will be required to settle the obligation; or
>   - The amount of the obligation cannot be measured with sufficient reliability.
>
> *(IAS 37)*

As a rule of thumb, probable means more than 50% likely. If an obligation is probable, it is not a contingent liability – instead, a provision is needed.

Treatment of contingent liabilities

Contingent liabilities **should not be recognised in financial statements** but they **should be disclosed**. The required disclosures are:

- A brief description of the nature of the contingent liability
- An estimate of its financial effect
- An indication of the uncertainties that exist
- The possibility of any reimbursement

Contingent assets

> IAS 37 defines a **contingent asset** as:
>
> A possible asset that arises from past events and whose existence will be confirmed by the occurrence or non-occurrence of one or more uncertain future events not wholly within control of the entity. *(IAS 37)*

A contingent asset must not be recognised. Only when the realisation of the related economic benefits is virtually certain should recognition take place. At that point, **the asset is no longer a contingent asset!**

Disclosure

Contingent assets must only be disclosed in the notes if they are **probable**. In that case a brief description of the contingent asset should be provided along with an estimate of its likely financial effect.

'Let out'

IAS 37 permits reporting entities to avoid disclosure requirements relating to provisions, contingent liabilities and contingent assets if they would be expected to **seriously prejudice** the position of the entity in dispute with other parties. However, this should only be employed in **extremely rare** cases. Details of the general nature of the provision/contingencies must still be provided, together with an explanation of why it has not been disclosed.

Inventories and construction contracts

9

1 Inventories and short-term WIP (IAS 2)

IAS 2 was revised in December 2003. It lays out the required accounting treatment for inventories (sometimes called stocks) under the historical cost system.

The following items are **excluded** from the scope of the standard.

- Work in progress under **construction contracts** (covered by IAS 11 *Construction contracts*, see Section 2)
- **Financial instruments** (ie shares, bonds)
- **Biological assets**

Certain inventories are exempt from the standard's **measurement rules**, ie those held by:

- Producers of **agricultural and forest products**
- **Commodity-broker traders**

The standard gives the following important definitions.

> - **Inventories** are assets:
>   - held for sale in the ordinary course of business;
>   - in the process of production for such sale; or
>   - in the form of materials or supplies to be consumed in the production process or in the rendering of services.
> - **Net realisable value** is the estimated selling price in the ordinary course of business less the estimated costs of completion and the estimated costs necessary to make the sale.
> - **Fair value** is the amount for which an asset could be exchanged or a liability settled between knowledgeable, willing parties in an arm's length transaction.
>
> *(IAS 2)*

Inventories can **include** any of the following.

- Goods purchased and held for resale, eg goods held for sale by a retailer, or land and buildings held for resale
- **Finished goods** produced
- **Work in progress** being produced
- Materials and supplies awaiting use in the production process (**raw materials**)

The standard states that '**Inventories should be measured at the lower of cost and net realisable value.**'

Cost of inventories

The cost of inventories will consist of all costs of:

*   **Purchase**
*   **Costs of conversion**
*   **Other costs** incurred in bringing the inventories to their **present location and condition**

The standard lists the following as comprising the costs of purchase of inventories:

*   **Purchase price** *plus*
*   **Import duties** and other *taxes plus*
*   Transport, handling and any other cost **directly attributable** to the acquisition of finished goods, services and materials less
*   **Trade discounts**, rebates and other similar amounts

Costs of conversion of inventories consist of two main parts.

(a)   Costs **directly related** to the units of production, eg direct materials, direct labour
(b)   Fixed and variable **production overheads** that are incurred in converting materials into finished goods, allocated on a systematic basis.

> *   **Fixed production overheads** are those indirect costs of production that remain relatively constant regardless of the volume of production, eg the cost of factory management and administration.
> *   **Variable production overheads** are those indirect costs of production that vary directly, or nearly directly, with the volume of production, eg indirect materials and labour.   (IAS 2)

The standard emphasises that fixed production overheads must be allocated to items of inventory on the basis of the **normal capacity of the production facilities**. This is an important point.

(a)   **Normal capacity** is the expected achievable production based on the average over several periods/seasons, under normal circumstances.
(b)   The above figure should take account of the capacity lost through **planned maintenance**.
(c)   If it approximates to the normal level of activity then the **actual level of production** can be used.
(d)   **Low production** or **idle plant** will *not* result in a higher fixed overhead allocation to each unit.
(e)   **Unallocated overheads** must be recognised as an expense in the period in which they were incurred.
(f)   When production is **abnormally high**, the fixed production overhead allocated to each unit will be reduced, so avoiding inventories being stated at more than cost.
(g)   The allocation of variable production overheads to each unit is based on the **actual use** of production facilities.

Any other costs should only be recognised if they are incurred in bringing the inventories to **their present location and condition**.

The standard lists types of cost which **would not be included** in cost of inventories. Instead, they should be recognised as an **expense** in the period they are incurred.

(a)   **Abnormal amounts** of wasted materials, labour or other production costs

(b)   **Storage costs** (except costs which are necessary in the production process before a further production stage)
(c)   **Administrative overheads** not incurred to bring inventories to their present location and conditions
(d)   **Selling costs**

Net realisable value (NRV)

As a general rule assets should not be carried at amounts greater than those expected to be realised from their sale or use. In the case of inventories this amount could fall below cost when items are **damaged or become obsolete**, or where the **costs to completion have increased** in order to make the sale.

In fact we can identify the principal situations in which NRV is likely to be less than cost, ie where there has been:

(a)   An **increase in costs** or a **fall in selling price**
(b)   A **physical deterioration** in the condition of inventory
(c)   **Obsolescence** of products
(d)   A decision as part of the company's marketing strategy to manufacture and sell products at a **loss**
(e)   **Errors in production or purchasing**

A write down of inventories would normally take place on an item by item basis, but similar or related items may be **grouped together**. This grouping together is acceptable for, say, items in the same product line, but it is not acceptable to write down inventories based on a whole classification (eg finished goods) or a whole business.

The assessment of NRV should take place **at the same time** as estimates are made of selling price, using the most reliable information available. Fluctuations of price or cost should be taken into account if they relate directly to **events after the reporting period**, which confirm conditions existing at the end of the period.

The reasons why inventory is held must also be taken into account. Some inventory, for example, may be held to satisfy a firm contract and its NRV will therefore be the **contract price**. Any additional inventory of the same type held at the period end will, in contrast, be assessed according to general sales prices when NRV is estimated.

Net realisable value must be reassessed at the end of each period and compared again with cost. If the NRV has risen for inventories held over the end of more than one period, then the previous write down must be **reversed** to the extent that the inventory is then valued at the lower of cost and the new NRV. This may be possible when selling prices have fallen in the past and then risen again.

On occasion a write down to NRV may be of such size, incidence or nature that it must be **disclosed separately**.

Cost formulae for inventories

IAS 2 allows two cost formulae (FIFO or weighted average cost) for inventories that are ordinarily interchangeable or are not produced and segregated for specific projects. The issue is whether an entity may use different cost formulae for different types of inventories.

IAS 2 provides that an entity should use **the same cost formula for all inventories having similar nature and use to the entity**. For inventories with different nature or use (for example, certain commodities used in one business segment and the same type of commodities used in another business segment), different cost formulae may be justified. A difference in geographical location of inventories (and in the respective tax rules), by itself, is not sufficient to justify the use of different cost formulae.

2 IAS 11: Construction contracts

A company is building a large tower block that will house offices, under a contract with an investment company. It will take three years to build the block and over that time it will obviously have to pay for building materials, wages of workers on the building, architects' fees and so on. It will receive periodic payments from the investment company at various predetermined stages of the construction. How does it decide, in each of the three years, **what to include as income and expenditure** for the contract in the statement of comprehensive income?

This is the problem tackled by IAS 11 *Construction contracts*.

Example: construction contract

A numerical example might help to illustrate the problem. Suppose that a contract is started on 1 January 20X5, with an estimated completion date of 31 December 20X6. The final contract price is $1,500,000. In the first year, to 31 December 20X5:

(a)   Costs incurred amounted to $600,000.
(b)   Half the work on the contract was completed.
(c)   Certificates of work completed have been issued, to the value of $750,000.
(d)   It is estimated with reasonable certainty that further costs to completion in 20X6 will be $600,000.

What is the contract profit in 20X5, and what entries would be made for the contract at 31 December 20X5 if:

(a)   Profits are deferred until the completion of the contract?
(b)   A proportion of the estimated revenue and profit is credited to profit or loss in 20X5?

Solution

(a)   If profits were deferred until the completion of the contract in 20X6, the revenue and profit recognised on the contract in 20X5 would be nil, and the value of work in progress on 31 December 20X5 would be $600,000. IAS 11 takes the view that this policy is unreasonable, because in 20X6, the total profit of $300,000 would be recorded. Since the contract revenues are earned throughout 20X5 and 20X6, a profit of nil in 20X5 and $300,000 in 20X6 would be contrary to the accruals concept of accounting.

(b)   **It is fairer to recognise revenue and profit throughout the duration of the contract.** As at 31 December 20X5 revenue of $750,000 should be matched with cost of sales of $600,000 in the statement of comprehensive income, leaving an attributable profit for 20X5 of $150,000.

The only entry in the statement of financial position as at 31 December 20X5 is a receivable of $750,000 recognising that the company is owed this amount for work done to date. No balance remains for work in progress, the whole $600,000 having been recognised in cost of sales.

What is a construction contract?

A contract which needs IAS 11 treatment does not have to last for a period of more than one year. The main point is that the contract activity **starts in one financial period and ends in another**, thus creating the problem: to which of two or more periods should contract income and costs be allocated? In fact the definition given in the IAS of a construction contract is very straightforward.

> **Construction contract**. A contract specifically negotiated for the construction of an asset or a combination of assets that are closely interrelated or interdependent in terms of their design, technology and function or their ultimate purpose or use.
>
> (IAS 11)

The standard differentiates between fixed price contracts and cost plus contracts.

> * **Fixed price contract**. A contract in which the contractor agrees to a fixed contract price, or a fixed rate per unit of output, which in some cases is subject to cost escalation clauses.
> * **Cost plus contract**. A construction contract in which the contractor is reimbursed for allowable or otherwise defined costs, plus a percentage of these costs or a fixed fee.
>
> (IAS 11)

Construction contracts may involve the building of one asset, eg a bridge, or a series of interrelated assets eg an oil refinery. They may also include **rendering of services** (eg architects) or restoring or demolishing an asset.

Contract revenue

Contract revenue will be the **amount specified in the contract**, subject to variations in the contract work, incentive payments and claims if these will probably give rise to revenue and if they can be reliably measured. The result is that contract revenue is measured at the **fair value** of received or receivable revenue.

The standard elaborates on the types of uncertainty, which depend on the outcome of future events, that affect the **measurement of contract revenue**.

* An **agreed variation** (increase/decrease)
* **Cost escalation clauses** in a fixed price contract (increase)
* **Penalties** imposed due to delays by the contractor (decrease)
* **Number of units** varies in a contract for fixed prices per unit (increase/decrease)

In the case of any variation, claim or incentive payment, two factors should be assessed to determine whether contract revenue should be recognised.

* Whether it is **probable** that the customer will accept the variation/claim, or that the contract is sufficiently advanced that the performance criteria will be met
* Whether the amount of the revenue can be **measured reliably**

Contract costs

Contract costs consist of:

* Costs relating **directly** to the contract
* Costs attributable to general contract activity which can be **allocated** to the contract, such as insurance, cost of design and technical assistance not directly related to a specific contract and construction overheads

- Any other costs which can be **charged to the customer** under the contract, which may include general administration costs and development costs

Costs that **relate directly** to a specific contract include the following.

- **Site labour costs**, including site supervision
- Costs of **materials** used in construction
- **Depreciation** of plant and equipment used on the contract
- Costs of **moving** plant, equipment and materials to and from the contract site
- Costs of **hiring** plant and equipment
- Costs of **design and technical assistance** that are directly related to the contract
- Estimated costs of **rectification and guarantee work**, including expected warranty costs
- **Claims from third parties**

General contract activity costs should be **allocated systematically and rationally**, and all costs with similar characteristics should be treated **consistently**. The allocation should be based on the **normal level** of construction activity. Borrowing costs may be attributed in this way (see IAS 23).

Some costs **cannot be attributed** to contract activity and so the following should be **excluded** from construction contract costs.

- **General administration costs** (unless reimbursement is specified in the contract)
- **Selling costs**
- **R&D** (unless reimbursement is specified in the contract)
- **Depreciation** of idle plant and equipment not used on any particular contract

Recognition of contract revenue and expenses

Revenue and costs associated with a contract should be recognised according to the stage of completion of the contract at the end of the reporting period, but *only when* the **outcome of the activity can be estimated reliably**. If a loss is predicted on a contract, then it should be recognised immediately. This is often known as the **percentage of completion method**.

A reliable estimate of the outcome of a construction contract can only be made when certain conditions have been met, and these conditions will be different for fixed price and cost plus contracts.

- **Fixed price contracts**
  - Probable that economic benefits of the contract will flow to the entity
  - Total contract revenue can be reliably measured
  - Stage of completion at the period end and costs to complete the contract can be reliably measured
  - Costs attributable to the contract can be identified clearly and be reliably measured (actual costs can be compared to previous estimates)

- **Cost plus contracts**
  - Probable that economic benefits of the contract will flow to the entity
  - Costs attributable to the contract (whether or not reimbursable) can be identified clearly and be reliably measured

The **percentage of completion method** is an application of the accruals assumption. Contract revenue is matched to the contract costs incurred in reaching the stage of completion, so revenue, costs and profit are attributed to the proportion of work completed.

We can **summarise** the treatment as follows.

- Recognise **contract revenue** as revenue in the accounting periods in which the work is performed
- Recognise **contract costs** as an expense in the accounting period in which the work to which they relate is performed
- Any **expected excess** of total contract costs over total contract revenue should be recognised as an expense immediately
- Any costs incurred which relate to **future activity** should be recognised as an asset if it is probable that they will be recovered (often called contract work in progress, ie amounts due from the customer)
- Where amounts have been recognised as contract revenue, but their **collectability** from the customer becomes doubtful, such amounts should be recognised as an expense, not a deduction from revenue

When can reliable estimates be made?

IAS 11 only allows contract revenue and costs to be recognised when the outcome of the contract can be predicted, ie when it is probable that the economic benefits attached to the contract will flow to the entity. IAS 11 states that this can only be when a contract has been agreed which establishes the following.

- The **enforceable rights** of each party in respect of the asset to be constructed
- The **consideration** that is to be exchanged
- **Terms and manner of settlement**

In addition, the entity should have an **effective internal financial budgeting and reporting system**, in order to review and revise the estimates of contract revenue and costs as the contract progresses.

Determining the stage of completion

How should you decide on the stage of completion of any contract? The standard lists several methods.

- **Proportion of contract costs incurred** for work carried out to date
- **Surveys** of work carried out
- **Physical proportion** of the contract work completed

When the stage of completion is determined using the contract costs incurred to date, only contract costs reflecting the work to date should be included in costs incurred to date.

- Exclude costs relating to **future activity,** eg cost of materials delivered but not yet used
- Exclude payments made to subcontractors **in advance** of work performed

Outcome of the contract cannot be reliably estimated

When the contract's outcome cannot be reliably estimated the following treatment should be followed.

- Only recognise revenue to the extent of contract costs incurred which are expected to be **recoverable**
- Recognise contract costs as an **expense** in the period they are incurred

This **no profit/no loss approach** reflects the situation near the beginning of a contract, ie the outcome cannot be reliably estimated, but it is likely that costs will be recovered.

Contract costs which **cannot be recovered** should be recognised as an expense straight away. IAS 11 lists the following situations where this might occur.

*   The contract is **not fully enforceable**, ie its validity is seriously questioned
*   The completion of the contract is subject to the outcome of **pending litigation or legislation**
*   The contract relates to properties which will probably be **expropriated or condemned**
*   The customer is **unable to meet its obligations** under the contract
*   The contractor **cannot complete** the contract or in any other way meet its obligations under the contract

Where these **uncertainties cease to exist**, contract revenue and costs should be recognised as normal, ie by reference to the stage of completion.

Recognition of expected losses

Any loss on a contract should be **recognised as soon as it is foreseen**. The loss will be the amount by which total expected contract revenue is exceeded by total expected contract costs. The loss amount is not affected by whether work has started on the contract, the stage of completion of the work or profits on other contracts (unless they are related contracts treated as a single contract).

The effect of any change in the estimate of contract revenue or costs or the outcome of a contract should be accounted for as a **change in accounting estimate** under IAS 8 *Accounting policies, changes in accounting estimates and errors*.

Summary of accounting treatment

Statement of comprehensive income (income statement)

(a) **Revenue and costs**

(i) Sales revenue and associated costs should be recorded in the income statement section as the contract activity progresses.

(ii) Include an appropriate proportion of total contract value as sales revenue in the income statement.

(iii) The costs incurred in reaching that stage of completion are matched with this sales revenue, resulting in the reporting of results which can be attributed to the proportion of work completed.

(iv) Sales revenue is the value of work carried out to date.

(b) **Profit recognised in the contract**

(i) It must reflect the proportion of work carried out.

(ii) It should take into account any known inequalities in profitability in the various stages of a contract.

Statement of financial position

(a) **Current assets**

	$
Costs to date	X
Plus recognised profits	(X)
	X
Less recognised losses	(X)
	X
Less progress billings	(X)
Amount due from customers for contract work	X

(b) **Receivables**

Unpaid progress billings	X

(c) **Current liabilities**. Where (a) gives a net 'amount due to customers' this amount should be included as 'Gross amounts due to customers for contract work'.

Example

P Co has the following construction contract in progress:

	$m
Total contract price	750
Costs incurred to date	225
Estimated costs to completion	340
Progress payments invoiced and received	290

Now we will calculate the amounts to be recognised for the contract in the income statement and statement of financial position assuming the contract completion is calculated using the proportion of costs incurred method.

1   *Estimated profit*

	$m
Total contract price	750
Less costs incurred to date	(225)
Less estimated costs to completion	(340)
Estimated profit	185

2   Percentage complete

Costs to date / total estimated costs: $225 / (225 + 340) = 40\%$

3   *Income statement*

	$m
Revenue (40% x $750)	300
Cost of sales (40% x (225 + 340))	(226)
Profit (40% x 185)	74

4   *Statement of financial position*

	$m
Costs incurred to date	225
Recognised profits	74
Less progress billings to date	(290)
Amounts due from customers for contract work	9

How would we account for this if it was a loss-making contract? We will reduce P Co's contract price to $550m.

1   *Estimated loss*

	$m
Total contract price	550
Less costs incurred to date	(225)
Less Estimated costs to completion	(340)
Estimated loss	(15)

2   *Percentage complete*

Costs to date / total estimated costs: 225 / (225 + 340) = 40%

3   *Income statement*

	$m
Revenue (40% x $550)	220
Cost of sales (balancing figure)	(235)
Loss	(15)

4   *Statement of financial position*

	$m
Costs incurred to date	225
Recognised loss	(15)
Less progress billings to date	(290)
Amounts due to customers for contract work	(80)

Accounting for leases

10

1 IAS 17: Leases

IAS 17 *Leases* standardises the accounting treatment and disclosure of assets held under lease.

In a leasing transaction there is a **contract** between the lessor and the lessee for the hire of an asset. The lessor retains legal ownership but conveys to the lessee the right to use the asset for an agreed period of time in return for specified rentals. IAS 17 defines a lease and recognises two types.

- **Lease**. An agreement whereby the lessor conveys to the lessee in return for rent the right to use an asset for an agreed period of time.
- **Finance lease**. A lease that transfers substantially all the risks and rewards incident to ownership of an asset. Title may or may not eventually be transferred.
- **Operating lease**. A lease other than a finance lease.   (*IAS 17*)

A **finance lease** may be a **hire purchase agreement**. (The difference is that under a hire purchase agreement the customer eventually, after paying an agreed number of instalments, becomes entitled to exercise an option to purchase the asset. Under other leasing agreements, ownership remains forever with the lessor.)

To expand on the definition above, a finance lease should be presumed if at the inception of a lease the **present value of the minimum lease payments** is approximately equal to the **fair value of the leased asset**.

The present value should be calculated by using the **interest rate implicit in the lease**.

- **Minimum lease payments**. The payments over the lease term that the lessee is or can be required to make, excluding contingent rent, costs for services and taxes to be paid by and be reimbursed to the lessor, together with:
  - (a) For a lessee, any amounts guaranteed by the lessee or by a party related to the lessee
  - (b) For a lessor, any residual value guaranteed to the lessor by one of the following.
    - (i)   The lessee
    - (ii)   A party related to the lessee
    - (iii) An independent third party financially capable of meeting this guarantee

However, if the lessee has the option to purchase the asset at a price which is expected to be sufficiently lower than fair value at the date the option becomes exercisable for it to be reasonably certain, at the inception of the lease, that the option will be exercised, the minimum lease payments comprise the minimum payments payable over the lease term to the expected date of exercise of this purchase option and the payment required to exercise it.

- **Interest rate implicit in the lease.**

  The discount rate that, at the inception of the lease, causes the aggregate present value of

  (a) The minimum lease payments, and
  (b) The unguaranteed residual value

  to be equal to the sum of

  (a) The fair value of the leased asset, and
  (b) Any initial direct costs.

- **Initial direct costs** are **incremental costs** that are directly attributable to **negotiating** and **arranging** a lease, except for such costs incurred by manufacturer or dealer lessors. Examples of initial direct costs include amounts such as **commissions, legal fees** and relevant internal costs.

- **Lease term.** The non-cancellable period for which the lessee has contracted to lease the asset together with any further terms for which the lessee has the option to continue to lease the asset, with or without further payment, when at the inception of the lease it is reasonably certain that the lessee will exercise the option.

- A non-cancellable lease is a lease that is cancellable only in one of the following situations.

  (a) Upon the occurrence of some remote contingency
  (b) With the permission of the lessor
  (c) If the lessee enters into a new lease for the same or an equivalent asset with the same lessor
  (d) Upon payment by the lessee of an additional amount such that, at inception, continuation of the lease is reasonably certain

- The **inception of the lease** is the earlier of the date of the lease agreement and the date of commitment by the parties to the principal provisions of the lease. As at this date:

  (a) A lease is classified as either an operating lease or a finance lease; and
  (b) In the case of a finance lease, the amounts to be recognised at the start of lease term are determined

- **Economic life** is either:

  (a) The period over which an asset is expected to be economically usable by one or more users, or
  (b) The number of production or similar units expected to be obtained from the asset by one or more users.

- **Useful life** is the estimated remaining period, from the beginning of the lease term, without limitation by the lease term, over which the economic benefits embodied in the asset are expected to be consumed by the entity.

- **Guaranteed residual value** is:

  (a) For a lessee, that part of the residual value which is guaranteed by the lessee or by a party related to the lessee (the amount of the guarantee being the maximum amount that could, in any event, become payable).
  (b) For a lessor, that part of the residual value which is guaranteed by the lessee or by a third party unrelated to the lessor who is financially capable of discharging the obligations under the guarantee.

- **Unguaranteed residual value** is that portion of the residual value of the leased asset, the realisation of which by the lessor is not assured or is guaranteed solely by a party related to the lessor.

- **Gross investment in the lease** is the aggregate of:

  (a) The minimum lease payments receivable by the lessor under a finance lease, and
  (b) Any unguaranteed residual value accruing to the lessor.

- **Net investment in the lease** is the gross investment in the lease discounted at the interest rate implicit in the lease.

- **Unearned finance income** is the difference between:

  (a) The gross investment in the lease, and
  (b) The net investment in the lease.

- The **lessee's incremental borrowing rate of interest** is the rate of interest the lessee would have to pay on a similar lease or, if that is not determinable, the rate that, at the inception of the lease, the lessee would incur to borrow over a similar term, and with a similar security, the funds necessary to purchase the asset.

- **Contingent rent** is that portion of the lease payments that is not fixed in amount but is based on a factor other than just the passage of time (eg percentage of sales, amount of usage, price indices, market rates of interest).   (IAS 17)

Accounting for operating leases

Operating leases do not really pose an accounting problem. The lessee pays amounts periodically to the lessor and these are **charged to the income statement**. The lessor treats the leased asset as a non-current asset and depreciates it in the normal way. Rentals received from the lessee are credited to the income statement in the lessor's books.

Where the lessee is offered an incentive such as a **rent-free period** or **cashback incentive**, this is effectively a discount, which will be spread over the period of the operating lease in accordance with the accruals principle. For instance, if a company entered into a 4-year operating lease but was not required to make any payments until year 2, the total payments to be made over years 2-4 should be charged evenly over years 1-4.

Where a cashback incentive is received, the total amount payable over the lease term, less the cashback, should be charged evenly over the term of the lease. This can be done by crediting the cashback received to deferred income and releasing it to profit or loss over the lease term.

Accounting for finance leases

For assets held under **finance leases** (including hire purchase) this accounting treatment would not disclose the reality of the situation. For the lessor, in reality, what he owns is a stream of cash flows receivable from the lessee. **The asset is an amount receivable rather than a non-current asset.**

For the lessee the **substance of the transaction is that he has acquired a non-current asset**, and this is reflected in the accounting treatment prescribed by IAS 17, even though in law the lessee may never become the owner of the asset.

The following summary diagram shows the points of distinction between an operating lease and and a finance lease.

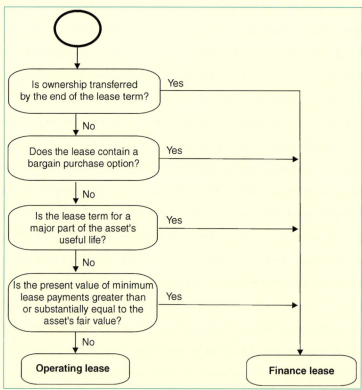

IAS 17 originally stated that when classifying a lease of **land and buildings** the **land** element is normally classified as an **operating lease unless title passes to the lessee** at the end of the contract.

This has now been amended. Effective from January 2010, entities now have the option to treat a long lease of land as a finance lease.

2 Lessees

Accounting treatment for finance leases

IAS 17 requires that, when an asset changes hands under a **finance lease, lessor and lessee should account for the transaction as though it were a credit sale.** In the lessee's books therefore the lease asset is capitalised:

DEBIT   Asset account
CREDIT   Lessor (liability) account

The amount to be recorded in this way is the **lower** of the **fair value** and the **present value** of the minimum lease payments.

IAS 17 states that it is not appropriate to show liabilities for leased assets as deductions from the leased assets. A distinction should be made between **current and non-current** lease liabilities, if the entity makes this distinction for other liabilities.

The asset should be **depreciated** (on the bases set out in IASs 16 and 38) over the shorter of the lease term and the useful life of the asset.

If there is reasonable certainty of eventual ownership of the asset, then it should be depreciated over its useful life.

Apportionment of rental payments

When the lessee makes a rental payment it will comprise two elements.

(a)   An **interest charge** on the finance provided by the lessor. This proportion of each payment is interest payable and interest receivable in the income statements of the lessee and lessor respectively.

(b)   A repayment of part of the **capital cost** of the asset. In the lessee's books this proportion of each rental payment must be debited to the lessor's account to reduce the outstanding liability. In the lessor's books, it must be credited to the lessee's account to reduce the amount owing (the debit of course is to cash).

The accounting problem is to decide what proportion of each instalment paid by the lessee represents interest, and what proportion represents a repayment of the capital advanced by the lessor.

The **actuarial method** is the best and most scientific method of doing this. It derives from the common-sense assumption that the interest charged by a lessor company will equal the rate of return desired by the company, multiplied by the amount of capital it has invested. This required rate of return is described as the **effective interest rate.**

(a)   At the beginning of the lease the capital invested is equal to the fair value of the asset (less any initial deposit paid by the lessee).

(b)   This amount reduces as each instalment is paid. It follows that the interest accruing is greatest in the early part of the lease term, and gradually reduces as capital is repaid.

Example

On 1 January 20X5 a company bought a machine under a finance lease. The cash price of the machine was $7,710 while the amount to be paid was $10,000. The agreement required the immediate payment of a $2,000 deposit with the balance being settled in four equal annual instalments commencing on 31 December 20X5. The charge of $2,290 represents interest of 15% per annum (the effective interest rate), calculated on the remaining balance of the liability during each accounting period. Depreciation on the plant is to be provided for at the rate of 20% per annum on a straight line basis assuming a residual value of nil.

Interest is calculated as 15% of the outstanding *capital* balance at the beginning of each year. The outstanding capital balance reduces each year by the capital element comprised in each instalment. This will appear as follows over the term of the lease:

	$
Cash price	7,710
Deposit	(2,000)
	5,710
Interest 15%	856
31 December 20X5 instalment	(2,000)
Balance at 31 December 20X5	4,566
Interest 15%	685
31 December 20X6 instalment	(2,000)
Balance at 31 December 20X6	3,251
Interest 15%	488
31 December 20X7 instalment	(2,000)
Balance at 31 December 20X7	1,739
Interest 15%	261
31 December 20X8 instalment	(2,000)
	–

Thus, at each year end the balance on the liability account will represent the outstanding capital liability. Future interest/finance charges are not a true liability as the capital could be paid off at any time, thus avoiding these charges.

Disclosure requirements for lessees

IAS 17 (revised) requires the following disclosures by lessees in respect of finance leases:

*   The **net carrying amount** at the reporting date for each class of asset
*   A **reconciliation** between the total of minimum lease payments at the reporting date, and their present value. In addition, an entity should disclose the total of minimum lease payments at the reporting date, and their present value, for each of the following periods:
    *   Not later than one year
    *   Later than one year and not later than five years
    *   Later than five years
*   **Contingent rents** recognised as income in the period
*   Total of **future minimum sublease payments** expected to be received under non-cancellable subleases at the reporting date
*   A **general description** of the lessee's material leasing arrangements

IAS 17 encourages (but does not require) further disclosures, as appropriate.

Example

In the case above, the company's financial statements for the first year of the lease, the year ended 31 December 20X5, would include the information given below.

STATEMENT OF FINANCIAL POSITION AS AT 31 DECEMBER 20X5 (EXTRACTS)

	$	$
Non-current assets		
Assets held under finance leases		
Plant and machinery at cost	7,710	
Less accumulated depreciation(20% × $7,710)	(1,542)	
		6,168
Non-current liabilities		
Obligations under finance leases		3,251
Current liabilities		
Obligations under finance leases (4,566 – 3,251)		1,315

Part
B

(Notice that only the outstanding **capital** element is disclosed under liabilities, ie the total of the minimum lease payments with future finance charges separately deducted.)

STATEMENT OF COMPREHENSIVE INCOME
FOR THE YEAR ENDED 31 DECEMBER 20X5 (EXTRACT)

	$
Interest payable and similar charges	
Interest on finance leases	856

Operating leases: disclosure requirements for lessees

For operating leases the disclosures are as follows.

(a)   The total of future minimum lease payments under non-cancellable operating leases for each of the following periods:
   (i)   Not later than one year
   (ii)   Later than one year and not later than five years
   (iii)   Later than five years
(b)   The total of any future minimum sublease payments expected to be received at the end of the reporting period
(c)   Lease and sublease payements recognised as an expense in the period
(d)   A general description of the lessees significant leasing arrangements

3 Lessors

To a certain extent at least, the accounting treatment of leases adopted by lessors will be a **mirror image** of that used by lessees.

Finance leases

Several of the definitions given earlier in this chapter are relevant to lessor accounting in particular:

*   Unguaranteed residual value

- Gross investment in the lease
- Unearned finance income
- Net investment in the lease

Accounting treatment

IAS 17 requires the **amount due from the lessee** under a finance lease to be recorded in the statement of financial position of a lessor as a receivable at the amount of the **net investment in the lease**.

The **recognition of finance income** under a finance lease should normally be based on a pattern to give a **constant periodic rate of return** on the lessor's net investment outstanding in respect of the finance lease in each period. In arriving at the constant periodic rate of return, a reasonable approximation may be made.

The lease payments (excluding costs for services) relating to the accounting period should be applied against the gross investment in the lease, so as to **reduce both the principal and the unearned finance income**.

The **estimated unguaranteed residual values** used to calculate the lessor's gross investment in a lease should be reviewed regularly. If there has been a reduction in the value, then the income allocation over the lease term must be revised. Any reduction in respect of amounts already accrued should be recognised immediately.

Initial direct costs incurred by lessors (eg commissions, legal fees and other costs that are directly attributable to negotiating and arranging a lease) are included in the initial measurement of the finance lease receivable.

Manufacturer/dealer lessors

IAS 17 (revised) looks at the situation where manufacturers or dealers offer customers the choice of either buying or leasing an asset. There will be two types of income under such a lease.

(a) Profit/loss equal to that from an **outright sale** (normal selling price less any discount)
(b) **Finance income** over the lease term

IAS 17 requires the following treatment.

(a) Recognise the **selling profit/loss** in income for the period as if it was an outright sale.
(b) If **interest rates are artificially low**, restrict the selling profit to that which would apply had a commercial rate been applied.
(c) Recognise **costs** incurred in connection with negotiating and arranging a lease as an **expense** when the **selling profit** is recognised (at the start of the lease term).

Lessors' disclosures for finance leases

The following should be disclosed.

- A **reconciliation** between the total gross investment in the lease at the year end, and the present value of minimum lease payments receivable at the year end. In addition, an entity should disclose the total gross investment in the lease and the present value of minimum lease payments receivable at the year end, for each of the following periods:
  - Not later than one year

- Later than one year and not later than five years
- Later than five years
- Unearned finance income
- The unguaranteed residual values accruing to the benefit of the lessor
- The accumulated allowance for uncollectible minimum lease payments receivable
- Contingent rents recognised in income
- A general description of the lessor's material leasing arrangements

Operating leases

Accounting treatment

An **asset** held for use in operating leases by a lessor should be recorded as a long-term asset and depreciated over its useful life. The basis for depreciation should be consistent with the lessor's policy on similar non-lease assets and follow the guidance in IAS 16.

Income from an operating lease, excluding charges for services such as insurance and maintenance, should be recognised on **a straight-line basis** over the period of the lease (even if the receipts are not on such a basis), unless another systematic and rational basis is more representative of the time pattern in which the benefit from the leased asset is receivable.

Initial direct costs incurred by lessors in negotiating and arranging an operating lease should be **added to the carrying amount** of the leased asset and recognised as an expense over the lease term on the same basis as lease income, ie capitalised and amortised over the lease term.

Lessors should refer to IAS 36 in order to determine whether a leased asset has become impaired.

A lessor who is a **manufacturer or dealer** should not recognise any selling profit on entering into an operating lease because it is not the equivalent of a sale.

Lessors' disclosures for operating leases

The following should be disclosed.

- For each class of asset, the **gross carrying amount**, the accumulated depreciation and accumulated impairment losses at the year end:
  - Depreciation recognised in income for the period
  - Impairment losses recognised in income for the period
  - Impairment losses reversed in income for the period
- The **future minimum lease payments** under non-cancellable operating leases in the aggregate and for each of the following periods:
  - Not later than one year
  - Later than one year and not later than five years
  - Later than five years
- Total **contingent rents** recognised in income
- A **general description** of the lessor's leasing arrangements

Sale and leaseback transactions

In a sale and leaseback transaction, an asset is sold by a vendor and then the same asset is **leased back** to the same vendor. The lease payment and sale price are normally interdependent because they are negotiated as part of the same package. The accounting treatment for the lessee or seller should be as follows, depending on the type of lease involved.

(a) In a sale and leaseback transaction which results in a **finance lease**, any apparent profit or loss (that is, the difference between the sale price and the previous carrying value) should be deferred and amortised in the financial statements of the seller/lessee over the lease term. It should not be recognised as income immediately.

(b) If the leaseback is an **operating lease**:

(i) Any profit or loss should be recognised immediately, provided it is clear that the transaction is established at a **fair value**.

(ii) Where the **sale price is below fair value**, any profit or loss should be recognised immediately except that if the apparent loss is compensated by future lease payments at below market price it should to that extent be deferred and amortised over the period for which the asset is expected to be used.

(iii) If the **sale price is above fair value**, the excess over fair value should be deferred and amortised over the period over which the asset is expected to be used.

In addition, for an operating lease where the fair value of the asset at the time of the sale is less than the **carrying amount**, the loss (carrying value less fair value) should be recognised immediately.

The buyer or lessor should account for a sale and leaseback in the **same way as other leases**.

The **disclosure requirements** for both lessees and lessors should force disclosure of sale and leaseback transactions.

Accounting for taxation

1 IAS 12: Income Taxes

IAS 12 does not deal with the detailed computation of corporate or personal tax. This will be done under a specific tax regime and is not the subject of any accounting standard. IAS 12 deals with current and deferred tax. The parts relating to current tax are fairly brief, because this is the simple and uncontroversial area of tax.

Definitions

These are some of the definitions given in IAS 12.

> - **Accounting profit**. Net profit or loss for a period before deducting tax expense.
> - **Taxable profit (tax loss)**. The profit (loss) for a period, determined in accordance with the rules established by the taxation authorities, upon which income taxes are payable (recoverable).
> - **Tax expense (tax income)**. The aggregate amount included in the determination of net profit or loss for the period in respect of current tax and deferred tax.
> - **Current tax**. The amount of income taxes payable (recoverable) in respect of the taxable profit (tax loss) for a period. (IAS 12)

It is important to distinguish between current and deferred tax.

(a) **Current tax** is the amount *actually payable* to the tax authorities in relation to the trading activities of the entity during the period.

(b) **Deferred tax** is an *accounting measure*, used to match the tax effects of transactions with their accounting impact and thereby produce less distorted results.

Recognition of current tax liabilities and assets

IAS 12 requires any **unpaid tax** in respect of the current or prior periods to be recognised as a liability.

Conversely, any **excess tax** paid in respect of current or prior periods over what is due should be recognised as an asset.

Example

In 20X8 D Co had taxable profits of $120,000. In the previous year (20X7) income tax on 20X7 profits had been estimated as $30,000.

Any under or over payments are not settled until the following year's tax payment is due.

What would be the tax payable and the charge for 20X8 if the tax due on 20X7 profits was subsequently agreed with the tax authorities as:

(a) $35,000? or
(b) $25,000?

The calculations are as follows:

(a)	$
Tax due on 20X8 profits ($120,000 × 30%)	36,000
Underpayment for 20X7	5,000
Tax charge and liability	41,000

(a)	$
Tax due on 20X8 profits (as above))	36,000
Overpayment for 20X7	(5,000)
Tax charge and liability	31,000

Alternatively, the rebate due could be shown separately as income in the statement of comprehensive income and as an asset in the statement of financial position. An offset approach like this is, however, most likely.

Taking this a stage further, IAS 12 also requires recognition as an asset of the benefit relating to any tax loss that can be **carried back** to recover current tax of a previous period. This is acceptable because it is probable that the benefit will flow to the entity and it can be reliably measured.

Measurement

Measurement of current tax liabilities (assets) for the current and prior periods is very simple. They are measured at the amount expected to be paid to (recovered from) the tax authorities. The tax rates (and tax laws) used should be those enacted (or substantively enacted) by the end of the reporting period.

Recognition of current tax

Normally, current tax is recognised as income or expense and included in the net profit or loss for the period, except in two cases.

(a)   Tax arising from a **business combination** which is an acquisition is treated differently.
(b)   Tax arising from a transaction or event which is recognised directly in equity (in the same or a different period).

The rule in (b) is logical. If a transaction or event is charged or credited directly to equity, rather than to the income statement, then the related tax should be also. An example of such a situation is where, under IAS 8, an adjustment is made to the **opening balance of retained earnings** due to either a change in accounting policy that is applied retrospectively, or to the correction of a material prior period error.

Presentation

In the statement of financial position, **tax assets and liabilities** should be shown separately from other assets and liabilities.

Current tax assets and liabilities can be **offset**, but this should happen only when certain conditions apply.

(a)   The entity has a **legally enforceable right** to set off the recognised amounts.

(b)   The entity intends to settle the amounts on a **net basis**, or to realise the asset and settle the liability at the same time.

The **tax expense (income)** related to the profit or loss from ordinary activities should be shown in the statement of comprehensive income.

The **disclosure requirements** of IAS 12 are extensive and we will look at these later in the chapter.

2 Deferred tax

Deferred tax gives rise to an accounting adjustment which allows for the fact that tax will be payable or reclaimable in the future.

When a company recognises an asset or liability, it expects to **recover or settle the carrying amount** of that asset or liability. In other words, it expects to sell or use up assets, and to pay off liabilities. What happens if that recovery or settlement is likely to make future tax payments larger (or smaller) than they would otherwise have been if the recovery or settlement had no tax consequences? In these circumstances, IAS 12 requires companies to recognise a **deferred tax liability** (or **deferred tax asset**).

Definitions

- **Deferred tax liabilities** are the amounts of income taxes payable in future periods in respect of taxable temporary differences.
- **Deferred tax assets** are the amounts of income taxes recoverable in future periods in respect of:
    - Deductible temporary differences
    - The carryforward of unused tax losses
    - The carryforward of unused tax credits
- **Temporary differences** are differences between the carrying amount of an asset or liability in the statement of financial position and its tax base. Temporary differences may be either:
    - **Taxable temporary differences**, which are temporary differences that will result in taxable amounts in determining taxable profit (tax loss) of future periods when the carrying amount of the asset or liability is recovered or settled
    - **Deductible temporary differences**, which are temporary differences that will result in amounts that are deductible in determining taxable profit (tax loss) of future periods when the carrying amount of the asset or liability is recovered or settled.
- The **tax base** of an asset or liability is the amount attributed to that asset or liability for tax purposes.   (*IAS 12*)

Tax base

We can expand on the definition given above by stating that the **tax base of an asset** is the amount that will be deductible for tax purposes against any taxable economic benefits that will flow to the entity when it recovers the carrying value of the asset. Where those economic benefits are not taxable, the tax base of the asset is the same as its carrying amount.

We can illustrate this with some examples:

(a)   A machine cost $10,000. For tax purposes, depreciation of $3,000 has already been deducted in the current and prior periods and the remaining cost will be deductible in future periods, either as tax-allowable depreciation or through a deduction on disposal. Revenue generated by using the machine is taxable, any gain on disposal of the machine will be taxable and any loss on disposal will be deductible for tax purposes.

The tax base of the machine is $7,000.

(b)   Interest receivable has a carrying amount of $1,000. The related interest revenue will be taxed on a cash basis.

The tax base of the interest receivable is nil.

(c)   Trade receivables have a carrying amount of $10,000. The related revenue has already been included in taxable profit (tax loss).

The tax base of the trade receivables is $10,000.

(d)   A loan receivable has a carrying amount of $1m. The repayment of the loan will have no tax consequences.

The tax base of the loan is $1m.

In the case of a **liability**, the tax base will be its carrying amount, less any amount that will be deducted for tax purposes in relation to the liability in future periods. For revenue received in advance, the tax base of the resulting liability is its carrying amount, less any amount of the revenue that will not be taxable in future periods.

Temporary differences

Accounting profits form the basis for computing **taxable profits**, on which the tax liability for the year is calculated; however, accounting profits and taxable profits are different. There are two reasons for the differences.

(a)   **Permanent differences**. These occur when certain items of revenue or expense are excluded from the computation of taxable profits (for example, entertainment expenses may not be allowable for tax purposes).

(b)   **Temporary differences**. These occur when items of revenue or expense are included in both accounting profits and taxable profits, but not for the same accounting period. For example, an expense which is allowable as a deduction in arriving at taxable profits for 20X7 might not be included in the financial accounts until 20X8 or later. In the long run, the total taxable profits and total accounting profits will be the same (except for permanent differences) so that temporary differences originate in one period and are capable of reversal in one or more subsequent periods. Deferred tax is the tax attributable to **temporary differences**.

The distinction made in the definition between **taxable temporary differences** and **deductible temporary differences** can be made clearer by looking at the explanations and examples given in the standard and its appendices.

3 Taxable temporary differences

All taxable temporary differences give rise to a deferred tax liability. The following are examples of circumstances that give rise to taxable temporary differences.

Transactions that affect the statement of comprehensive income

(a) **Interest revenue** received in arrears and included in accounting profit on the basis of time apportionment. It is included in taxable profit, however, on a cash basis.

(b) **Sale of goods revenue** is included in accounting profit when the goods are delivered, but only included in taxable profit when cash is received.

(c) **Depreciation** of an asset is accelerated for tax purposes. When new assets are purchased, allowances may be available against taxable profits which exceed the amount of depreciation chargeable on the assets in the financial accounts for the year of purchase.

(d) **Development costs** which have been capitalised will be amortised in the statement of comprehensive income, but they were deducted in full from taxable profit in the period in which they were incurred.

(e) **Prepaid expenses** have already been deducted on a cash basis in determining the taxable profit of the current or previous periods.

Transactions that affect the statement of financial position

(a) **Depreciation of an asset** is not deductible for tax purposes. No deduction will be available for tax purposes when the asset is sold/scrapped.

(b) A borrower records a **loan** at proceeds received (amount due at maturity) less transaction costs. The carrying amount of the loan is subsequently increased by amortisation of the transaction costs against accounting profit. The transaction costs were, however, deducted for tax purposes in the period when the loan was first recognised.

Fair value adjustments and revaluations

(a) **Current investments** or financial instruments are carried at fair value. This exceeds cost, but no equivalent adjustment is made for tax purposes.

(b) Property, plant and equipment is **revalued** by an entity (under IAS 16), but no equivalent adjustment is made for tax purposes. This also applies to long-term investments. As the tax base remains at the original value, there will be a difference between the carrying value and the tax base, leading to an increase in the deferred tax provision.

The reasoning behind this is as follows:

(a) **When an asset is recognised**, it is expected that its carrying amount will be recovered in the form of economic benefits that flow to the entity in future periods.

(b) If the carrying amount of the asset is greater than its tax base, then taxable economic benefits will also be **greater than** the amount that will be allowed as a deduction for tax purposes.

(c) The difference is therefore a **taxable temporary difference** and the obligation to pay the resulting income taxes in future periods is a **deferred tax liability**.

(d) As the entity recovers the carrying amount of the asset, the taxable temporary difference will **reverse** and the entity will have taxable profit.

(e) It is then probable that economic benefits will flow from the entity in the form of **tax payments**, and so the recognition of all deferred tax liabilities is required by IAS 12.

Example: taxable temporary differences

A company purchased an asset costing $1,500. At the end of 20X8 the carrying amount is $1,000. The cumulative depreciation for tax purposes is $900 and the current tax rate is 25%.

What is the deferred tax liability for the asset?

Firstly, what is the tax base of the asset? It is $1,500 – $900 = $600.

In order to recover the carrying value of $1,000, the entity must earn taxable income of $1,000, but it will only be able to deduct $600 as a taxable expense. The entity must therefore pay income tax of $400 × 25% = $100 when the carrying value of the asset is recovered.

The entity must therefore recognise a deferred tax liability of $400 × 25% = $100, recognising the difference between the carrying amount of $1,000 and the tax base of $600 as a taxable temporary difference.

Timing differences

Some temporary differences are often called **timing differences**, when income or expense is included in accounting profit in one period, but is included in taxable profit in a different period. The main types of taxable temporary differences which are timing differences and which result in deferred tax liabilities are:

- **Interest received** which is accounted for on an accruals basis, but which for tax purposes is included on a cash basis.
- **Accelerated depreciation** for tax purposes.
- Capitalised and amortised **development costs**.

Revalued assets

Under IAS 16 assets may be revalued. If this affects the taxable profit for the current period, the tax base of the asset changes and **no temporary difference** arises.

If, however (as in some countries), the revaluation does not affect current taxable profits, the tax base of the asset is not adjusted. Consequently, the taxable flow of economic benefits to the entity as the carrying value of the asset is recovered will differ from the amount that will be deductible for tax purposes.

The difference between the carrying amount of a revalued asset and its tax base is a temporary difference and gives rise to a **deferred tax liability or asset**.

Initial recognition of an asset or liability

A temporary difference can arise on initial recognition of an asset or liability, eg if part or all of the cost of an asset will not be deductible for tax purposes. The **nature of the transaction** which led to the initial recognition of the asset is important in determining the method of accounting for such temporary differences.

If the transaction affects either accounting profit or taxable profit, an entity will **recognise any deferred tax liability** or asset. The resulting deferred tax expense or income will be recognised in profit or loss.

Where a transaction affects **neither accounting profit nor taxable profit** IAS 12 does not permit the recognition of a deferred tax asset or liability as it would make the financial statements less transparent. This will be the case both on initial recognition and subsequently.

Example: initial recognition

Suppose a company intends to use an asset which cost $10,000 in 20X1 through its useful life of five years. Its residual value will then be nil. The tax rate is 40%. Any capital gain on disposal would not be taxable (and any capital loss not deductible). Depreciation of the asset is not deductible for tax purposes.

What are the deferred tax consequences in each of years 20X1 and 20X2?

As at 20X1, as it recovers the carrying amount of the asset, the company will earn taxable income of $10,000 and pay tax of $4,000. The resulting deferred tax liability of $4,000 would not be recognised because it results from the initial recognition of the asset.

As at 20X2, the carrying value of the asset is now $8,000. In earning taxable income of $8,000, the entity will pay tax of $3,200. Again, the resulting deferred tax liability of $3,200 is not recognised, because it results from the initial recognition of the asset.

4 Deductible temporary differences

The rule to remember here is that all **deductible temporary differences give rise to a deferred tax asset**. There is a proviso, however. The deferred tax asset must also satisfy the **recognition criteria** given in IAS 12. This is that a deferred tax asset should be recognised for all deductible temporary differences to the extent that it is **probable that taxable profit will be available** against which it can be utilised. This is an application of prudence. Before we look at this issue in more detail, let us consider the examples of deductible temporary differences given in the standard.

Transactions that affect the statement of comprehensive income

(a) **Retirement benefit costs** (pension costs) are deducted from accounting profit as service is provided by the employee. They are not deducted in determining taxable profit until the entity pays either retirement benefits or contributions to a fund. (This may also apply to similar expenses.)

(b) **Accumulated depreciation** of an asset in the financial statements is greater than the accumulated depreciation allowed for tax purposes up to the end of the reporting period.

(c) The **cost of inventories** sold before the end of the reporting period is deducted from accounting profit when goods/services are delivered, but is deducted from taxable profit when the cash is received. (Note. There is also a taxable temporary difference associated with the related trade receivable, as noted in Section 3 above.)

(d) The carrying amount of inventory, or the **recoverable amount** of an item of property, plant and equipment falls and the carrying value is therefore **reduced**, but that reduction is ignored for tax purposes until the asset is sold.

(e) **Research costs** (or organisation/other start-up costs) are recognised as an expense for accounting purposes but are not deductible against taxable profits until a later period.

(f)   Income is **deferred** in the statement of financial position, but has already been
       included in taxable profit in current/prior periods.

(g)   A **government grant** is included in the statement of financial position as deferred
       income, but it will not be taxable in future periods. (Note. A deferred tax asset
       may not be recognised here according to the standard.)

Fair value adjustments and revaluations

Current investments or **financial instruments** may be carried at fair value which is less
than cost, but no equivalent adjustment is made for tax purposes.

Recognition of deductible temporary differences

We looked at the important recognition criteria above. As with temporary taxable
differences, there are also circumstances where the overall rule for recognition of
deferred tax asset is not allowed.

(a)   Where the deferred tax asset arises from **negative goodwill** which is treated as
       deferred income.

(b)   Where the deferred tax asset arises from **initial recognition** of an asset or liability
       in a transaction which:
       (i)   Is not a business combination, and
       (ii)   At the time of the transaction, affects neither accounting nor taxable profit/tax
               loss.

Let us lay out the reasoning behind the recognition of deferred tax assets arising from
deductible temporary differences.

(a)   When a **liability is recognised**, it is assumed that its carrying amount will be settled
       in the form of outflows of economic benefits from the entity in future periods.

(b)   When these resources flow from the entity, part or all may be deductible in
       determining taxable profits of a **period later** than that in which the liability is
       recognised.

(c)   A **temporary tax difference** then exists between the carrying amount of the liability
       and its tax base.

(d)   A **deferred tax asset** therefore arises, representing the income taxes that will be
       recoverable in future periods when that part of the liability is allowed as a
       deduction from taxable profit.

(e)   Similarly, when the carrying amount of an asset is **less than its tax base**, the
       difference gives rise to a deferred tax asset in respect of the income taxes that will
       be recoverable in future periods.

Example: deductible temporary differences

X Co recognises a liability of $10,000 for accrued product warranty costs on 31
December 20X7. These product warranty costs will not be deductible for tax purposes
until the entity pays claims. The tax rate is 25%.

What are the deferred tax implications of this situation?

What is the tax base of the liability? It is nil (carrying amount of $10,000 less the amount
that will be deductible for tax purposes in respect of the liability in future periods).

When the liability is settled for its carrying amount, the entity's future taxable profit will
be reduced by $10,000 and so its future tax payments by $10,000 $\times$ 25% = $2,500.

The difference of $10,000 between the carrying amount ($10,000) and the tax base (nil) is a deductible temporary difference. The entity should therefore recognise a deferred tax asset of $10,000 × 25% = $2,500 **provided that** it is probable that the entity will earn sufficient taxable profits in future periods to benefit from a reduction in tax payments.

Taxable profits in future periods

When can we be sure that sufficient taxable profit will be available against which a deductible temporary difference can be utilised? IAS 12 states that this will be assumed when sufficient **taxable temporary differences** exist which relate to the same taxation authority and the same taxable entity. These should be expected to reverse:

(a) In the same period as the expected reversal of the deductible temporary difference, or

(b) In periods into which a tax loss arising from the deferred tax asset can be carried back or forward.

Only in these circumstances is the deferred tax asset **recognised**, in the period in which the deductible temporary differences arise.

Unused tax losses and unused tax credits

An entity may have unused tax losses or credits (ie which it can offset against taxable profits) at the end of a period. Should a deferred tax asset be recognised in relation to such amounts? IAS 12 states that a deferred tax asset may be recognised in such circumstances **to the extent that it is probable future taxable profit will be available against which the unused tax losses/credits can be utilised**.

Reassessment of unrecognised deferred tax assets

For *all* unrecognised deferred tax assets, at the end of each reporting period an entity should **reassess the availability of future taxable profits** and whether part or all of any unrecognised deferred tax assets should now be recognised. This may be due to an improvement in trading conditions which is expected to continue.

5 Measurement and recognition of deferred tax

The full provision method as used in IAS 12 has the advantage that it recognises that each timing difference at the end of the reporting period has an effect on future tax payments. If a company claims an accelerated tax allowance on an item of plant, future tax assessments will be bigger than they would have been otherwise. Future transactions may well affect those assessments still further, but that is not relevant in assessing the position at the end of the reporting period.

Example

Suppose that V Co begins trading on 1 January 20X7. In its first year it makes profits of $5m, the depreciation charge is $1m and the tax allowances on those assets is $1.5m. The rate of income tax is 30%.

The tax liability is $1.35m (30% × $m(5.0 + 1.0 −1.5), but the debit to profit or loss is increased by the deferred tax liability of 30% × $0.5m = $150,000. The total charge to profit or loss is therefore $1.5m which is an effective tax rate of 30% on accounting profits (ie 30% × $5.0m).

Changes in tax rates

Where the corporate rate of income tax **fluctuates from one year to another**, a problem arises in respect of the amount of deferred tax to be credited (debited) to the statement of comprehensive income in later years.

IAS 12 requires deferred tax assets and liabilities to be measured at the tax rates expected to apply in the period **when the asset is realised or liability settled**, based on tax rates and laws enacted (or substantively enacted) at the end of the reporting period.

Discounting

Discounting is used to allow for the effect of the time value of money.

IAS 12 states that deferred tax assets and liabilities **should not be discounted** because of the complexities and difficulties involved. Discounting is applied to other non-current liabilities such as provisions and deferred payments.

Carrying amount of deferred tax assets

The carrying amount of deferred tax assets should be **reviewed at the end of each reporting period** and reduced where appropriate (insufficient future taxable profits). Such a reduction may be reversed in future years.

Recognition

As with current tax, deferred tax should normally be recognised as income or an expense and included in the net profit or loss for the period in the **statement of comprehensive income**. The exception is where the tax arises from a transaction or event which is recognised (in the same or a different period) **directly in equity**.

The figures shown for deferred tax in the statement of comprehensive income will consist of **two components**.

(a)   Deferred tax relating to **timing differences**.
(b)   Adjustments relating to **changes in the carrying amount of deferred tax assets/liabilities** (where there is no change in timing differences), eg changes in tax rates/laws, reassessment of the recoverability of deferred tax assets, or a change in the expected recovery of an asset.

Items in (b) will be recognised in profit or loss, unless they relate to items previously charged/credited to equity.

Deferred tax (and current tax) should be charged/credited directly to equity if the tax relates to items also charged/credited directly to equity (in the same or a different period).

Examples of IASs which allow certain items to be credited/charged directly to equity include:

(a)   **Revaluations** of property, plant and equipment (IAS 16), and
(b)   The effect of a **change in accounting policy** (applied retrospectively) or correction of a **material error** (IAS 8)

Example

Z Co owns a property which has a carrying value at the beginning of 20X9 of $1,500,000. At the year end it has entered into a contract to sell the property for $1,800,000. The tax rate is 30%. How will this be shown in the financial statements?

STATEMENT OF COMPREHENSIVE INCOME (EXTRACT)

	$'000
Profit for the year	X
Other comprehensive income:	
Gains on property revaluation	300
Income tax relating to components of other comprehensive income (300 × 30%)	(90)
Other comprehensive income for the year net of tax	210

The amounts will be posted as follows:

	Dr $'000	Cr $'000
Property, plant and equipment	300	
Deferred tax		90
Revaluation surplus		210

Why do we recognise deferred tax?

(a) Adjustments for deferred tax are made in accordance with the **accruals concept** and in accordance with the definition of a **liability** in the Framework, ie a past event has given rise to an obligation in the form of increased taxation which will be payable in the future. The amount can be reliably estimated. A deferred tax asset similarly meets the definition of an **asset**.

(b) If the future tax consequences of transactions are not recognised, profit can be overstated, leading to overpayment of dividends and distortion of share price and EPS.

6 Taxation in financial statements

Taxation in the statement of comprehensive income

The tax on profit on ordinary activities is calculated by aggregating:

(a) **Income tax** on taxable profits
(b) **Transfers to or from deferred taxation**
(c) Any **under-provision or over-provision** of income tax on profits of previous years

When income tax on profits is calculated, **the calculation is only an estimate of what the company thinks its tax liability will be. In subsequent dealings with the tax authorities, a different income tax charge might eventually be agreed**.

The difference between the estimated tax on profits for one year and the actual tax charge finally agreed for the year is made as an adjustment to taxation on profits in the following year, **resulting in the disclosure of either an under-provision or an over-provision of tax.**

Example

In the accounting year to 31 December 20X3, S Co made an operating profit before taxation of $110,000.

Income tax on the operating profit has been estimated as $45,000. In the previous year (20X2) income tax on 20X2 profits had been estimated as $38,000 but it was subsequently agreed at $40,500.

A transfer to the credit of the deferred taxation account of $16,000 will be made in 20X3.

What will be:

(a)   The tax on profits for 20X3 for disclosure in the accounts?
(b)   The amount of tax payable?

The calculations are as follows:

(a)	$
Income tax on profits (liability in the statement of FP)	45,000
Deferred taxation	16,000
Under-provision of tax in previous year $(40,500 – 38,000)	2,500
Tax on profits for 20X3 (income statement charge)	63,500

(b)	$
Tax payable on 20X3 profits (liability)	45,000

Taxation in the statement of financial position

It should already be apparent from the previous examples that the income tax charge in the statement of comprehensive income will not be the same as income tax liabilities in the statement of financial position.

In the statement of financial position, there are several items which we might expect to find.

(a)   **Income tax may be payable** in respect of (say) interest payments paid in the last accounting return period of the year, or accrued.
(b)   If no tax is payable (or very little), then there might be an **income tax recoverable asset** disclosed in current assets (income tax is normally recovered by offset against the tax liability for the year).
(c)   There will usually be a **liability for tax**, possibly including the amounts due in respect of previous years but not yet paid.
(d)   We may also find a **liability on the deferred taxation account**. Deferred taxation is shown under 'non-current liabilities' in the statement of financial position.

Presentation of tax assets and liabilities

These should be **presented separately** from other assets and liabilities in the statement of financial position. Deferred tax assets and liabilities should be distinguished from current tax assets and liabilities.

In addition, deferred tax assets/liabilities should not be classified as current assets/liabilities, where an entity makes such a distinction.

There are only limited circumstances where **current tax assets** and liabilities may be **offset**. This should only occur if two things apply

(a)   The entity has a legally enforceable right to set off the recognised amounts.
(b)   The entity intends either to settle on a net basis, or to realise the asset and settle the liability simultaneously.

Similar criteria apply to the **offset of deferred tax assets and liabilities**.

Financial instruments

12

1 Financial assets and liabilities

If you read the financial press you will probably be aware of **rapid international expansion** in the use of financial instruments. These vary from straightforward, traditional instruments, eg bonds, through to various forms of so-called 'derivative instruments'.

We can perhaps summarise the reasons why a project on the accounting for financial instruments was considered necessary as follows.

(a) The **significant growth of financial instruments** over recent years has outstripped the development of guidance for their accounting.

(b) The topic is of **international concern**, other national standard-setters are involved as well as the IASB.

(c) There have been recent **high-profile disasters** involving derivatives (eg Barings) which, while not caused by accounting failures, have raised questions about accounting and disclosure practices.

There are four Standards on financial instruments:

(a) IAS 32 *Financial instruments: Presentation*, which deals with:
  (i) The classification of financial instruments between liabilities and equity
  (ii) Presentation of certain compound instruments

(b) IFRS 7 *Financial instruments: Disclosures*, which revised, simplified and incorporated disclosure requirements previously in IAS 32.

(c) IAS 39 *Financial instruments: Recognition and measurement*, which deals with:
  (i) Recognition and derecognition
  (ii) The measurement of financial instruments
  (iii) Hedge accounting

(d) IFRS 9 *Financial Instruments*, which replaces the provisions of IAS 39 regarding the classification and measurement of financial assets (not liabilities).

The most important definitions are common to all four Standards.

Financial instrument. Any contract that gives rise to both a financial asset of one entity and a financial liability or equity instrument of another entity.

Financial asset. Any asset that is:

(a) Cash
(b) An equity instrument of another entity

(c) A contractual right to receive cash or another financial asset from another entity; or to exchange financial instruments with another entity under conditions that are potentially favourable to the entity, or

(d) A contract that will or may be settled in the entity's own equity instruments and is:

    (i) A non-derivative for which the entity is or may be obliged to receive a variable number of the entity's own equity instruments; or

    (ii) A derivative that will or may be settled other than by the exchange of a fixed amount of cash or another financial asset for a fixed number of the entity's own equity instruments.

Financial liability. Any liability that is:

(a) A contractual obligation:

    (i) To deliver cash or another financial asset to another entity, or

    (ii) To exchange financial instruments with another entity under conditions that are potentially unfavourable; or

(b) A contract that will or may be settled in the entity's own equity instruments and is:

    (i) A non-derivative for which the entity is or may be obliged to deliver a variable number of the entity's own equity instruments; or

    (ii) a derivative that will or may be settled other than by the exchange of a fixed amount of cash or another financial asset for a fixed number of the entity's own equity instruments.

Equity instrument. Any contract that evidences a residual interest in the assets of an entity after deducting all of its liabilities.

Fair value is the amount for which an asset could be exchanged, or a liability settled, between knowledgeable, willing parties in an arm's length transaction

Derivative. A financial instrument or other contract with all three of the following characteristics:

(a) Its value changes in response to the change in a specified interest rate, financial instrument price, commodity price, foreign exchange rate, index of prices or rates, credit rating or credit index, or other variable (sometimes called the 'underlying')

(b) It requires no initial net investment or an initial net investment that is smaller than would be required for other types of contracts that would be expected to have a similar response to changes in market factors; and

(c) It is settled at a future date.   (IAS 32 and IAS 39)

We should clarify some points arising from these definitions. Firstly, one or two terms above should be themselves defined.

(a) A '**contract**' need not be in writing, but it must comprise an agreement that has 'clear economic consequences' and which the parties to it cannot avoid, usually because the agreement is enforceable in law.

(b) An '**entity**' here could be an individual, partnership, incorporated body or government agency.

The definitions of **financial assets and financial liabilities** may seem rather circular, referring as they do to the terms financial asset and financial instrument. The point is that there may be a chain of contractual rights and obligations, but it will lead ultimately to the receipt or payment of cash or the acquisition or issue of an equity instrument.

Examples of **financial assets** include:

(a)   Trade receivables
(b)   Options
(c)   Shares (when used as an investment).

Examples of **financial liabilities** include:

(a)   Trade payables
(b)   Debenture loans payable
(c)   Redeemable preference (non-equity) shares
(d)   Forward contracts standing at a loss.

As we have already noted, financial instruments include both of the following.

(a)   **Primary instruments**: eg receivables, payables and equity securities
(b)   **Derivative instruments**: eg financial options, futures and forwards, interest rate swaps and currency swaps, **whether recognised or unrecognised**

IAS 32 makes it clear that the following items are not financial instruments.

*   **Physical assets**, eg inventories, property, plant and equipment, leased assets and intangible assets (patents, trademarks etc)
*   **Prepaid expenses**, deferred revenue and most warranty obligations
*   Liabilities or assets that are **not contractual** in nature
*   Contractual rights/obligations that **do not involve transfer of a financial asset**, eg commodity futures contracts, operating leases

Contingent rights and obligations meet the definition of financial assets and financial liabilities respectively, even though many do not qualify for recognition in financial statements. This is because the contractual rights or obligations exist because of a past transaction or event (eg assumption of a guarantee).

Derivatives

A **derivative** is a financial instrument that **derives** its value from the price or rate of an underlying item. Common **examples** of derivatives include:

(a)   **Forward contracts**: agreements to buy or sell an asset at a fixed price at a fixed future date
(b)   **Futures contracts**: similar to forward contracts except that contracts are standardised and traded on an exchange
(c)   **Options**: rights (but not obligations) for the option holder to exercise at a pre-determined price; the option writer loses out if the option is exercised
(d)   **Swaps**: agreements to swap one set of cash flows for another (normally interest rate or currency swaps)

The nature of derivatives often gives rise to **particular problems**. The **value** of a derivative (and the amount at which it is eventually settled) depends on **movements** in an underlying item (such as an exchange rate). This means that settlement of a derivative can lead to a very different result from the one originally envisaged. A company which has derivatives is exposed to **uncertainty and risk** (potential for gain or loss) and this can have a very material effect on its financial performance, financial position and cash flows.

Yet because a derivative contract normally has **little or no initial cost**, under traditional accounting it **may not be recognised** in the financial statements at all. Alternatively it may be recognised at an amount which bears no relation to its current value. This is clearly **misleading** and leaves users of the financial statements unaware of the **level of risk** that the company faces. IASs 32 and 39 were developed in order to correct this situation.

2 IAS 32: Financial instruments: Presentation

The objective of IAS 32 is:

'to enhance financial statement users' understanding of the significance of on-balance sheet and off-balance sheet financial instruments to an entity's financial position, performance and cash flows.'

IAS 32 should be applied in the presentation of all types of financial instruments, whether recognised or unrecognised.

Certain items are **excluded**.

- Interests in subsidiaries (IAS 27)
- Interests in associates (IAS 28)
- Interests in joint ventures (IAS 31)
- Pensions and other post-retirement benefits (IAS 19)
- Insurance contracts
- Contracts for contingent consideration in a business combination
- Contracts that require a payment based on climatic, geological or other physical variables
- Financial instruments, contracts and obligations under share-based payment transactions (IFRS 2)

Liabilities and equity

The main thrust of IAS 32 here is that financial instruments should be presented according to their **substance, not merely their legal form**. In particular, entities which issue financial instruments should classify them (or their component parts) as **either financial liabilities, or equity**.

The classification of a financial instrument as a liability or as equity depends on the following.

- The substance of the contractual arrangement on initial recognition
- The definitions of a financial liability and an equity instrument

How should a **financial liability be distinguished from an equity instrument**? The critical feature of a **liability** is an **obligation** to transfer economic benefit. Therefore a financial instrument is a financial liability if there is a **contractual obligation** on the issuer either to deliver cash or another financial asset to the holder or to exchange another financial instrument with the holder under potentially unfavourable conditions to the issuer.

The financial liability exists **regardless of the way in which the contractual obligation will be settled**. The issuer's ability to satisfy an obligation may be restricted, eg by lack of access to foreign currency, but this is irrelevant as it does not remove the issuer's obligation or the holder's right under the instrument.

Where the above critical feature is *not* met, then the financial instrument is an **equity instrument**. IAS 32 explains that although the holder of an equity instrument may be entitled to a pro rata share of any distributions out of equity, the issuer does *not* have a contractual obligation to make such a distribution.

Although substance and legal form are often **consistent with each other**, this is not always the case. In particular, a financial instrument may have the legal form of equity, but in substance it is in fact a liability. Other instruments may combine features of both equity instruments and financial liabilities.

For example, many entities issue **preference shares** which must be **redeemed** by the issuer for a fixed (or determinable) amount at a fixed (or determinable) future date. Alternatively, the holder may have the right to require the issuer to redeem the shares at or after a certain date for a fixed amount. In such cases, the issuer has an **obligation**. Therefore the instrument is a **financial liability** and should be classified as such.

The classification of the financial instrument is made when it is **first recognised** and this classification will continue until the financial instrument is removed from the entity's statement of financial position.

Contingent settlement provisions

An entity may issue a financial instrument where the way in which it is settled depends on:

(a) The occurrence or non-occurrence of uncertain future events, or
(b) The outcome of uncertain circumstances,

that are beyond the control of both the holder and the issuer of the instrument. For example, an entity might have to deliver cash instead of issuing equity shares. In this situation it is not immediately clear whether the entity has an equity instrument or a financial liability.

Such financial instruments should be classified as **financial liabilities** unless the possibility of settlement is remote.

Settlement options

When a derivative financial instrument gives one party a **choice** over how it is settled (eg, the issuer can choose whether to settle in cash or by issuing shares) the instrument is a **financial asset** or a **financial liability** unless **all the alternative choices** would result in it being an equity instrument.

Compound financial instruments

Some financial instruments contain both a liability and an equity element. In such cases, IAS 32 requires the component parts of the instrument to be **classified separately**, according to the substance of the contractual arrangement and the definitions of a financial liability and an equity instrument.

One of the most common types of compound instrument is **convertible debt**. This creates a primary financial liability of the issuer and grants an option to the holder of the instrument to convert it into an equity instrument (usually ordinary shares) of the issuer. This is the economic equivalent of the issue of conventional debt plus a warrant to acquire shares in the future.

Although in theory there are several possible ways of calculating the split, the following method is recommended by IAS 32:

(a)   Calculate the value for the liability component.
(b)   Deduct this from the instrument as a whole to leave a residual value for the equity component.

The reasoning behind this approach is that an entity's equity is its residual interest in its assets amount after deducting all its liabilities.

The **sum of the carrying amounts** assigned to liability and equity will always be equal to the carrying amount that would be ascribed to the instrument **as a whole**.

Example: valuation of compound instruments

Z Co issues 2,000 convertible bonds at the start of 20X2. The bonds have a three year term, and are issued at par with a face value of $1,000 per bond, giving total proceeds of $2,000,000. Interest is payable annually in arrears at a nominal annual interest rate of 6%. Each bond is convertible at any time up to maturity into 250 common shares.

When the bonds are issued, the prevailing market interest rate for similar debt without conversion options is 9%. At the issue date, the market price of one common share is $3. The dividends expected over the three year term of the bonds amount to 14c per share at the end of each year. The risk-free annual interest rate for a three year term is 5%.

What is the value of the equity component in the bond?

The liability component is valued first, and the difference between the proceeds of the bond issue and the fair value of the liability is assigned to the equity component. The present value of the liability component is calculated using a discount rate of 9%, the market interest rate for similar bonds having no conversion rights, as shown.

	$
Present value of the principal: $2,000,000 payable at the end of three years ($2m × 0.772)*	1,544,000
Present value of the interest: $120,000 payable annually in arrears for three years ($120,000 × 2.531)*	303,725
Total liability component	1,847,720
Equity component (balancing figure)	152,280
Proceeds of the bond issue	2,000,000

* These figures can be obtained from discount and annuity tables.

The split between the liability and equity components remains the same throughout the term of the instrument, even if there are changes in the **likelihood of the option being exercised**. This is because it is not always possible to predict how a holder will behave. The issuer continues to have an obligation to make future payments until conversion, maturity of the instrument or some other relevant transaction takes place.

Treasury shares

If an entity reacquires its own equity instruments, those instruments ('treasury shares') shall be deducted from equity. No gain or loss shall be recognised in profit or loss on the purchase, sale, issue or cancellation of an entity's own equity instruments. Consideration paid or received shall be recognised directly in equity.

Interest, dividends, losses and gains

As well as looking at statement of financial position presentation, IAS 32 considers how financial instruments affect the profit or loss (and movements in equity). The treatment varies according to whether interest, dividends, losses or gains relate to a financial liability or an equity instrument.

(a)   Interest, dividends, losses and gains relating to a financial instrument (or component part) classified as a **financial liability** should be recognised as **income** or **expense** in profit or loss.

(b)   Distributions to holders of a financial instrument classified as an **equity instrument** should be **debited directly to equity** by the issuer.

(c)   **Transaction costs** of an equity transaction shall be accounted for as a **deduction from equity** (unless they are directly attributable to the acquisition of a business, in which case they are accounted for under IFRS 3).

Offsetting a financial asset and a financial liability

A financial asset and financial liability should **only** be **offset**, with the net amount reported in the statement of financial position, when an entity:

(a)   Has a legally enforceable right of set off, and

(b)   Intends to settle on a net basis, or to realise the asset and settle the liability simultaneously, ie at the same moment.

This will reflect the expected **future cash flows** of the entity in these specific circumstances. In all other cases, financial assets and financial liabilities are presented separately.

Amendment to IAS 32: Puttable financial instruments and obligations arising on liquidation

This amendment was issued in February 2008. The changes deal with puttable financial instruments and the effect obligations that arise on liquidation have on determining whether an instrument is debt or equity.

IAS 32 requires that if the holder of a financial instrument can require the issuer to redeem it for cash it should be classified as a liability. Some ordinary shares and partnership interests allow the holder to 'put' the instrument (that is to require the issuer to redeem it in cash). Such shares might more usually be considered as equity, but application of IAS 32 results in their being classified as liabilities.

The amendment would requires entities to classify such instruments as equity, so long as they meet certain conditions. The amendment further requires that instruments imposing an obligation on an entity to deliver to another party a pro rata share of the net assets only on liquidation should be classified as equity.

3   IAS 39: Financial instruments: Recognition and measurement

IAS 39 applies to **all entities** and to **all types of financial instruments except** those specifically excluded, as listed below.

(a) Investments in **subsidiaries, associates, and joint ventures** that are accounted for under IASs 27, 28 and 31
(b) **Leases** covered in IAS 17
(c) **Employee benefit plans** covered in IAS 19
(d) **Insurance contracts**
(e) Equity instruments **issued by the entity** eg ordinary shares issued, or options and warrants
(f) **Financial guarantee** contracts
(g) **Contracts for contingent consideration** in a business combination, covered in IFRS 3
(h) Contracts requiring payment based on climatic, geological or other **physical variables**
(i) **Loan commitments** that cannot be settled net in cash or another financial instrument
(j) Financial instruments, contracts and obligations under **share based payment transactions**, covered in IFRS 2

Initial recognition

Financial instruments should be recognised in the statement of financial position when the entity becomes a party to the **contractual provisions of the instrument**.

Notice that this is **different** from the recognition criteria in the *Framework* and in most other standards. Items are normally recognised when there is a probable inflow or outflow of resources and the item has a cost or value that can be measured reliably.

Example: initial recognition

An entity has entered into two separate contracts.

(a) A firm commitment (an order) to buy a specific quantity of iron.
(b) A forward contract to buy a specific quantity of iron at a specified price on a specified date, provided delivery of the iron is not taken.

Contract (a) is a normal trading contract. The entity does not recognise a liability for the iron until the goods have actually been delivered. (Note that this contract is not a financial instrument because it involves a physical asset, rather than a financial asset.)

Contract (b) is a financial instrument. Under IAS 39, the entity recognises a financial liability (an obligation to deliver cash) on the commitment date, rather than waiting for the closing date on which the exchange takes place.

Note that planned future transactions, no matter how likely, are not assets and liabilities of an entity – the entity has not yet become a party to the contract.

Derecognition

Derecognition is the removal of a previously recognised financial instrument from an entity's statement of financial position.

An entity should derecognise a **financial asset** when:

(a) The contractual rights to the cash flows from the financial asset expire, or
(b) The entity transfers substantially all the risks and rewards of ownership of the financial asset to another party.

An entity should derecognise a **financial liability** when it is **extinguished** – ie, when the obligation specified in the contract is discharged or cancelled or expires.

It is possible for only **part** of a financial asset or liability to be derecognised. This is allowed if the part comprises:

(a)   only specifically identified cash flows; or

(b)   only a fully proportionate (pro rata) share of the total cash flows.

For example, if an entity holds a bond it has the right to two separate sets of cash inflows: those relating to the principal and those relating to the interest. It could sell the right to receive the interest to another party while retaining the right to receive the principal.

On derecognition, the amount to be included in net profit or loss for the period is calculated as follows:

	$	$
Carrying amount of asset/liability (or the portion of asset/liability) transferred		X
Less: Proceeds received/paid	X	
Any cumulative gain or loss reported in equity	X	
		(X)
Difference to net profit/loss		X

Where only part of a financial asset is derecognised, the carrying amount of the asset should be allocated between the part retained and the part transferred based on their relative fair values on the date of transfer. A gain or loss should be recognised based on the proceeds for the portion transferred.

4 Measurement of financial instruments

Financial instruments are initially measured at the **fair value** of the consideration given or received (ie, **cost**) **plus** (in most cases) **transaction costs** that are **directly attributable** to the acquisition or issue of the financial instrument.

The **exception** to this rule is where a financial instrument is designated as **at fair value through profit or loss** (this term is explained below). In this case, **transaction costs** are **not** added to fair value at initial recognition.

The fair value of the consideration is normally the transaction price or market prices. If market prices are not reliable, the fair value may be **estimated** using a valuation technique (for example, by discounting cash flows).

Subsequent measurement

For the purposes of measuring a financial instrument held subsequent to initial recognition, IAS 39 classifies financial assets or liabilities into four categories defined here. IFRS 9 has now been issued which will simplify the treatment of financial assets, but it is not yet generally adopted, so we will begin with the IAS 39 provisions. Note particularly the criteria for a financial asset or liability at fair value through profit and loss.

A financial asset or liability at fair value through profit or loss meets either of the following conditions:

(a) It is classified as held for trading. A financial instrument is classified as held for trading if it is:

    (i) Acquired or incurred principally for the purpose of selling or repurchasing it in the near term

    (ii) Part of a portfolio of identified financial instruments that are managed together and for which there is evidence of a recent actual pattern of short-term profit-taking, or

    (iii) A derivative (unless it is a designated and effective hedging instrument).

(b) Upon initial recognition it is designated by the entity as at fair value through profit or loss. An entity may only use this designation in severely restricted circumstances:

    (i) It **eliminates** or significantly **reduces** a measurement or recognition **inconsistency** (mismatch) that would otherwise arise.

    (ii) A **group of** financial assets or liabilities is managed and its performance is evaluated **on a fair value basis.**

Held-to-maturity investments are non-derivative financial assets with fixed or determinable payments and fixed maturity that an entity has the positive intent and ability to hold to maturity other than:

(a) Those that the entity upon initial recognition designates as at fair value through profit or loss

(b) Those that the entity designates as available for sale

(c) Those that meet the definition of loans and receivables

Loans and receivables are non-derivative financial assets with fixed or determinable payments that are not quoted in an active market, other than:

(a) Those that the entity intends to sell immediately or in the near term, which should be classified as held for trading and those that the entity upon initial recognition designates as at fair value through profit or loss

(b) Those that the entity upon initial recognition designates as available-for-sale, or

(c) Those for which the holder may not recover substantially all of the initial investment, other than because of credit deterioration, which shall be classified as available for sale

An interest acquired in a pool of assets that are not loans or receivables (for example, an interest in a mutual fund or a similar fund) is not a loan or a receivable.

Available-for-sale financial assets are those financial assets that are not:

(a) Loans and receivables originated by the entity,

(b) Held-to-maturity investments, or

(c) Financial assets at fair value through profit or loss.   (IAS 39)

After initial recognition, all financial assets should be **remeasured to fair value**, without any deduction for transaction costs that may be incurred on sale or other disposal, except for:

(a) Loans and receivables
(b) Held to maturity investments
(c) Investments in unquoted equity instruments whose fair value cannot be reliably measured and derivatives linked to such instruments

Loans and receivables and **held to maturity investments** should be measured at **amortised cost** using the **effective interest method**.

> **Amortised cost** of a financial asset or financial liability is the amount at which the financial asset or liability is measured at initial recognition minus principal repayments, plus or minus the cumulative amortisation of any difference between that initial amount and the maturity amount, and minus any write-down (directly or through the use of an allowance account) for impairment or uncollectability.
>
> The **effective interest method** is a method of calculating the amortised cost of a financial instrument and of allocating the interest income or interest expense over the relevant period.
>
> The **effective interest rate** is the rate that exactly discounts estimated future cash payments or receipts through the expected life of the financial instrument to the net carrying amount of the financial asset or liability. (IAS 39)

Example: Amortised cost

On 1 January 20X1 X Co purchases a debt instrument for its fair value of $1,000. The debt instrument is due to mature on 31 December 20X5. The instrument has a principal amount of $1,250 and the instrument carries fixed interest at 4.72% that is paid annually. (The effective interest rate is 10%.)

How should X Co account for the debt instrument over its five year term?

X Co will receive interest of $59 (1,250 × 4.72%) each year and $1,250 when the instrument matures.

X Co must allocate the discount of $250 and the interest receivable over the five year term at a constant rate on the carrying amount of the debt. To do this, it must apply the effective interest rate of 10%.

The following table shows the allocation over the years:

Year	Amortised cost at beginning of year $	Profit or loss: Interest income for year (@10%) $	Interest received during year (cash inflow) $	Amortised cost at end of year $
20X1	1,000	100	(59)	1,041
20X2	1,041	104	(59)	1,086
20X3	1,086	109	(59)	1,136
20X4	1,136	113	(59)	1,190
20X5	1,190	119	(1,250 + 59)	–

Each year the carrying amount of the financial asset is increased by the interest income for the year and reduced by the interest actually received during the year.

Investments whose **fair value cannot be reliably measured** should be measured at cost.

Classification – IAS 39

There is a certain amount of flexibility in that **any** financial instrument can be designated as fair value through profit or loss. However, this is a **once and for all choice** and has to be made on initial recognition. Once a financial instrument has been classified in this way it **cannot be reclassified**, even if it would otherwise be possible to measure it at cost or amortised cost.

In contrast, it is quite difficult for an entity **not** to remeasure financial instruments to fair value.

Note that derivatives **must** be remeasured to fair value. This is because it would be misleading to measure them at cost.

For a financial instrument to be held to maturity it must meet several extremely narrow criteria. The entity must have a **positive intent** and a **demonstrated ability** to hold the investment to maturity. These conditions are not met if:

(a) The entity intends to hold the financial asset for an undefined period
(b) The entity stands ready to sell the financial asset in response to changes in interest rates or risks, liquidity needs and similar factors (unless these situations could not possibly have been reasonably anticipated)
(c) The issuer has the right to settle the financial asset at an amount significantly below its amortised cost (because this right will almost certainly be exercised)
(d) It does not have the financial resources available to continue to finance the investment until maturity
(e) It is subject to an existing legal or other constraint that could frustrate its intention to hold the financial asset to maturity

In addition, an **equity** instrument is **unlikely** to meet the criteria for classification as held to maturity.

There is a **penalty** for selling or reclassifying a 'held-to-maturity' investment other than in certain very tightly defined circumstances. If this has occurred during the **current** financial year or during the **two preceding** financial years **no** financial asset can be classified as held-to-maturity.

If an entity can no longer hold an investment to maturity, it is no longer appropriate to use amortised cost and the asset must be re-measured to fair value. **All** remaining held-to-maturity investments must also be re-measured to fair value and classified as available-for-sale.

Note: This penalty has now been removed by IFRS 9. Entities are no longer forced to reclassify to fair value all instruments in a class of assets classified as held to maturity in the event that one of those instruments is sold.

Subsequent measurement of financial liabilities

After initial recognition, all financial liabilities should be measured at **amortised cost**, with the exception of financial liabilities at fair value through profit or loss (including most derivatives). These should be measured at fair value, but where the fair value is not capable of reliable measurement, they should be measured at cost.

Example

B Co issues a bond for $503,778 on 1 January 20X2. No interest is payable on the bond, but it will be held to maturity and redeemed on 31 December 20X4 for $600,000. The bond has **not** been designated as at fair value through profit or loss.

What is the charge to profit or loss of B Co for the year ended 31 December 20X2 and the balance outstanding at 31 December 20X2?

The bond is a 'deep discount' bond and is a financial liability of B Co. It is measured at amortised cost. Although there is no interest as such, the difference between the initial cost of the bond and the price at which it will be redeemed is a finance cost. This must be allocated over the term of the bond at a constant rate on the carrying amount.

To calculate amortised cost we need to calculate the effective interest rate of the bond:

$$\frac{600,000}{503,778} = 1.191 \text{ over three years}$$

To calculate an annual rate, we take the cube root, $(1.191)^{1/3} = 1.06$, so the annual interest rate is 6%.

The charge to the income statement is $30,226 (503,778 x 6%)

The balance outstanding at 31 December 20X2 is $534,004 (503,778 + 30,226)

Gains and losses

Instruments at **fair value through profit or loss**: gains and losses are recognised **in profit or loss**.

Available for sale financial assets: gains and losses are recognised **directly in equity** through the statement of changes in equity. When the asset is derecognised the cumulative gain or loss previously recognised in equity should be recognised in profit and loss.

Financial instruments carried at **amortised cost**: gains and losses are recognised **in profit and loss** as a result of the amortisation process and when the asset is derecognised.

Financial assets and financial liabilities that are **hedged items**: special rules apply. (See section 7)

Impairment and uncollectability of financial assets

At each year end, an entity should assess whether there is any objective evidence that a financial asset or group of assets is impaired.

What are the indications that a financial asset or group of assets may be impaired?

IAS 39 lists the following:

(a) Significant financial difficulty of the issuer
(b) A breach of contract, such as a default in interest or principal payments
(c) The lender granting a concession to the borrower that the lender would not otherwise consider, for reasons relating to the borrower's financial difficulty
(d) It becomes probable that the borrower will enter bankruptcy

(e)   The disappearance of an active market for that financial asset because of
        financial difficulties

Where there is objective evidence of impairment, the entity should determine the
amount of any impairment loss.

Financial assets carried at amortised cost

The impairment loss is the **difference** between the asset's **carrying amount** and its
recoverable amount. The asset's recoverable amount is the present value of estimated
future cash flows, discounted at the financial instrument's **original** effective interest rate.

The amount of the loss should be **recognised in profit or loss**.

If the impairment loss decreases at a later date (and the decrease relates to an event
occurring **after** the impairment was recognised) the reversal is recognised in profit or
loss. The carrying amount of the asset must not exceed the original amortised cost.

Note: Under IFRS 9 **only** financial assets measured at amortised cost are subject to
impairment and all impairments can be reversed.

Financial assets carried at cost

Unquoted equity instruments are carried at cost if their fair value cannot be reliably
measured. The impairment loss is the difference between the asset's **carrying amount**
and the **present value of estimated future cash flows**, discounted at the current market
rate of return for a similar financial instrument. Such impairment losses cannot be
reversed.

Available for sale financial assets

Available for sale financial assets are carried at fair value and gains and losses are
recognised directly in equity. Any impairment loss on an available for sale financial
asset should be **removed from equity** and **recognised in net profit or loss for the period**
even though the financial asset has not been derecognised.

The impairment loss is the difference between its **acquisition cost** (net of any principal
repayment and amortisation) and **current fair value** (for equity instruments) or
recoverable amount (for debt instruments), less any impairment loss on that asset
previously recognised in profit or loss.

Impairment losses relating to equity instruments cannot be reversed. Impairment losses
relating to debt instruments may be reversed if, in a later period, the fair value of the
instrument increases and the increase can be objectively related to an event occurring
after the loss was recognised.

5 IFRS 9: Financial Instruments

IFRS 9 *Financial Instruments* was issued in November 2009. It prescribes the
classification and measurement of financial assets (not liabilities) and is the first phase
of a project to replace IAS 39. The final date for mandatory adoption of IFRS 9 is 1
January 2013, so IAS 39 may continue to be used by some entities for a few more years.

The intention of the IASB in issuing IFRS 9 was to reduce the complexity associated with
IAS 39 and make it easier for users of financial statements to assess the amounts,
timing and uncertainty of cash flows arising from financial assets. For this reason it has
reduced the four measurement categories above to two.

Under IFRS 9 financial assets are classified based on the objective of the entity's business model for managing the instrument and its contractual cash flow terms.

At initial recognition an entity measures all financial assets at fair value. Subsequently assets can be measured at **amortised cost** or **fair value**.

A financial asset is measured at amortised cost if both of the following conditions are met:

(a)   The objective of the entity's business model is to hold the financial asset in order to collect the contractual cash flows; and

(b)   The contractual terms of the financial asset give rise on specified dates to cash flows that are solely repayments of principal and payments of interest on the principal outstanding.

If a financial asset does not meet these conditions it is measured at fair value. Reclassification between the fair value category and amortised cost is required when, and only when, and entity changes its business model for managing its financial assets. This is expected to be infrequent.

6 Embedded derivatives

Certain contracts that are not themselves derivatives (and may not be financial instruments) include derivative contracts that are 'embedded' within them. These non-derivatives are called **host contracts**.

> An **embedded derivative** is a derivative instrument that is combined with a non-derivative host contract to form a single hybrid instrument.

Examples of host contracts

Possible examples include:

(a)   A lease
(b)   A debt or equity instrument
(c)   An insurance contract
(d)   A sale or purchase contract
(e)   A construction contract

Examples of embedded derivatives

Possible examples include:

(a)   A term in a lease of retail premises that provides for contingent rentals based on sales:

'Host' contract	Lease	➡	Accounted for as normal
Embedded derivative	Contingent rentals	➡	Treat as derivative, ie re-measured to FV with changes recognised in profit or loss

(b)   A bond which is redeemable in five years' time with part of the redemption price being based on the increase in the FTSE 100 index.

(c)   Construction contract priced in a foreign currency. The construction contract is a non-derivative contract, but the change in foreign exchange rate is the embedded derivative.

Accounting treatment of embedded derivatives

IAS 39 requires that an embedded derivative be separated from its host contract and accounted for as a derivative when the following conditions are met.

(a)   The economic characteristics and risks of the embedded derivative are not closely related to the economic characteristics and risks of the host contract.

(b)   A separate instrument with the same terms as the embedded derivative would meet the definition of a derivative.

(c)   The hybrid (combined) instrument is not measured at fair value with changes in fair value recognised in the profit or loss (a derivative embedded in a financial asset or financial liability need not be separated out if the entity holds the combined instrument at fair value through profit or loss).

7 Hedging

IAS 39 **requires hedge accounting** where there is a **designated hedging relationship** between a hedging instrument and a hedged item. It is **prohibited otherwise**.

Hedging, for accounting purposes, means designating one or more hedging instruments so that their change in fair value is an offset, in whole or in part, to the change in fair value or cash flows of a hedged item.

A **hedged item** is an asset, liability, firm commitment, or forecasted future transaction that:

(a)   exposes the entity to risk of changes in fair value or changes in future cash flows, and that

(b)   is designated as being hedged.

A **hedging instrument** is a designated derivative or (in limited circumstances) another financial asset or liability whose fair value or cash flows are expected to offset changes in the fair value or cash flows of a designated hedged item. (A non-derivative financial asset or liability may be designated as a hedging instrument for hedge accounting purposes only if it hedges the risk of changes in foreign currency exchange rates.)

Hedge effectiveness is the degree to which changes in the fair value or cash flows of the hedged item attributable to a hedged risk are offset by changes in the fair value or cash flows of the hedging instrument.   (IAS 39)

In simple terms, entities hedge to reduce their exposure to risk and uncertainty, such as changes in prices, interest rates or foreign exchange rates. Hedge accounting recognises hedging relationships by allowing (for example) losses on a hedged item to be offset against gains on a hedging instrument.

Generally only assets, liabilities etc that involve external parties can be designated as hedged items. The foreign currency risk of an intragroup monetary item (eg payable/receivable between two subsidiaries) may qualify as a hedged item in the group financial statements if it results in an exposure to foreign exchange rate gains or losses that are not fully eliminated on consolidation. This can happen (per IAS 21) when the transaction is between entities with different functional currencies.

In addition the foreign currency risk of a highly probable group transaction may qualify as a hedged item if it is in a currency other than the functional currency of the entity and the foreign currency risk will affect profit or loss.

Example: Hedging

A company owns inventories of 20,000 gallons of oil which cost $400,000 on 1 December 20X3.

In order to hedge the fluctuation in the market value of the oil the company signs a futures contract to deliver 20,000 gallons of oil on 31 March 20X4 at the futures price of $22 per gallon.

The market price of oil on 31 December 20X3 is $23 per gallon and the futures price for delivery on 31 March 20X4 is $24 per gallon.

What is the impact of these transactions on the financial statements of the company:

(a) Without hedge accounting?
(b) With hedge accounting?

The futures contract was intended to protect the company from a fall in oil prices (which would have reduced the profit when the oil was eventually sold). However, oil prices have actually risen, so that the company has made a loss on the contract.

Without hedge accounting:

The futures contract is a derivative and therefore must be remeasured to fair value under IAS 39. The loss on the futures contract is recognised in profit or loss:

DEBIT	Profit or loss (20,000 × 24–22)	$40,000	
CREDIT	Financial liability		$40,000

With hedge accounting:

The loss on the futures contract is recognised in profit or loss as before.

The inventories are revalued to fair value:

	$
Fair value at 31 December 20X4 (20,000 × 23)	460,000
Cost	(400,000)
Gain	60,000

The gain is also recognised in profit or loss:

DEBIT	Inventory	$60,000	
CREDIT	Profit or loss		$60,000

The net effect on profit or loss is a gain of $20,000 compared with a loss of $40,000 without hedging.

The **standard** identifies three types of **hedging relationship**.

> **Fair value hedge:** a hedge of the exposure to changes in the fair value of a recognised asset or liability, or an identified portion of such an asset or liability, that is attributable to a particular risk and could affect profit or loss.
>
> **Cash flow hedge:** a hedge of the exposure to variability in cash flows that
>
> (a) Is attributable to a particular risk associated with a recognised asset or liability (such as all or some future interest payments on variable rate debt) or a highly probable forecast transaction (such as an anticipated purchase or sale), and that
>
> (b) Could affect profit or loss.
>
> **Hedge of a net investment in a foreign operation:** IAS 21 defines a net investment in a foreign operation as the amount of the reporting entity's interest in the net assets of that operation. *(IAS 39)*

The hedge in the example above is a **fair value hedge** (it hedges exposure to changes in the fair value of a recognised asset: the oil).

Conditions for hedge accounting

Before a hedging relationship qualifies for hedge accounting, all of the following conditions must be met.

(a)   The hedging relationship must be **designated at its inception as a hedge** based on the entity's risk management objective and strategy. There must be formal documentation (including identification of the hedged item, the hedging instrument, the nature of the risk that is to be hedged and how the entity will assess the hedging instrument's effectiveness in offsetting the exposure to changes in the hedged item's fair value or cash flows attributable to the hedged risk).

(b)   The hedge is expected to be **highly effective** in achieving offsetting changes in fair value or cash flows attributable to the hedged risk. (Note: the hedge need not necessarily be fully effective. A highly effective hedge must be 80%-125% effective)

(c)   For **cash flow hedges**, a **forecast transaction** that is the subject of the hedge must be **highly probable** and must present an exposure to variations in cash flows that could ultimately affect profit or loss.

(d)   The effectiveness of the hedge can be **measured reliably.**

(e)   The hedge is assessed on an ongoing basis (annually) and has been **effective during the reporting period.**

Accounting treatment

Fair value hedges

The **gain or loss** resulting from **re-measuring** the hedging instrument at fair value is **recognised in profit or loss.**

The gain or loss on the hedged item attributable to the **hedged risk** should **adjust the carrying amount** of the hedged item and be **recognised in profit or loss.**

Cash flow hedges

The portion of the gain or loss on the hedging instrument that is determined to be an **effective** hedge shall be **recognised directly in equity** through the statement of changes in equity.

The **ineffective portion** of the gain or loss on the hedging instrument should be **recognised in profit or loss**.

When a hedging transaction results in the recognition of an asset or liability, changes in the value of the hedging instrument recognised in equity either:

(a) Are adjusted against the carrying value of the asset or liability, or
(b) Affect the profit or loss at the same time as the hedged item (for example, through depreciation or sale).

Example: Cash flow hedge

W Co signs a contract on 1 November 20X1 to purchase an asset on 1 November 20X2 for €60,000,000. W Co reports in US$ and hedges this transaction by entering into a forward contract to buy €60,000,000 on 1 November 20X2 at US$1: €1.5.

Spot and forward exchange rates at the following dates are:

	Spot	Forward (for delivery on 1.11.X2)
1.11.X1	US$1: €1.45	US$1: €1.5
31.12.X1	US$1: €1.20	US$1: €1.24
1.11.X2	US$1: €1.0	US$1: €1.0 (actual)

What are the double entries relating to these transactions at 1 November 20X1, 31 December 20X1 and 1 November 20X2?

Entries at 1 November 20X1

The value of the forward contract at inception is zero so no entries recorded (other than any transaction costs), but risk disclosures will be made.

The contractual commitment to buy the asset would be disclosed if material (IAS 16).

Entries at 31 December 20X1

Gain on forward contract:

	$
Value of contract at 31.12.X1 (€60,000,000/1.24)	48,387,097
Value of contract at 1.11.X1 (€60,000,000/1.5)	40,000,000
Gain on contract	8,387,097

Compare to movement in value of asset (unrecognised):

Increase in $ cost of asset

(€60,000,000/1.20 – €60,000,000/1.45) $8,620,690

As this is higher, the hedge is deemed fully effective at this point:

DEBIT	Financial asset (Forward a/c)	$8,387,097	
CREDIT	Equity		$8,387,097

Entries at 1 November 20X2

Additional gain on forward contract

	$
Value of contract at 1.11.X2 (€60,000,000/1.0)	60,000,000
Value of contract at 31.12.X1 (€60,000,000/1.24)	48,387,097
Gain on contract	11,612,903

Compare to movement in value of asset (unrecognised):

	$
Increase in $ cost of asset	
(€60,000,000/1.0 – €60,000,000/1.2)	$10,000,000

Therefore, the hedge is not fully effective during this period, but is still highly effective (and hence hedge accounting can be used):

$10,000,000/ $11,612,903 = 86% which is within the 80% – 125% bandings.

DEBIT	Financial asset (Forward a/c)	$11,612,903	
CREDIT	Equity		$10,000,000
CREDIT	Profit or loss		$1,612,903

Purchase of asset at market price

DEBIT	Asset (€60,000,000/1.0)	$60,000,000	
CREDIT	Cash		$60,000,000

Settlement of forward contract

DEBIT	Cash	$20,000,000	
CREDIT	Financial asset (Forward a/c)		$20,000,000

Realisation of gain on hedging instrument

The cumulative gain of $18,387,097 recognised in equity:

- Is transferred to profit or loss as the asset is used, ie over the asset's useful life; or
- Adjusts the initial cost of the asset (reducing future depreciation).

8 Reducing complexity

In March 2008, the IASB issued a Discussion Paper *Reducing complexity in reporting financial instruments*. The Discussion Paper is also being considered for comment by the US Financial Accounting Standards Board (FASB). In fact this is a joint project between the IASB and FASB.

The objective of the joint project is to **develop less complex and principle-based standards** on accounting for financial instruments. The Discussion Paper aims to gather information in order to assist with this project.

The Discussion Paper covers the following matters.

(a) The main **causes of complexity** in financial instrument accounting: multiple measurement methods

(b)   **A long-term solution** for reducing complexity and improving financial instrument accounting: measure all financial instruments at **fair value**

(c)   Three possible approaches for the medium term:

(i)   Amending the current measurement requirements

(ii)   Replacing the existing measurement requirements

(iii) Simplifying hedge accounting requirements

The determination of fair value and the classification of financial instruments as debt or equity are not discussed, as these matters are dealt with in separate projects.

As the Discussion Paper acknowledges, the main reason for complexity in accounting for financial instruments is the **many different ways in which they can be measured**.

The Discussion Paper maintains the view that **fair value is the only measure that is appropriate for all types of financial instruments**, and that a full fair value model would be much simpler to apply than the current mixed model.

IFRS 9 has now been issued as the first step in reducing complexity. It applies only to assets and stops short of bringing in a requirement to measure all financial assets at fair value.

9   Amended reclassification rules

In October 2008, the IASB published amendments to IAS 39 *Financial instruments: recognition and measurement* and IFRS 7 *Financial instruments: disclosures*. The IASB had come under pressure, to bring the reclassification of financial assets into line with US GAAP, thus creating a 'level playing field'. The amendments were effective from 1 July 2008.

The amendment only applies to reclassification of some non-derivative financial assets recognised in accordance with IAS 39. Reclassification is not permitted for financial liabilities, derivatives and financial assets that are designated as fair value through profit or loss (FVTPL) on initial recognition under the 'fair value option'.

The amendments therefore **only permit reclassification of debt and equity financial assets** subject to meeting specified criteria. They **do not permit reclassification into FVTPL**.

What are the criteria for reclassification out of FVTPL and available for sale (AFS)?

The criteria vary depending on whether the asset would have met the definition of 'loans and receivables' if it had not been classified as FVTPL or available for sale (AFS) on initial recognition.

(a)   If the debt instrument would have met the definition of loans and receivables, had it not been required to be classified as held for trading at initial recognition, it may be classified out of FVTPL **provided the entity has the intention and ability to hold the asset for the foreseeable future or until maturity**.

(b)   If a debt instrument was classified as AFS, but would have met the definition of loans and receivables if it had not been designated as AFS, it may be reclassified to the loans and receivables category **provided the entity has the intention and ability to hold the financial asset for the foreseeable future or until maturity**.

(c)   Other debt instruments or any equity instruments may be reclassified from FVTPL to AFS or, in the case of debt instruments only from FVTPL to held to maturity (HTM) **if the financial assets are no longer held for selling in the short term**. Such cases will be rare.

Reclassified assets must be measured at the reclassification date at the **fair value of the financial asset at the date of reclassification**.

(a)   Previously recognised gains and losses cannot be reversed.

(b)   The fair value at the date of reclassification becomes the new cost, or amortised cost of the financial asset.

Measurement after the reclassification date

After the reclassification date, **the normal IAS 39 requirements apply**. For example, in the case of financial assets measured at amortised cost, a **new effective interest rate** will be determined. If a fixed rate debt is reclassified as loans and receivables and held to maturity, this effective interest rate will be used as the discount rate for future impairment calculations.

For assets reclassified out of AFS, amounts previously recognised in other comprehensive income must be reclassified to profit or loss.

Exception

Reclassified debt instruments are treated differently. If, after the instrument has been reclassified, an entity increases its estimate of recoverability of future cash flows, the carrying amount is not adjusted upwards (in accordance with existing IAS 39 rules). Instead, a **new effective interest rate must be applied from that date** on. This enables the increase in recoverability of cash flows to be recognised over the expected life of the financial asset.

Disclosures

IFRS 7 has been amended to require additional disclosures for reclassifications that fall within the scope of the above amendments. They relate to the amounts reclassified in and out of each category, the fair values of reclassified assets, fair value gains or losses recognised in the period of reclassification and any new effective interest rate.

10   IFRS 7: Financial Instruments: Disclosures

The IASB maintains that users of financial instruments need information about an entity's exposures to risks and how those risks are managed, as this information can **influence a user's assessment of the financial position and financial performance of an entity** or of the amount, timing and uncertainty of its **future cash flows**.

There have been new techniques and approaches to measuring risk management, which highlighted the need for guidance.

Accordingly, IFRS 7 *Financial instruments: Disclosures* was issued in August 2005.

General requirements

The extent of disclosure required depends on the extent of the entity's use of financial instruments and of its exposure to risk. IFRS 7 **adds to the requirements previously in IAS 32** by requiring:

*   Enhanced statement of financial position and statement of comprehensive income disclosures

*   Disclosures about an allowance account when one is used to reduce the carrying amount of impaired financial instruments.

The standard requires **qualitative and quantitative disclosures about exposure to risks** arising from financial instruments, and specifies minimum disclosures about **credit risk, liquidity risk** and **market risk.**

The objective of the IFRS is to require entities to provide disclosures in their financial statements that enable users to evaluate:

(a) The significance of financial instruments for the entity's financial position and performance

(b) The nature and extent of risks arising from financial instruments to which the entity is exposed during the period and at the reporting date, and how the entity manages those risks.

The principles in IFRS 7 complement the principles for recognising, measuring and presenting financial assets and financial liabilities in IAS 32 *Financial instruments: Presentation* and IAS 39 *Financial instruments: Recognition and Measurement.*

Classes of financial instruments and levels of disclosure

The entity must group financial instruments into classes **appropriate to the nature of the information disclosed**. An entity must decide in the light of its circumstances how much detail it provides. Sufficient information must be provided to permit reconciliation to the line items presented in the statement of financial position.

Statement of financial position

The following must be disclosed.

(a) **Carrying amount** of financial assets and liabilities by IAS 39 category

(b) **Reason for any reclassification** between fair value and amortised cost (and vice versa)

(c) **Details** of the assets and exposure to risk where the entity has made a **transfer** such that part or all of the financial assets do not qualify for derecognition.

(d) The **carrying amount** of financial assets the entity has **pledged as collateral** for liabilities or contingent liabilities and the associated terms and conditions.

(e) When financial assets are impaired by credit losses and the entity records the impairment in a separate account (eg an **allowance account** used to record individual impairments or a similar account used to record a collective impairment of assets) rather than directly reducing the carrying amount of the asset, it must disclose a **reconciliation** of changes in that account during the period for each class of financial assets.

(f) The **existence of multiple embedded derivatives**, where compound instruments contain these.

(g) Defaults and breaches.

Statement of comprehensive income

The entity must disclose the following **items of income, expense, gains or losses**, either on the face of the financial statements or in the notes.

(a) Net gains/losses by IAS 39 category (broken down as appropriate: eg interest, fair value changes, dividend income)

(b) Interest income/expense

(c) Impairments losses by class of financial asset

Other disclosures

Entities must disclose in the summary of **significant accounting policies** the measurement basis used in preparing the financial statements and the other accounting policies that are relevant to an understanding of the financial statements.

Disclosures must be made relating to **hedge accounting**, as follows:

(a) Description of hedge
(b) Description of financial instruments designated as hedging instruments and their fair value at the reporting date
(c) The nature of the risks being hedged
(d) For cash flow hedges, periods when the cash flows will occur and when will affect profit or loss
(e) For fair value hedges, gains or losses on the hedging instrument and the hedged item
(f) The ineffectiveness recognised in profit or loss arising from cash flow hedges and net investments in foreign operations

Disclosures must be made relating to fair value:

(a) **By class** in a way that allows comparison to statement of financial position value in the statement of financial position. (Financial assets and liabilities may only be offset to the extent that their carrying amounts are offset in the statement of financial position.)
(b) The **methods and assumptions** used, for example by reference to an active market, and any change in these assumptions. If the market for a financial instrument is not active, a valuation technique, as per IAS 39, must be used. There could be a difference between the fair value at initial recognition and the amount that would be determined using the valuation technique. The accounting policy for recognising that difference in profit or loss, the aggregate difference yet to be recognised in profit or loss at the beginning and end of the period and a reconciliation of the changes in the balance of this difference, should be disclosed, as in the following example.

Example: Fair value disclosures

Background

On 1 January 20X1 an entity purchases for $15 million financial assets that are not traded in an active market. The entity has only one class of such financial assets.

The transaction price of $15 million is the fair value at initial recognition.

After initial recognition, the entity will apply a valuation technique to establish the financial assets fair value. This valuation technique includes variables other than data from observable markets.

At initial recognition, the same valuation technique would have resulted in an amount of $14 million, which differs from fair value by $1 million.

The entity has existing differences of $5 million at 1 January 20X1.

Application of requirements

The entity's 20X2 disclosure would include the following:

Accounting policies

The entity uses the following valuation technique to determine the fair value of financial instruments that are not traded in an active market: [description of technique, not included in this example]. Differences may arise between the fair value at initial recognition (which, in accordance with IAS 39, is generally the transaction price) and the amount determined at initial recognition using the valuation technique. Any such differences are [description of the entity's accounting policy].

In the notes to the financial statements

As discussed in note X, the entity uses [name of valuation technique] to measure the fair value of the following financial instruments that are not traded in an active market. However, in accordance with IAS 39, the fair value of an instrument at inception is generally the transaction price. If the transaction price differs from the amount determined at inception using the valuation technique, that difference is [description of the entity's accounting policy]. The differences yet to be recognised in profit or loss are as follows:

	31 Dec 20X2	31 Dec 20X1
	$m	$m
Balance at beginning of year	5.3	5.0
New transactions		1.0
Amounts recognised in profit or loss during the year	(0.7)	(0.8)
Other increases		0.2
Other decreases	(0.1)	(0.1)
Balance at end of year	4.5	5.3

Disclosures of fair value are **not required** if carrying value is a reasonable approximation to fair value, or if fair value cannot be measured reliably.

Nature and extent of risks arising from financial instruments

In undertaking transactions in financial instruments, an entity may assume or transfer to another party one or more of **different types of financial risk** as defined below. The disclosures required by the standard show the extent to which an entity is exposed to these different types of risk, relating to both recognised and unrecognised financial instruments.

Credit risk	The risk that one party to a financial instrument will cause a financial loss for the other party by failing to discharge an obligation.
Currency risk	The risk that the fair value or future cash flows of a financial instrument will fluctuate because of changes in foreign exchange rates.
Interest rate risk	The risk that the fair value or future cash flows of a financial instrument will fluctuate because of changes in market interest rates.
Liquidity risk	The risk that an entity will encounter difficulty in meeting obligations associated with financial liabilities.
Loans payable	Loans payable are financial liabilities, other than short-term trade payables on normal credit terms.
Market risk	The risk that the fair value or future cash flows of a financial instrument will fluctuate because of changes in market prices. Market risk comprises three types of risk: currency risk, interest rate risk and other price risk.
Other price risk	The risk that the fair value or future cash flows of a financial instrument will fluctuate because of changes in market prices (other than those arising from interest rate risk or currency risk), whether those changes are caused by factors specific to the individual financial instrument or its issuer, or factors affecting all similar financial instruments traded in the market.
Past due	A financial asset is past due when a counterparty has failed to make a payment when contractually due.

Qualitative disclosures

For each type of risk arising from financial instruments, an entity must disclose:

(a) The **exposures to risk** and how they arise
(b) Its objectives, policies and processes for managing the risk and the methods used to measure the risk
(c) Any **changes** in (a) or (b) from the previous period

Quantitative disclosures

For each financial instrument risk, **summary quantitative data** about risk exposure must be disclosed. This should be based on the information provided internally to key management personnel. More information should be provided if this is unrepresentative.

Information about **credit risk** must be disclosed by class of financial instrument:

(a) Maximum exposure at the year end
(b) Any collateral pledged as security
(c) In respect of the amount disclosed in (b), a description of collateral held as security and other credit enhancements
(d) Information about the credit quality of financial assets that are neither past due nor impaired
(e) Financial assets that are past due or impaired, giving an age analysis and a description of collateral held by the entity as security.
(f) Collateral and other credit enhancements obtained, including the nature and carrying amount of the assets and policy for disposing of assets not readily convertible into cash

For **liquidity risk** entities must disclose:

(a) A maturity analysis of financial liabilities
(b) A description of the way risk is managed

Disclosures required in connection with **market risk** are:

(a) Sensitivity analysis, showing the effects on profit or loss of changes in each market risk
(b) If the sensitivity analysis reflects interdependencies between risk variables, such as interest rates and exchange rates the method, assumptions and limitations must be disclosed

Capital disclosures

Certain disclosures about **capital** are required. An entity's capital does not relate solely to financial instruments, but has more general relevance. Accordingly, those disclosures are included in IAS 1, rather than in IFRS 7.

Earnings per share

13

1 IAS 33: Earnings per share

The objective of IAS 33 is to improve the **comparability** of the performance of different entities in the same period and of the same entity in different accounting periods by prescribing methods for determining the number of shares to be included in the calculation of earnings per share and other amounts per share and by specifying their presentation.

The following definitions are given in IAS 33, some of which are given in other IASs.

> **Ordinary share:** an equity instrument that is subordinate to all other classes of equity instruments.
>
> **Potential ordinary share:** a financial instrument or other contract that may entitle its holder to ordinary shares.
>
> **Warrants or options:** financial instruments that give the holder the right to purchase ordinary shares.
>
> **Financial instrument:** any contract that gives rise to both a financial asset of one entity and a financial liability or equity instrument of another entity.
>
> **Equity instrument:** any contract that evidences a residual interest in the assets of an entity after deducting all of its liabilities. (IAS 33)

There may be more than one class of ordinary shares, but ordinary shares of the same class will have the same rights to receive dividends. Ordinary shares participate in the net profit for the year **only after other types of shares**, eg preference shares.

Potential ordinary shares

IAS 33 identifies the following examples of financial instruments and other contracts generating potential ordinary shares.

(a) **Debt or equity instruments**, including preference shares, that are convertible into ordinary shares
(b) **Share warrants and options**
(c) **Employee plans** that allow employees to receive ordinary shares as part of their remuneration and other share purchase plans
(d) Shares that would be issued upon the satisfaction of **certain conditions** resulting from contractual arrangements, such as the purchase of a business or other assets

IAS 33 has the following scope restrictions.

(a) Only companies with (potential) ordinary shares which are **publicly traded** need to present EPS (including companies in the process of being listed).
(b) EPS need only be presented on the basis of **consolidated results** where the parent's results are shown as well.

(c)   Where companies **choose** to present EPS, even when they have no (potential) ordinary shares which are traded, they must do so in accordance with IAS 33.

2 Basic EPS

Measurement

Basic EPS should be calculated by dividing the **net profit** or loss for the period attributable to ordinary shareholders by the **weighted average number of ordinary shares** outstanding during the period.

$$\text{Basic EPS} = \frac{\text{Net profit /(loss) attributable to ordinary shareholders}}{\text{Weighted average number of ordinary shares outstanding during the period}}$$

Earnings

Earnings includes **all items of income and expense** (including tax and minority interests) less net profit attributable to **preference shareholders**, including preference dividends.

Preference dividends deducted from net profit consist of:

(a)   Preference dividends on non-cumulative preference shares declared in respect of the period

(b)   The full amount of the required preference dividends for cumulative preference shares for the period, whether or not they have been declared (excluding those paid/declared during the period in respect of previous periods)

Per share

The number of ordinary shares used should be the weighted average number of ordinary shares during the period. This figure (for all periods presented) should be **adjusted for events**, other than the conversion of potential ordinary shares, that have changed the number of shares outstanding without a corresponding change in resources.

The **time-weighting factor** is the number of days the shares were outstanding compared with the total number of days in the period; a reasonable approximation is usually adequate.

Example: weighted average number of shares

J Co, a listed company, has the following share transactions during 20X7.

Date	Details	Shares issued	Treasury shares*	Shares outstanding
1 January 20X7	Balance at beginning of year	200,000	30,000	170,000
31 May 20X7	Issue of new shares for cash	80,000	–	250,000
1 December 20X7	Purchase of treasury shares	–	25,000	225,000
31 December 20X7	Balance at year end	280,000	55,000	225,000

* Treasury shares are an entity's own shares acquired. In some countries own shares cannot be held, but must be cancelled on acquisition.

What is the weighted average number of shares outstanding for 20X7?

The weighted average number of shares can be calculated in two ways.

(a) $(170,000 \times 5/12) + (250,000 \times 6/12) + (225,000 \times 1/12) = 214,583$ shares

(b) $(170,000 \times 12/12) + (80,000 \times 7/12) - (25,000 \times 1/12) = 214,583$ shares

Consideration

Shares are usually included in the weighted average number of shares from the **date consideration is receivable** which is usually the date of issue; in other cases consider the specific terms attached to their issue (consider the substance of any contract). The treatment for the issue of ordinary shares in different circumstances is as follows.

Consideration	Start date for inclusion
In exchange for cash	When cash is receivable
On the voluntary reinvestment of dividends on ordinary or preferred shares	The dividend payment date
As a result of the conversion of a debt instrument to ordinary shares	Date interest ceases accruing
In place of interest or principal on other financial instruments	Date interest ceases accruing
In exchange for the settlement of a liability of the entity	The settlement date
As consideration for the acquisition of an asset other than cash	The date on which the acquisition is recognised
For the rendering of services to the entity	As services are rendered

Ordinary shares issued as **purchase consideration** in an acquisition should be included as of the date of acquisition because the acquired entity's results will also be included from that date.

If ordinary shares are **partly paid**, they are treated as a fraction of an ordinary share to the extent they are entitled to dividends relative to fully paid ordinary shares.

Contingently issuable shares (including those subject to recall) are included in the computation when all necessary conditions for issue have been satisfied.

3 Effect on EPS of changes in capital structure

We looked at the effect of issues of new shares or buy-backs of shares on basic EPS above. In these situations, the corresponding figures for EPS for the previous year will be comparable with the current year because, as the weighted average number of shares has risen or fallen, there has been a **corresponding increase or decrease in resources.** Money has been received when shares were issued, and money has been paid out to repurchase shares. It is assumed that the sales or purchases have been made at full market price.

Example: earnings per share with a new issue

On 30 September 20X2, B Co made an issue at full market price of 1,000,000 ordinary shares. The company's accounting year runs from 1 January to 31 December. Relevant information for 20X1 and 20X2 is as follows.

	20X2	20X1
Shares in issue as at 31 December	9,000,000	8,000,000
Profits after tax and preference dividend	$3,300,000	$3,280,000

What is the EPS for 20X2 and the corresponding figure for 20X1?

Weighted average number of shares	20X2	20X1
9 months × 8 million	6,000,000	
3 months × 9 million	2,250,000	
	8,250,000	8,000,000
Earnings	$3,300,000	$3,280,000
EPS	40 cents	41 cents

In spite of the increase in total earnings by $20,000 in 20X2, the EPS is not as good as in 20X1, because there was extra capital employed for the final 3 months of 20X2.

There are other events, however, which change the number of shares outstanding, **without a corresponding change in resources**. In these circumstances it is necessary to make adjustments so that the current and prior period EPS figures are comparable.

Four such events are considered by IAS 33.

(a) **Capitalisation or bonus issue** (sometimes called a stock dividend)
(b) Bonus element in any other issue, eg a rights issue to existing shareholders
(c) **Share split**
(d) **Reverse share split** (consolidation of shares)

Capitalisation/bonus issue and share split/reverse share split

These two types of event can be considered together as they have a similar effect. In both cases, ordinary shares are issued to existing shareholders for **no additional consideration**. The number of ordinary shares has increased without an increase in resources.

This problem is solved by **adjusting the number of ordinary shares outstanding before the event** for the proportionate change in the number of shares outstanding as if the event had occurred at the beginning of the earliest period reported.

Example: earnings per share with a bonus issue

G Co had 400,000 shares in issue, until on 30 September 20X2 it made a bonus issue of 100,000 shares. Total earnings were $80,000 in 20X2 and $75,000 in 20X1. The company's accounting year runs from 1 January to 31 December.

EPS will be:

	20X2	20X1
Earnings	$80,000	$75,000
Shares at 1 January	400,000	400,000
Bonus issue	100,000	100,000
	500,000 shares	500,000 shares
EPS	16c	15c

The number of shares for 20X1 must also be adjusted if the figures for EPS are to remain comparable.

Rights issue

A rights issue of shares is an issue of new shares to existing shareholders **at a price below the current market value**. The offer of new shares is made on the basis of x new shares for every y shares currently held; eg a 1 for 3 rights issue is an offer of 1 new share at the offer price for every 3 shares currently held. This means that there is a bonus element included.

To arrive at figures for EPS when a rights issue is made, we need to calculate first of all the **theoretical ex rights price**. This is a weighted average value per share, and is perhaps explained most easily with a numerical example.

Example: theoretical ex-rights price

Suppose that E Co has 10,000,000 shares in issue. It now proposes to make a 1 for 4 rights issue at a price of $3 per share. The market value of existing shares on the final day before the issue is made is $3.50 (this is the 'with rights' value). What is the theoretical ex rights price per share?

	$
Before issue 4 shares, value $3.50 each	14.00
Rights issue 1 share, value $3	3.00
Theoretical value of 5 shares	17.00

$$\text{Theoretical ex rights price} = \frac{\$17.00}{5} = \$3.40 \text{ per share}$$

Note that this calculation can alternatively be performed using the total value and number of outstanding shares.

Procedures

The procedures for calculating the EPS for the current year and a corresponding figure for the previous year are now as follows.

(a)   The **EPS for the corresponding previous period** should be multiplied by the following fraction. (Note. The market price on the last day of quotation is taken as the fair value immediately prior to exercise of the rights, as required by the standard.)

$$\frac{\text{Theoretical ex-rights price}}{\text{Market price on last day of quotation (with rights)}}$$

(b)   To obtain the **EPS for the current year**:

(i)   Multiply the number of shares before the rights issue by the fraction of the year before the date of issue and by the following fraction

$$\frac{\text{Market price on last day of quotation (with rights)}}{\text{Theoretical ex-rights price}}$$

(ii)   Multiply the number of shares after the rights issue by the fraction of the year after the date of issue and add to the figure arrived at in (i)

The total earnings should then be divided by the total number of shares so calculated.

Example: earnings per share with a rights issue

B Co had 100,000 shares in issue, but then makes a 1 for 5 rights issue on 1 October 20X2 at a price of $1. The market value on the last day of quotation with rights was $1.60.

Total earnings are $50,000 in 20X2 and $40,000 in 20X1.

What is the EPS for 20X2 and the corresponding figure for 20X1?

Calculation of theoretical ex rights price:

	$
Before issue 5 shares, value × $1.60	8.00
Rights issue 1 share, value × $1.00	1.00
Theoretical value of 6 shares	9.00

Theoretical ex rights price $= \dfrac{\$9}{6} = \$1.50$

EPS for 20X1

EPS as calculated before taking into account the rights issue = 40c ($40,000 divided by 100,000 shares).

$$EPS = \frac{1.50}{1.60} \times 40c = 37\tfrac{1}{2}c$$

(This is the corresponding value for 20X1 which will be shown in the financial statements for B Co at the end of 20X2.)

EPS for 20X2

Number of shares before the rights issue was 100,000. 20,000 shares were issued.

Stage 1:	$100,000 \times 9/12 \times \dfrac{1.60}{1.50}$	=	80,000
Stage 2:	$120,000 \times 3/12$	=	30,000
			110,000

$$EPS = \frac{\$50,000}{110,000} = 45\tfrac{1}{2}c$$

The figure for total earnings is the actual earnings for the year.

4 Diluted EPS

At the end of an accounting period, a company may have in issue some **securities** which do not (at present) have any 'claim' to a share of equity earnings, but **may give rise to such a claim in the future**. These securities include:

(a) A **separate class of equity shares** which at present is not entitled to any dividend, but will be entitled after some future date

(b) **Convertible loan stock** or **convertible preference shares** which give their holders the right at some future date to exchange their securities for ordinary shares of the company, at a pre determined conversion rate

(c) Options or warrants

In such circumstances, the future number of ordinary shares in issue might increase, which in turn results in a fall in the EPS. In other words, a **future increase** in the **number of ordinary shares will cause a dilution or 'watering down' of equity**, and it is possible to calculate a **diluted earnings per share** (ie the EPS that would have been obtained during the financial period if the dilution had already taken place). This will indicate to investors the possible effects of a future dilution.

Earnings

The earnings calculated for basic EPS should be adjusted by the **post-tax** (including deferred tax) effect of:

(a) Any **dividends** on dilutive potential ordinary shares that were deducted to arrive at earnings for basic EPS
(b) **Interest recognised** in the period for the dilutive potential ordinary shares
(c) Any **other changes in income or expenses** (fees and discount, premium accounted for as yield adjustments) that would result from the conversion of the dilutive potential ordinary shares

The conversion of some potential ordinary shares may lead to changes in **other income or expenses**. For example, the reduction of interest expense related to potential ordinary shares and the resulting increase in net profit for the period may lead to an increase in the expense relating to a non-discretionary employee profit-sharing plan. When calculating diluted EPS, the net profit or loss for the period is adjusted for any such consequential changes in income or expense.

Per share

The number of ordinary shares is the weighted average number of ordinary shares calculated for basic EPS plus the weighted average number of ordinary shares that would be issued on the conversion of all the **dilutive potential ordinary shares** into ordinary shares.

It should be assumed that dilutive ordinary shares were converted into ordinary shares at the **beginning of the period** or, if later, at the actual date of issue. There are two other points.

(a) The computation assumes the most **advantageous conversion rate** or exercise rate from the standpoint of the holder of the potential ordinary shares.
(b) **Contingently issuable** (potential) ordinary shares are treated as for basic EPS; if the conditions have not been met, the number of contingently issuable shares included in the computation is based on the number of shares that would be issuable if the end of the reporting period was the end of the contingency period. Restatement is not allowed if the conditions are not met when the contingency period expires.

Example: diluted EPS

In 20X7 F Co had a basic EPS of 105c based on earnings of $105,000 and 100,000 ordinary $1 shares. It also had in issue $40,000 15% Convertible Loan Stock which is convertible in two years' time at the rate of 4 ordinary shares for every $5 of stock. The rate of tax is 30%. In 20X7 gross profit of $200,000 and expenses of $50,000 were recorded, including interest payable of $6,000.

What is the diluted EPS?

Diluted EPS is calculated as follows.

Step 1 **Number of shares:** the additional equity on conversion of the loan stock will be $40,000 \times 4/5 = 32,000$ shares

Step 2 **Earnings:** F Co will save interest payments of $6,000 but this increase in profits will be taxed. Hence the earnings figure may be recalculated:

	$
Gross profit	200,000
Expenses (50,000 – 6,000)	(44,000)
Profit before tax	156,000
Tax expense (30%)	(46,800)
Earnings	109,200

Step 3 **Calculation:** Diluted EPS = $\dfrac{\$109{,}200}{132{,}000}$ = 82.7c

Step 4 **Dilution:** the dilution in earnings would be 105c – 82.7c = 22.3c per share.

Dilutive potential ordinary shares

According to IAS 33, potential ordinary shares should be treated as dilutive when, and only when, their conversion to ordinary shares would **decrease net profit per share** from continuing operations. It is important to only include in the diluted EPS calculation those potential ordinary shares which are actually dilutive.

Example:

A Co has 5,000,000 ordinary shares of 25 cents each in issue, and also had in issue in 20X4:

(a) $1,000,000 of 14% convertible loan stock, convertible in three years' time at the rate of 2 shares per $10 of stock;

(b) $2,000,000 of 10% convertible loan stock, convertible in one year's time at the rate of 3 shares per $5 of stock.

The total earnings in 20X4 were $1,750,000.

The rate of income tax is 35%.

What is the basic EPS and diluted EPS?

(a)   Basic EPS = $\dfrac{\$1{,}750{,}000}{5 \text{ million}}$ = 35 cents

(b)   We must decide which of the potential ordinary shares (ie the loan stocks) are dilutive (ie would decrease the EPS if converted).

For the 14% loan stock, incremental EPS = $\dfrac{0.65 \times \$140{,}000}{200{,}000 \text{ shares}}$ = 45.5c

For the 10% loan stock, incremental EPS $= \dfrac{0.65 \times \$200{,}000}{1.2\text{m shares}} = 10.8\text{c}$

The effect of converting the 14% loan stock is therefore to increase the EPS figure, since the incremental EPS of 45.5c is greater than the basic EPS of 35c. The 14% loan stock is not dilutive and is therefore excluded from the diluted EPS calculation.

The 10% loan stock is dilutive.

Diluted EPS $= \dfrac{\$1.75\text{m} + \$0.13\text{m}}{5\text{m} + 1.2\text{m}} = 30.3\text{c}$

Restatement

If the number of ordinary or potential ordinary shares outstanding **increases** as a result of a capitalisation, bonus issue or share split, or decreases as a result of a reverse share split, the calculation of basic and diluted EPS for all periods presented should be **adjusted retrospectively**.

If these changes occur **after the reporting date** but before the financial statements are authorised for issue, the calculations per share for the financial statements and those of any prior period should be based on the **new number of shares** (and this should be disclosed).

In addition, basic and diluted EPS of all periods presented should be adjusted for the effects of **material errors**, and adjustments resulting from **changes** in **accounting policies**, dealt with in accordance with IAS 8.

An entity **does not restate diluted EPS** of any prior period for changes in the assumptions used or for the conversion of potential ordinary shares into ordinary shares outstanding.

Entities are encouraged to disclose a description of ordinary share transactions or potential ordinary share transactions, other than capitalisation issues and share splits, which occur **after the reporting date** when they are of such importance that non-disclosure would affect the ability of the users of the financial statements to make proper evaluations and decisions (see IAS 10). Examples of such transactions include the following.

(a) Issue of shares for cash
(b) Issue of shares when the proceeds are used to repay debt or preferred shares outstanding at the reporting date
(c) Redemption of ordinary shares outstanding
(d) Conversion or exercise of potential ordinary shares, outstanding at the reporting date, into ordinary shares
(e) Issue of warrants, options or convertible securities
(f) Achievement of conditions that would result in the issue of contingently issuable shares

EPS amounts are not adjusted for such transactions occurring after the reporting date because such transactions **do not affect the amount of capital used** to produce the net profit or loss for the period.

5 Presentation, disclosure and other matters

Basic and diluted EPS should be presented by an entity on the **face of the statement of comprehensive income** for each class of ordinary share that has a different right to share in the net profit for the period. The basic and diluted EPS should be presented with **equal prominence** for all periods presented.

Disclosure must still be made where the EPS figures (basic and/or diluted) are **negative** (ie a loss per share).

An entity should disclose the following.

(a) The amounts used as the **numerators** in calculating basic and diluted EPS, and a reconciliation of those amounts to the net profit or loss for the period

(b) The weighted average number of ordinary shares used as the **denominator** in calculating basic and diluted EPS, and a **reconciliation** of these denominators to each other.

Significance of earnings per share

Earnings per share (EPS) is one of the most frequently quoted statistics in financial analysis. Because of the widespread use of the price earnings **(P/E) ratio** as a yardstick for investment decisions, it became increasingly important.

Reported and forecast EPS can, through the P/E ratio, have a **significant effect on a company's share price**. Thus, a share price might fall if it looks as if EPS is going to be low. This is not very rational, as EPS can depend on many, often subjective, assumptions used in preparing a historical statement such as the income statement. It does not necessarily bear any relation to the value of a company, and of its shares. Nevertheless, the market is sensitive to EPS.

EPS has also served as a means of assessing the **stewardship and management** role performed by company directors and managers. Remuneration packages might be linked to EPS growth, thereby increasing the pressure on management to improve EPS. The danger of this, however, is that management effort may go into distorting results to produce a favourable EPS.

14

---

1 IAS 7: Statement of cash flows

The aim of IAS 7 is to provide information to users of financial statements about the entity's **ability to generate cash and cash equivalents**, as well as indicating the cash needs of the entity. The statement of cash flows provides *historical* information about cash and cash equivalents, classifying cash flows between operating, investing and financing activities.

A statement of cash flows should be presented as an **integral part** of an entity's financial statements. All types of entity can provide useful information about cash flows as the need for cash is universal, whatever the nature of their revenue-producing activities. Therefore **all entities are required by the standard to produce a statement of cash flows**.

Benefits of cash flow information

The use of statements of cash flows is very much **in conjunction** with the rest of the financial statements. Users can gain further appreciation of the change in net assets, of the entity's financial position (liquidity and solvency) and the entity's ability to adapt to changing circumstances by affecting the amount and timing of cash flows. Statements of cash flows **enhance comparability** as they are not affected by differing accounting policies used for the same type of transactions or events.

Cash flow information of a historical nature can be used as an indicator of the amount, timing and certainty of future cash flows. Past forecast cash flow information can be **checked for accuracy** as actual figures emerge. The relationship between profit and cash flows can be analysed as can changes in prices over time.

Definitions

The standard gives the following definitions, the most important of which are **cash** and **cash equivalents**.

- **Cash** comprises cash on hand and demand deposits.
- **Cash equivalents** are short-term, highly liquid investments that are readily convertible to known amounts of cash and which are subject to an insignificant risk of changes in value.
- **Cash flows** are inflows and outflows of cash and cash equivalents.
- **Operating activities** are the principal revenue-producing activities of the entity and other activities that are not investing or financing activities.
- **Investing activities** are the acquisition and disposal of non-current assets and other investments not included in cash equivalents.
- **Financing activities** are activities that result in changes in the size and composition of the equity capital and borrowings of the entity. (IAS 7)

Cash and cash equivalents

The standard expands on the definition of cash equivalents: they are not held for investment or other long-term purposes, but rather to meet short-term cash commitments. To fulfil the above definition, an investment's **maturity date should normally be within three months from its acquisition date**. It would usually be the case then that equity investments (ie shares in other companies) are *not* cash equivalents. An exception would be where preferred shares were acquired with a very close maturity date.

Loans and other borrowings from banks are classified as investing activities. In some countries, however, **bank overdrafts** are repayable on demand and are treated as part of an entity's total cash management system. In these circumstances an overdrawn balance will be included in cash and cash equivalents. Such banking arrangements are characterised by a balance which fluctuates between overdrawn and credit.

Movements between different types of cash and cash equivalent are not included in cash flows. The investment of surplus cash in cash equivalents is part of cash management, not part of operating, investing or financing activities.

The manner of presentation of cash flows between operating, investing and financing activities **depends on the nature of the entity**. By classifying cash flows between different activities in this way users can see the impact on cash and cash equivalents of each one, and their relationships with each other. We can look at each in more detail.

Operating activities

This is perhaps the key part of the statement of cash flows because it shows whether, and to what extent, companies can **generate cash from their operations**. It is these operating cash flows which must, in the end pay for all cash outflows relating to other activities, ie paying loan interest, dividends and so on.

Most of the components of cash flows from operating activities will be those items which **determine the net profit or loss of the entity**, ie they relate to the main revenue-producing activities of the entity. The standard gives the following as examples of cash flows from operating activities.

(a)   Cash receipts from the sale of goods and the rendering of services
(b)   Cash receipts from royalties, fees, commissions and other revenue
(c)   Cash payments to suppliers for goods and services
(d)   Cash payments to and on behalf of employees

Certain items may be included in the net profit or loss for the period which do not relate to operational cash flows, for example the profit or loss on the sale of a piece of plant will be included in net profit or loss, but the cash flows will be classed as **investing**.

Investing activities

The cash flows classified under this heading show the extent of new investment in **assets which will generate future profit and cash flows**. The standard gives the following examples of cash flows arising from investing activities.

(a)   Cash payments to acquire property, plant and equipment, intangibles and other non-current assets, including those relating to capitalised development costs and self-constructed property, plant and equipment
(b)   Cash receipts from sales of property, plant and equipment, intangibles and other non-current assets
(c)   Cash payments to acquire shares or debentures of other entities

(d)   Cash receipts from sales of shares or debentures of other entities
(e)   Cash advances and loans made to other parties
(f)   Cash receipts from the repayment of advances and loans made to other parties

Financing activities

This section of the statement of cash flows shows the share of cash which the entity's capital providers have claimed during the period. This is an indicator of **likely future interest and dividend payments**. The standard gives the following examples of cash flows which might arise under this heading.

(a)   Cash proceeds from issuing shares
(b)   Cash payments to owners to acquire or redeem the entity's shares
(c)   Cash proceeds from issuing debentures, loans, notes, bonds, mortgages and other short or long-term borrowings
(d)   Principal repayments of amounts borrowed under finance leases

Item (d) needs more explanation. Where the reporting entity uses an asset held under a finance lease, the amounts to go in the statement of cash flows as financing activities are repayments of the **principal (capital)** rather than the **interest**. The interest paid will be shown under operating activities.

Example: finance lease rental

The notes to the financial statements of H Co show the following in respect of obligations under finance leases.

Year ended 30 June	20X5	20X4
	$'000	$'000
Amounts payable within one year	12	8
Within two to five years	110	66
	122	74
Less finance charges allocated to future periods	(14)	(8)
	108	66

Interest paid on finance leases in the year to 30 June 20X5 amounted to $6m. Additions to tangible non-current assets acquired under finance leases were shown in the non-current asset note at $56,000.

What is the capital repayment to be shown in the statement of cash flows of H Co for the year to 30 June 20X5?

OBLIGATIONS UNDER FINANCE LEASES

	$'000		$'000
Capital repayment (bal fig)	14	Bal 1.7.X4	66
Bal 30.6.X5	108	Additions	56
	122		122

Reporting cash flows from operating activities

The standard offers a choice of method for this part of the statement of cash flows.

(a)   **Direct method:** disclose major classes of gross cash receipts and gross cash payments

(b) **Indirect method:** net profit or loss is adjusted for the effects of transactions of a non-cash nature, any deferrals or accruals of past or future operating cash receipts or payments, and items of income or expense associated with investing or financing cash flows

The **direct method is the preferred method** because it discloses information, not available elsewhere in the financial statements, which could be of use in estimating future cash flows. The example below shows both methods.

Using the direct method

The direct method requires **information about gross cash receipts and payments**. There are different ways in which this can be obtained. The most obvious way is simply to extract the information from the accounting records. This may be a laborious task, however, and the indirect method is probably more widely used.

Using the indirect method

This method is undoubtedly **easier** from the point of view of the preparer of the statement of cash flows. The net profit or loss for the period is adjusted for the following.

(a) Changes during the period in inventories, operating receivables and payables
(b) Non-cash items, eg depreciation, provisions, profits/losses on the sales of assets
(c) Other items, the cash flows from which should be classified under investing or financing activities.

A **proforma** of such a calculation, taken from the IAS, is as follows. (The proforma has been amended to reflect changes to IFRS.)

	$
Cash flows from operating activities	
Profit before taxation	X
Adjustments for:	
Depreciation	X
Foreign exchange loss	X
Investment income	(X)
Interest expense	X
	X
Increase in trade and other receivables	(X)
Decrease in inventories	X
Decrease in trade payables	(X)
Cash generated from operations	X
Interest paid	(X)
Income taxes paid	(X)
Net cash from operating activities	X

It is important to understand why **certain items are added and others subtracted**. Note the following points.

(a) Depreciation is not a cash expense, but is deducted in arriving at profit. It makes sense, therefore, to eliminate it by adding it back.
(b) By the same logic, a loss on a disposal of a non-current asset (arising through underprovision of depreciation) needs to be added back and a profit deducted.

(c)   An increase in inventories means less cash – you have spent cash on buying inventory.
(d)   An increase in receivables means the company's debtors have not paid as much, and therefore there is less cash.
(e)   If we pay off payables, causing the figure to decrease, again we have less cash.

The direct method is encouraged where the necessary information is not too costly to obtain, but IAS 7 does not require it. In practice the indirect method is more commonly used, since it is quicker and easier.

Interest and dividends

Cash flows from interest and dividends received and paid should each be **disclosed separately**. Each should be classified in a consistent manner from period to period as either operating, investing or financing activities.

Dividends paid by the entity can be classified in **one of two ways**.

(a)   As a **financing cash flow**, showing the cost of obtaining financial resources.
(b)   As a component of **cash flows from operating activities** so that users can assess the entity's ability to pay dividends out of operating cash flows.

Taxes on income

Cash flows arising from taxes on income should be **separately disclosed** and should be classified as cash flows from operating activities unless they can be specifically identified with financing and investing activities.

Taxation cash flows are often **difficult to match** to the originating underlying transaction, so most of the time all tax cash flows are classified as arising from operating activities.

Components of cash and cash equivalents

The components of cash and cash equivalents should be disclosed and a **reconciliation** should be presented, showing the amounts in the statement of cash flows reconciled with the equivalent items reported in the statement of financial position.

It is also necessary to disclose the **accounting policy** used in deciding the items included in cash and cash equivalents, in accordance with IAS 1 *Presentation of Financial Statements*, but also because of the wide range of cash management practices worldwide.

Other disclosures

All entities should disclose, together with a **commentary by management**, any other information likely to be of importance, for example:

(a)   Restrictions on the use of or access to any part of cash equivalents
(b)   The amount of undrawn borrowing facilities which are available
(c)   Cash flows which increased operating capacity compared to cash flows which merely maintained operating capacity
(d)   Cash flows arising from each reported industry and geographical segment

Example of a statement of cash flows

This example is adapted from the example given in the standard. Note that 'net cash from operating activities' is the same under both methods.

Direct method

STATEMENT OF CASH FLOWS

YEAR ENDED 31 DECEMBER 20X7

	$m	$m
Cash flows from operating activities		
Cash receipts from customers	30,330	
Cash paid to suppliers and employees	(27,600)	
Cash generated from operations	2,730	
Interest paid	(270)	
Income taxes paid	(900)	
Net cash from operating activities		1,560
Cash flows from investing activities		
Purchase of property, plant and equipment	(900)	
Proceeds from sale of equipment	20	
Interest received	200	
Dividends received	200	
Net cash used in investing activities		(480)
Cash flows from financing activities		
Proceeds from issue of share capital	250	
Proceeds from long-term borrowings	250	
Dividends paid*	(1,290)	
Net cash used in financing activities		(790)
Net increase in cash and cash equivalents		290
Cash and cash equivalents at beginning of period (Note)		120
Cash and cash equivalents at end of period (Note)		410

* This could also be shown as an operating cash flow

Net cash from operating activities can also be calculated using the **indirect method**.

Indirect method

STATEMENT OF CASH FLOWS (extract)

YEAR ENDED 31 DECEMBER 20X7

	$m	$m
Cash flows from operating activities		
Profit before taxation	3,570	
Adjustments for:		
Depreciation	450	
Investment income	(500)	
Interest expense	400	
	3,920	
Increase in trade and other receivables	(500)	
Decrease in inventories	1,050	
Decrease in trade payables	(1,740)	
Cash generated from operations	2,730	
Interest paid	(270)	
Income taxes paid	(900)	
Net cash from operating activities		1,560

2 Preparing a statement of cash flows

In essence, preparing a statement of cash flows under IAS 7 is very straightforward. We will now go through a full example.

D CO

STATEMENT OF COMPREHENSIVE INCOME FOR THE YEAR ENDED 31 DECEMBER 20X2

	$'000
Revenue	2,553
Cost of sales	(1,814)
Gross profit	739
Other income: interest received	25
Distribution costs	(125)
Administrative expenses	(264)
Finance costs	(75)
Profit before tax	300
Income tax expense	(140)
Profit for the year	160
Other comprehensive income:	
Revaluation gain on property	9
Total comprehensive income for the year	169

D CO

STATEMENTS OF FINANCIAL POSITION AS AT 31 DECEMBER

	20X2	20X1
Assets	$'000	$'000
Non-current assets		
Property, plant and equipment	380	305
Intangible assets	250	200
Investments	–	25
Current assets		
Inventories	150	102
Receivables	390	315
Short-term investments	50	–
Cash in hand	2	1
Total assets	1,222	948
Equity and liabilities		
Equity		
Share capital ($1 ordinary shares)	200	150
Share premium account	160	150
Revaluation surplus	100	91
Retained earnings	260	180
Non-current liabilities		
Long-term loan	170	50
Current liabilities		
Trade payables	127	119
Bank overdraft	85	98
Taxation	120	110
Total equity and liabilities	1,222	948

The following information is available.

(a) The proceeds of the sale of non-current asset investments amounted to $30,000.

(b) Fixtures and fittings, with an original cost of $85,000 and a carrying amount of $45,000, were sold for $32,000 during the year.

(c) The following information relates to property, plant and equipment.

	31.12.20X2	31.12.20X1
	$'000	$'000
Cost	720	595
Accumulated depreciation	(340)	(290)
Carrying amount	380	305

(d) 50,000 $1 ordinary shares were issued during the year at a premium of 20c per share.

(e) The short-term investments are highly liquid and are close to maturity.

(f) Dividends of $80,000 were paid during the year.

The statement of cash flows will be as follows:

D CO

STATEMENT OF CASH FLOWS FOR THE YEAR ENDED 31 DECEMBER 20X2

	$'000	$'000
Cash flows from operating activities		
Profit before tax	300	
Depreciation charge (W1)	90	
Loss on sale of property, plant and equipment (45 – 32)	13	
Profit on sale of non-current asset investments	(5)	
Interest expense (net)	50	
(Increase)/decrease in inventories	(48)	
(Increase)/decrease in receivables	(75)	
Increase/(decrease) in payables	8	
	333	
Interest paid	(75)	
Dividends paid	(80)	
Tax paid (110 + 140 – 120)	(130)	
Net cash from operating activities		48
Cash flows from investing activities		
Payments to acquire property, plant and equipment (W2)	(201)	
Payments to acquire intangible non-current assets	(50)	
Receipts from sales of property, plant and equipment	32	
Receipts from sale of non-current asset investments	30	
Interest received	25	
Net cash used in investing activities		(164)
Cash flows from financing activities		
Issue of share capital	60	
Long-term loan	120	
Net cash flows from financing activities		180
Increase in cash and cash equivalents		64
Cash and cash equivalents at 1.1.X2 (1 – 98)		(97)
Cash and cash equivalents at 31.12.X2 (50 + 2 – 85)		(33)

Part
B

Single entity financial statements

191

Workings

1. *Depreciation charge*

	$'000	$'000
Depreciation at 31 December 20X2		340
Depreciation 31 December 20X1	290	
Depreciation on assets sold (85 – 45)	40	
		250
Charge for the year		90

2. *Purchase of property, plant and equipment*

PROPERTY, PLANT AND EQUIPMENT (COST)

	$'000		$'000
1.1.X2 Balance b/d	595	Disposals	85
Revaluation (100 – 91)	9		
Purchases (bal figure)	201	31.12.X2 Balance c/d	720
	805		805

Examples of other items that may arise are:

*   Share capital issues. The proceeds will be split between share capital and share premium.

*   Bonus issues. These do not involve cash.

*   Revaluation of non-current assets. This must be taken into account in calculating acquisitions and disposals.

*   Movement on deferred tax. This must be taken into account in calculating tax paid.

*   Finance leases. Assets acquired under finance leases must be adjusted for in non-current asset calculations and the amount paid under the finance lease must appear as a cash flow.

3 Interpretation of statements of cash flows

So what kind of information does the statement of cash flows, along with its notes, provide?

Some of the main areas where IAS 7 should provide information not found elsewhere in the financial statements are as follows.

(a) The **relationships between profit and cash** can be seen clearly and analysed accordingly.

(b) **Cash equivalents** are highlighted, giving a better picture of the liquidity of the company.

(c) **Financing inflows and outflows must be shown, rather than simply passed through reserves.**

One of the most important things to realise at this point is that it is wrong to try to assess the health or predict the death of a reporting entity solely on the basis of a single indicator. When analysing cash flow data, **the comparison should not just be between cash flows and profit, but also between cash flows over a period of time** (say three to five years).

The **relationship between profit and cash flows will vary constantly**. Healthy companies do not always have reported profits exceeding operating cash flows. Similarly, unhealthy companies can have operating cash flows well in excess of reported profit. The value of comparing them is in determining the extent to which earned profits are being converted into the necessary cash flows.

Profit is not as important as the extent to which a company can **convert its profits into cash on a continuing basis**. This process should be judged over a period longer than one year. The cash flows should be compared with profits over the same periods to decide how successfully the reporting entity has converted earnings into cash.

Cash flow figures should also be considered in terms of their specific relationships with each other over time. A form of '**cash flow gearing**' can be determined by comparing operating cash flows and financing flows, particularly borrowing, to establish the extent of dependence of the reporting entity on external funding.

Other relationships can be examined.

(a) Operating cash flows and investment flows can be related to match cash recovery from investment to investment.
(b) Investment can be compared to distribution to indicate the proportion of total cash outflow designated specifically to investor return and reinvestment.
(c) A comparison of tax outflow to operating cash flow minus investment flow will establish a 'cash basis tax rate'.

The 'ratios' mentioned above can be monitored **inter– and intra-firm** and the analyses can be undertaken in monetary, general price-level adjusted, or percentage terms.

Criticisms of IAS 7

The inclusion of **cash equivalents** has been criticised because it does not reflect the way in which businesses are managed: in particular, the requirement that to be a cash equivalent an investment has to be within three months of maturity is considered **unrealistic**.

The management of assets similar to cash (ie 'cash equivalents') is not distinguished from other investment decisions.

1 IAS 24: Related party disclosures

In the absence of information to the contrary, it is assumed that a reporting entity has **independent discretionary power** over its resources and transactions and pursues its activities independently of the interests of its individual owners, managers and others. Transactions are presumed to have been undertaken on an **arm's length basis**, ie on terms such as could have obtained in a transaction with an external party, in which each side bargained knowledgeably and freely, unaffected by any relationship between them.

These assumptions may not be justified when **related party relationships** exist, because the requisite conditions for competitive, free market dealings may not be present. Whilst the parties may endeavour to achieve arm's length bargaining the very nature of the relationship may preclude this occurring.

This is the related parties issue and IAS 24 tackles it by ensuring that financial statements contain the disclosures necessary to draw attention to the possibility that the reported financial position and results may have been affected by the existence of related parties and by material transactions with them. In other words, this is a standard which is primarily concerned with **disclosure**.

Scope

The standard requires disclosure of related party transactions and outstanding balances in the **separate financial statements** of a parent, venturer or investor presented in accordance with IAS 27 as well as in consolidated financial statements.

This is a **change** from the previous version of IAS 24, which did not require disclosure in the separate financial statements of a parent or wholly-owned subsidiary that are made available or published with consolidated financial statements for the group.

An entity's financial statements disclose related party transactions and outstanding balances with other entities in a group. **Intragroup** transactions and balances are **eliminated** in the preparation of consolidated financial statements.

Definitions

The following important definitions are given by the standard which was subjected to minor amendment in November 2009. Note that the definitions of **control** and **significant influence** are now the same as those given in IASs 27, 28 and 31.

Related party. A party is related to an entity if:

(a) directly, or indirectly through one or more intermediaries, it:
   (i) Controls, is controlled by, or is under common control with, the entity (this includes parents, subsidiaries and fellow subsidiaries)

    (ii)   Has an interest in the entity that gives it significant influence over the entity; or

    (iii)   Has joint control over the entity

(b)   it is an associate

(c)   it is a joint venture in which the entity is a venturer

(d)   it is a member of the key management personnel of the entity or its parent

(e)   it is a close member of the family of any individual referred to in (a) or (d)

(f)   it is an entity that is controlled, jointly controlled or significantly influenced by; or for which significant voting power in such entity resides with, directly or indirectly, any individual referred to in (d) or (e); or

(g)   both entities are joint ventures of the same third party

(h)   one is a joint venture and the other an associate of the same third party

(i)   it is a post-employment benefit plan for the benefit of employees of the entity, or of any entity that is a related party of the entity.

Related party transaction. A transfer of resources, services or obligations between related parties, regardless of whether a price is charged.

Control is the power to govern the financial and operating policies of an entity so as to obtain benefits from its activities.

Significant influence is the power to participate in the financial and operating policy decisions of an entity, but is not control over these policies. Significant ownership may be gained by share ownership, statute or agreement.

Joint control is the contractually agreed sharing of control over an economic activity.

Key management personnel are those persons having authority and responsibility for planning, directing and controlling the activities of the entity, directly or indirectly, including any director (whether executive or otherwise) of that entity.

Close members of the family of an individual are those family members who may be expected to influence, or be influenced by, that individual in their dealings with the entity. They may include:

(a)   The individual's domestic partner and children

(b)   Children of the domestic partner; and

(c)   Dependants of the individual or the domestic partner.   *(IAS 24)*

The most important point to remember here is that, when considering each possible related party relationship, attention must be paid to the **substance of the relationship, not merely the legal form**.

IAS 24 lists the following which are **not necessarily related parties**.

(a)   Two entities simply because they have a director or other key management in common (notwithstanding the definition of related party above, although it is necessary to consider how that director would affect both entities).

(b)   **Two venturers, simply because they share joint control over a joint venture.**

(c)   Certain other bodies, simply as a result of their **role in normal business dealings with the entity**

    (i)   Providers of finance

    (ii)   Trade unions

(iii)   Public utilities

(iv)   Government departments and agencies

(d)   **Any single customer, supplier, franchisor, distributor, or general agent** with whom the entity transacts a significant amount of business, simply by virtue of the resulting economic dependence.

Disclosure

As noted above, IAS 24 is almost entirely concerned with disclosure and its provisions are meant to **supplement** those disclosure requirements required by national company legislation and other IASs (particularly IASs 1, 22, 27 and 28).

The standard lists some **examples** of transactions that are disclosed if they are with a related party:

- Purchases or sales of goods (finished or unfinished)
- Purchases or sales of property and other assets
- Rendering or receiving of services
- Leases
- Transfer of research and development
- Transfers under licence agreements
- Provision of finance (including loans and equity contributions in cash or in kind)
- Provision of guarantees and collateral security
- Settlement of liabilities on behalf of the entity or by the entity on behalf of another party

Parents and subsidiaries

Relationships between **parents and subsidiaries** must be **disclosed irrespective** of **whether** any **transactions** have **taken place between** the related parties. An entity must disclose the **name** of its **parent** and, if different, the **ultimate controlling party**. This will enable a reader of the financial statements to be able to form a view about the effects of a related party relationship on the reporting entity.

If neither the parent nor the ultimate controlling party produces financial statements available for public use, the name of the next most senior parent that does so shall also be disclosed.

If there are transactions between a parent and subsidiary then they may benefit one of the parties in a way that would not occur in an arms-length transaction. For example, the subsidiary may sell goods to the parent at lower than market price which means that the subsidiary's profits will be lower than if it were a stand alone entity.

If the parent is putting the subsidiary up for sale then a potential purchaser will have to assess the subsidiary's financial statements and understand the impact that related party transactions have had. It is more likely in this circumstance that the parent will wish to make the subsidiary's financial statements as attractive as possible in order to ensure a sale.

There are a number of areas that the purchaser may need to consider:

- The terms of trading between the entities to assess how much of the subsidiary's trade is recurring and whether it is on fair market terms. In a sale situation the parent may sell goods to the subsidiary at below market price to make the subsidiary look more attractive.

- The existence of debt between the parties. Possible the parent could loan money to the subsidiary at below the market interest rate which may not be possible to maintain once the subsidiary is sold.
- The level of dividends payable as the subsidiary may have paid large dividends to the parent which may not be sustainable post sale.

Management personnel

An entity should disclose **key management personnel compensation** in **total** and for **each** of the following **categories**:

(a) **Short-term employee benefits** (eg wages, salaries, social security contributions, paid annual leave and paid sick-leave, profit sharing and bonuses and non-monetary benefits such as medical care, housing, cars and free or subsidised goods or services)

(b) **Post-employment benefits** (eg pensions, other retirement benefits, life insurance and medical care)

(c) **Other long-term benefits** (eg long-service leave, sabbatical leave, long-term disability benefits and, if they are not payable within twelve months after the end of the period, profit sharing, bonuses and deferred compensation)

(d) **Termination benefits**; and

(e) **Equity compensation benefits**

Compensation includes amounts paid on behalf of a parent of the entity in respect of the entity.

Disclosures

Where **transactions have taken place** between related parties, the entity should disclose the **nature** of the related party relationships, as well as information about the **transactions and outstanding balances** necessary for an understanding of the potential effect of the relationship on the financial statements. As a minimum, disclosures must include:

(a) The **amount of the transactions**

(b) The **amount of outstanding balances** and
   (i) their terms and conditions, including whether they are secured, and the nature of the consideration to be provided in settlement
   (ii) details of any guarantees given or received

(c) Provisions for **doubtful debts** related to the amount of outstanding balances

(d) The **expense** recognised during the period in respect of **bad or doubtful debts** due from related parties.

The above disclosures shall be made separately for **each** of the following categories:

(a) The parent
(b) Entities with joint control or significant influence over the entity
(c) Subsidiaries
(d) Associates
(e) Joint ventures in which the entity is a venturer
(f) Key management personnel of the entity or its parent; and
(g) Other related parties.

Items of a similar nature may be **disclosed in aggregate** *unless* separate disclosure is necessary for an understanding of the effect on the financial statements.

Disclosures that related party transactions were made on terms equivalent to those that prevail in arm's length transactions are made only if such disclosures can be substantiated.

2 IFRS 8: Operating segments

Large entities produce a wide range of products and services, often in several different countries. Further information on how the overall results of entities are made up from each of these product or geographical areas will help the users of the financial statements. This is the reason for **segment reporting**.

- The entity's **past performance** will be better understood
- The entity's **risks and returns** may be better assessed
- More **informed judgements** may be made about the entity as a whole

Risks and returns of a **diversified, multi-national company** can only be assessed by looking at the individual risks and rewards attached to groups of products or services or in different groups of products or services or in different geographical areas. These are subject to differing rates of profitability, opportunities for growth, future prospects and risks.

Segment reporting is covered by IFRS 8 *Operating segments*, which replaced IAS 14 *Segment reporting* in November 2006.

An entity must disclose information to enable users of its financial statements to evaluate the nature and financial effects of the business activities in which it engages and the economic environments in which it operates.

Only entities whose **equity or debt securities are publicly traded** (ie on a stock exchange) need disclose segment information. In group accounts, only **consolidated** segmental information needs to be shown. (The statement also applies to entities filing or in the process of filing financial statements for the purpose of issuing instruments.)

Definition of operating segment

> **Operating segment:** This is a component of an entity:
>
> (a) That engages in business activities from which it may earn revenues and incur expenses (including revenues and expenses relating to transactions with other components of the same entity)
> (b) Whose operating results are regularly reviewed by the entity's chief operating decision maker to make decisions about resources to be allocated to the segment and assess its performance, and
> (c) For which discrete financial information is available. *IFRS 8*

The term 'chief operating decision maker' identifies a function, not necessarily a manager with a specific title. That function is to allocate resources and to assess the performance of the entity's operating segments.

Aggregation

Two or more operating segments may be **aggregated** if the segments have **similar economic characteristics**, and the segments are similar in each of the following respects:

- The **nature of the products or services**
- The **nature of the production process**
- The **type or class of customer for their products or services**

- The **methods used to distribute their products or provide their services**, and
- If applicable, the **nature of the regulatory environment**

Determining reportable segments

An entity must report separate information about **each operating segment** that:

(a)   Has been identified as meeting the **definition of an operating segment**; and
(b)   Segment total is **10% or more of total**:
    (i)   **Revenue** (internal and external), or
    (ii)   **Profit** of **all segments not reporting a loss** (or all segments in loss if greater), or
    (iii)   **Assets**

At least **75% of the entity's total external revenue** must be reported by the operating segments identified. Where this is not the case, additional segments must be identified (even if they do not meet the 10% thresholds).

Two or more operating segments **below** the thresholds may be aggregated to produce a reportable segment if the segments have similar economic characteristics, and the segments are similar in a **majority** of the aggregation criteria above.

Operating segments that do not meet **any of the quantitative thresholds** may be reported separately if management believes that information about the segment would be useful to users of the financial statements.

The following decision tree will assist in identifying reportable segments.

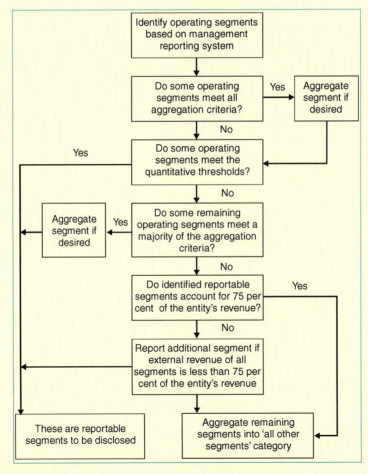

IFRS 8 disclosures are of:

- Operating segment profit or loss
- Segment assets
- Segment liabilities
- Certain income and expense items

Disclosures are also required about the revenues derived from products and services and about the countries in which revenues are earned or assets held, even if that information is not used by management in making decisions.

Here is an example taken from the *Implementation Guidance* to IFRS 8, which is presented for illustration purposes only.

	Car parts $	Motor vessels $	Software $	Electronics $	Finance $	All other $	Totals $
Revenues from external customers	3,000	5,000	9,500	12,000	5,000	(a) 1,000	35,500
Intersegment revenues	–	–	3,000	1,500	–	–	4,500
Interest revenue	450	800	1,000	1,500	–	–	3,750
Interest expense	350	600	700	1,100	–	–	2,750
Net interest revenue (b)	–	–	–	–	1,000	–	1,000
Depreciation and amortisation	200	100	50	1,500	1,100	–	2,950
Reportable segment profit	200	70	900	2,300	500	100	4,070
Other material non-cash items:							
Impairment of assets	–	200	–	–	–	–	200
Reportable segment assets	2,000	5,000	3,000	12,000	57,000	2,000	81,000
Expenditure for reportable segment non-current assets	300	700	500	800	600	–	2,900
Reportable segment liabilities	1,050	3,000	1,800	8,000	30,000	–	43,850

(a) Revenues from segments below the quantitative thresholds are attributable to four operating segments of the company. Those segments include a small property business, an electronics equipment rental business, a software consulting practice and a warehouse leasing operation. None of those segments has ever met any of the quantitative thresholds for determining reportable segments.

(b) The finance segment derives a majority of its revenue from interest. Management primarily relies on net interest revenue, not the gross revenue and expense amounts, in managing that segment. Therefore, as permitted by IFRS 8, only the net amount is disclosed.

In April 2009 under the annual IFRS Improvements, IFRS 8 was amended to state that segment assets no longer have to be disclosed if they are not reported internally. This is effective from January 2010.

Constitution of a group

16

1 Group accounts

There are many reasons for businesses to operate as groups; for the goodwill associated with the names of the subsidiaries, for tax or legal purposes and so forth. In many countries, company law requires that the results of a group should be presented as a whole. In traditional accounting terminology, a group of **companies** consists of a **parent company** and one or more **subsidiary companies** which are controlled by the parent company.

We will be looking at three accounting standards in this and the next three chapters.

- IAS 27 *Consolidated and separate financial statements*
- IFRS 3 *Business combinations*
- IAS 28 *Investments in associates*

These standards are all concerned with different aspects of group accounts, but there is some overlap between them, particularly between IFRS 3 and IAS 27.

In this and the next chapter we will concentrate on IAS 27, which covers the basic group definitions and consolidation procedures of a parent-subsidiary relationship. First of all, however, we will look at all the important definitions involved in group accounts, which **determine how to treat each particular type of investment** in group accounts.

Definitions

- **Control.** The power to govern the financial and operating policies of an entity so as to obtain benefits from its activities.   *(IFRS 3, IASs 27, 28)*
- **Subsidiary**. An entity that is controlled by another entity (known as the parent).   *(IFRS 3, IASs 27, 28)*
- **Parent.** An entity that has one or more subsidiaries.   *(IFRS 3, IAS 27)*
- **Group.** A parent and all its subsidiaries.   *(IAS 27)*
- **Associate.** An entity, including an unincorporated entity such as a partnership, in which an investor has significant influence and which is neither a subsidiary nor a joint venture of the investor.   *(IAS 28)*
- **Significant influence** is the power to participate in the financial and operating policy decisions of an investee or an economic activity but is not control or joint control over those policies.   *(IAS 28)*

We can summarise the different types of investment and the required accounting for them as follows.

Investment	Criteria	Required treatment in group accounts
Subsidiary	Control	Full consolidation
Associate	Significant influence	Equity accounting
Investment which is none of the above	Asset held for accretion of wealth	As for single company accounts per IAS 39

Investments in subsidiaries

The important point here is **control**. In most cases, this will involve the holding company or parent owning a majority of the ordinary shares in the subsidiary (to which normal voting rights are attached). There are circumstances, however, when the parent may own only a minority of the voting power in the subsidiary, *but* the parent still has control.

IAS 27 states that control can usually be assumed to exist when the parent **owns more than half (ie over 50%) of the voting power** of an entity *unless* it can be clearly shown that **such ownership does not constitute control** (these situations will be very rare).

What about situations where this ownership criterion does not exist? IAS 27 lists the following situations where control exists, even when the parent owns only 50% or less of the voting power of an entity.

(a)   The parent has power over more than 50% of the voting rights by virtue of **agreement with other investors**

(b)   The parent has power to **govern the financial and operating policies** of the entity by statute or under an agreement

(c)   The parent has the power to **appoint or remove a majority of members of the board of directors** (or equivalent governing body)

(d)   The parent has power to cast a **majority of votes at meetings of the board of directors**

IAS 27 also states that a parent loses control when it loses the power to govern the financial and operating policies of an investee. Loss of control can occur without a change in ownership levels. This may happen if a subsidiary becomes subject to the control of a government, court administrator or regulator (for example, in bankruptcy).

IAS 27 requires a parent to present consolidated financial statements, in which the accounts of the parent and subsidiary (or subsidiaries) are combined and presented as **a single entity**.

Investments in associates

This type of investment is something less than a subsidiary, but more than a simple investment. The key criterion here is **significant influence**. This is defined as the 'power to participate', but not to 'control' (which would make the investment a subsidiary).

Significant influence can be determined by the holding of voting rights (usually attached to shares) in the entity. IAS 28 states that if an investor holds **20% or more** of the voting power of the investee, it can be presumed that the investor has significant influence over the investee, unless it can be clearly shown that this is not the case.

Significant influence can be presumed not to exist if the investor holds **less than 20%** of the voting power of the investee, unless it can be demonstrated otherwise.

The **existence of significant influence** is evidenced in one or more of the following ways.

(a)   Representation on the **board of directors** (or equivalent) of the investee

(b)   Participation in the **policy making process**
(c)   **Material transactions** between investor and investee
(d)   Interchange of management personnel
(e)   Provision of essential technical information

2 IAS 27: Consolidated and separate financial statements

> **Consolidated financial statements**. The financial statements of a group presented as those of a single economic entity.   (*IAS 27*)

When a parent issues consolidated financial statements, it should consolidate **all subsidiaries**, both foreign and domestic.

Exemption from preparing group accounts

A parent **need not present** consolidated financial statements if and only if **all** of the following hold:

(a)   The parent is itself a **wholly-owned subsidiary** or it is a **partially owned subsidiary** of another entity and its other owners, including those not otherwise entitled to vote, have been informed about, and do not object to, the parent not presenting consolidated financial statements
(b)   Its securities are **not publicly traded**
(c)   It is **not in the process of issuing securities** in public securities markets; and
(d)   The **ultimate or intermediate parent** publishes consolidated financial statements that comply with International Financial Reporting Standards

A parent that does not present consolidated financial statements must comply with the IAS 27 rules on separate financial statements (discussed later in this section).

Potential voting rights

An entity may own share warrants, share call options, or other similar instruments that are **convertible into ordinary shares** in another entity. If these are exercised or converted they may give the entity voting power or reduce another party's voting power over the financial and operating policies of the other entity (potential voting rights). The **existence and effect** of potential voting rights, including potential voting rights held by another entity, should be considered when assessing whether an entity has control over another entity (and therefore has a subsidiary).

In assessing whether potential voting rights give rise to control, the entity examines all facts and circumstances that affect the rights (for example, terms and conditions), except the intention of management and the financial ability to exercise the rights or convert them into equity shares.

Exclusion of a subsidiary from consolidation

The rules on exclusion of subsidiaries from consolidation are necessarily strict, because this is a common method used by entities to manipulate their results. If a subsidiary which carries a large amount of debt can be excluded, then the gearing of the group as a whole will be improved. In other words, this is a way of taking debt **out of the statement of financial position**.

IAS 27 did originally allow a subsidiary to be excluded from consolidation where **control is intended to be temporary**. This exclusion was then removed by IFRS 5.

Subsidiaries held for sale are accounted for in accordance with IFRS 5 *Non-current assets held for sale and discontinued operations*.

It has been argued in the past that subsidiaries should be excluded from consolidation on the grounds of *dissimilar activities*, ie the activities of the subsidiary are so different to the activities of the other companies within the group that to include its results in the consolidation would be misleading. IAS 27 rejects this argument: exclusion on these grounds is not justified because better (relevant) information can be provided about such subsidiaries by consolidating their results and then giving additional information about the different business activities of the subsidiary.

The previous version of IAS 27 permitted exclusion where the subsidiary operates under **severe long-term restrictions** and these significantly impair its ability to transfer funds to the parent. This exclusion has now been **removed**. Control must actually be lost for exclusion to occur.

Different reporting dates

In most cases, all group companies will prepare accounts to the same reporting date. One or more subsidiaries may, however, prepare accounts to a different reporting date from the parent and the bulk of other subsidiaries in the group.

In such cases the subsidiary may prepare additional statements to the reporting date of the rest of the group, for consolidation purposes. If this is not possible, the subsidiary's accounts may still be used for the consolidation, provided that the gap between the reporting dates is **three months or less**.

Where a subsidiary's accounts are drawn up to a different accounting date, **adjustments should be made** for the effects of significant transactions or other events that occur between that date and the parent's reporting date.

Uniform accounting policies

Consolidated financial statements should be prepared using **the same accounting policies** for like transactions and other events in similar circumstances.

Adjustments must be made where members of a group use different accounting policies, so that their financial statements are suitable for consolidation.

Date of inclusion/exclusion

The results of subsidiary undertakings are included in the consolidated financial statements from:

(a)   the date of 'acquisition', ie the **date control passes to the parent**, to
(b)   the date of 'disposal', ie the **date control passes from the parent**.

Once an investment is no longer a subsidiary, it should be treated as an associate under IAS 28 (if applicable) or as an investment under IAS 39 *Financial instruments: recognition and measurement*.

Accounting for subsidiaries and associates in the parent's separate financial statements

A parent company will usually produce its own single company financial statements. In these statements, investments in subsidiaries and associates included in the consolidated financial statements should be *either*:

(a)   Accounted for at **cost**, or
(b)   In accordance with **IAS 39**

Where subsidiaries are **classified as held for sale** in accordance with IFRS 5 they should be accounted for in accordance with IFRS 5.

Disclosure

The disclosure requirements for **consolidated financial statements** are as follows.

(a)   **Summarised financial information** of **subsidiaries** that are **not consolidated**, either individually or in groups, including the amounts of total assets, total liabilities, revenues and profit or loss
(b)   The nature of the **relationship** between the parent and a **subsidiary** of which the **parent** does **not own**, directly or indirectly through subsidiaries, **more than half of the voting power**
(c)   For an investee of which more than half of the voting or potential voting power is owned, directly or indirectly through subsidiaries, but which, because of the absence of control, is not a subsidiary, the reasons **why** the **ownership** does **not constitute control**
(d)   The reporting date of the financial statements of a subsidiary when such financial statements are used to prepare consolidated financial statements and are as of a reporting date or for a period that is different from that of the parent, and the **reason** for using a **different reporting date or different period**
(e)   The nature and extent of any restrictions on the ability of subsidiaries to **transfer funds** to the parent in the form of cash dividends, repayment of loans or advances (ie borrowing arrangements, regulatory restraints etc)

Where a parent chooses to take advantage of the exemptions from preparing consolidated financial statements (see above) the **separate financial statements** must disclose:

(a)   The fact that the financial statements are separate financial statements; that the exemption from consolidation has been used; the name and country of incorporation of the entity whose consolidated financial statements that comply with IFRSs have been published; and the address where those consolidated financial statements are obtainable
(b)   A list of significant investments in subsidiaries, jointly controlled entities and associates, including the name, country of incorporation, proportion of ownership interest and, if different, proportion of voting power held
(c)   A description of the method used to account for the investments listed under (b)

When a parent prepares separate financial statements in addition to consolidated financial statements, the separate financial statements must disclose:

(a)   The fact that the statements are separate financial statements and the reasons why they have been prepared if not required by law
(b)   Information about investments and the method used to account for them, as above.

Part

C

Group financial statements

3 Content of group accounts and group structure

In simple terms a set of consolidated accounts is prepared by **adding together** the assets and liabilities of the parent company and each subsidiary. The **whole** of the assets and liabilities of each company are included, even though some subsidiaries may be only partly owned. The 'equity and liabilities' section of the statement of financial position will indicate how much of the net assets are attributable to the group and how much to outside investors in partly owned subsidiaries. These **outside investors** are known as the **non-controlling interest**.

> **Non-controlling interest**. The equity in a subsidiary not attributable, directly or indirectly, to a parent.   *(IFRS 3, IAS 27)*

Non-controlling interest should be presented in the consolidated statement of financial position **within equity, separately from the parent shareholders' equity**.

Most parent companies present their own individual accounts and their group accounts in a single **package**. The package typically comprises the following.

- **Parent company financial statements**, which will include 'investments in subsidiary undertakings' as an asset in the statement of financial position, and income from subsidiaries (dividends) in the statement of comprehensive income
- **Consolidated statement of financial position**
- **Consolidated statement of comprehensive income** (or separate income statement)
- **Consolidated statement of cash flows**

It may not be necessary to publish all of the parent company's financial statements, depending on local or national regulations.

Group structure

With the difficulties of definition and disclosure dealt with, let us now look at group structures. The simplest are those in which a parent company has only a **direct interest** in the shares of its subsidiary companies. For example:

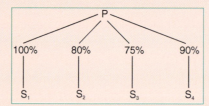

S1 Co is a wholly owned subsidiary of P Co. S2 Co, S3 Co and S4 Co are partly owned subsidiaries; a proportion of the shares in these companies is held by outside investors.

Often a parent will have **indirect holdings** in its subsidiary companies. This can lead to more complex group structures.

(a)

P Co owns 51% of the equity shares in S Co, which is therefore its subsidiary. S Co in its turn owns 51% of the equity shares in SS Co. SS Co is therefore a subsidiary of S Co and consequently a subsidiary of P Co. SS Co would describe S Co as its parent (or holding) company and P Co as its ultimate parent company.

Note that although P Co can control the assets and business of SS Co by virtue of the chain of control, its interest in the assets of SS Co is only 26%. This can be seen by considering a dividend of $100 paid by SS Co: as a 51% shareholder, S Co would receive $51; P Co would have an interest in 51% of this $51 = $26.01.

(b)

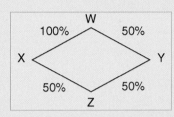

W Co owns 100% of the equity of X Co and 50% of the equity of Y Co. X Co and Y Co each own 50% of the equity of Z Co. Assume that:

(i)   W Co does not control the composition of Y Co's board, nor can it cast a majority of votes on the board
(ii)   W Co does not hold or control more than 50% of the **voting rights** in Y Co, either directly or by agreement with other investors
(iii)   W Co does not have the power to govern the financial or operating policies of Y Co by virtue of statute or an agreement
(iv)   None of the above apply to either X Co's or Y Co's holdings in Z Co

In other words, because W Co is not in co operation with the holder(s) of the other 50% of the shares in Y Co, neither Y nor Z can be considered subsidiaries.

In that case:

(i)   X Co is a subsidiary of W Co
(ii)   Y Co is not a subsidiary of W Co
(iii)   Z Co is not a subsidiary of either X Co or Y Co. Consequently, it is not a subsidiary of W Co

If Z Co pays a dividend of $100, X Co and Y Co will each receive $50. The interest of W Co in this dividend is as follows.

	$
Through X Co (100% × $50)	50
Through Y Co (50% × $50)	25
	75

Although W Co has an interest in 75% of Z Co's assets, Z Co is not a subsidiary of W Co.

(c)

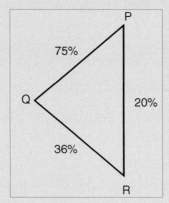

Q Co is a subsidiary of P Co. P Co therefore has indirect control over 36% of R Co's equity. P Co also has direct control over 20% of R Co's equity. R Co is therefore a subsidiary of P Co, although P Co's interest in R Co's assets is only 20% + (75% x 36%) = 47%.

Examples (b) and (c) illustrate an important point: in deciding whether a company A holds more than 50% of the equity (or equivalent) of an entity B it is necessary to aggregate:

- Shares (or equivalent) in B held directly by A
- Shares (or equivalent) in B held by entities which are subsidiaries of A

4 Group accounts: the related parties issue

IAS 24 draws attention to the significance of related party relationships and transactions – that transactions between the parties may not be 'at arm's length' and that users of the accounts must be made aware of this, as it may affect their view of the financial statements.

Individual company accounts

The relationship between a parent and a subsidiary is the most obvious example of a related party relationship and it offers a number of opportunities for manipulating results. Some of these may be aimed at improving the parent's individual financial statements.

Any of the following could take place:

- The subsidiary sells goods to the parent company at an artificially low price. This increases parent company profit while reducing profit in the subsidiary, thus increasing profit available for distribution to parent company shareholders at the expense of the non-controlling interest.
- The parent sells goods to the subsidiary at an artificially high price. This has the same result as above.
- The subsidiary makes a loan to the parent at an artificially low rate of interest or the parent makes a loan to the subsidiary at an artificially high rate of interest. The loans will be cancelled on consolidation but the interest payments will transfer profits from the subsidiary to the parent.
- The parent can sell an asset to the subsidiary at an amount in excess of its carrying amount. This again serves to transfer profit (and cash) to the parent.

Consolidated accounts

The transactions above seek to improve the **individual** parent company accounts at the expense of the individual subsidiary accounts. Dividends are paid to shareholders on the basis of these individual company financial statements, not the consolidated financial statements.

The tightening up of the opportunities for excluding a subsidiary from consolidation under IAS 27 have reduced the opportunities for improving the appearance of the **consolidated** financial statements. Prior to this, a number of possibilities could be exploited:

- A group could obtain loans via a subsidiary, which was not then consolidated. The loan would not appear in the consolidated statement of financial position and group gearing (% of capital provided by loans) would appear lower than it actually was.
- Sale and leaseback transactions could be carried out in which assets were sold to a non-consolidated subsidiary and leased back under an operating lease. This enabled the asset and its associated borrowings to be removed from the statement of financial position.

Disposal of subsidiaries

While the situations above are all concerned with improving the appearance of the parent company or group financial statements at the expense of those of the subsidiary, there may be occasions where the **opposite** is the intention.

For instance, when a parent company has decided to dispose of its shares in a poorly-performing subsidiary, it may seek to enhance the results of that subsidiary for the purpose of selling at a profit. In this case, transactions such as those above may be undertaken in the other direction – to transfer profit from the parent to the subsidiary.

Effect on trading

Even where no related party transactions have taken place, the parent/subsidiary relationship can still affect how the parties do business. For instance if, prior to acquisition by the parent, the subsidiary had a major customer or supplier who was a competitor of the parent, that trading arrangement can be expected to cease. The subsidiary may itself have been a competitor of the parent, in which case it may now have had to withdraw from certain markets in favour of the parent.

Part
C

Group financial statements

The consolidated statement of financial position

17

1 IAS 27: Summary of consolidation procedures

The financial statements of a parent and its subsidiaries are **combined on a line-by-line basis** by adding together like items of assets, liabilities, equity, income and expenses.

The following steps are then taken, in order that the consolidated financial statements should **show financial information about the group as if it was a single entity**.

(a) The carrying amount of the parent's **investment in each subsidiary** and the parent's **portion of equity** of each subsidiary are eliminated or cancelled

(b) **Non-controlling interests in the net income of consolidated subsidiaries** are adjusted against group income, to arrive at the net income attributable to the owners of the parent

(c) **Non-controlling interests in the net assets of consolidated subsidiaries** should be presented separately in the consolidated statement of financial position

Other matters to be dealt with include the following.

(a) **Goodwill on consolidation** should be dealt with according to IFRS 3

(b) **Dividends paid** by a subsidiary must be accounted for

IAS 27 states that all intra group balances and transactions, and the resulting **unrealised profits**, should be **eliminated in full. Unrealised losses** resulting from intragroup transactions should also be eliminated unless cost can be recovered.

Cancellation and part cancellation

The preparation of a consolidated statement of financial position, in a very simple form, consists of two procedures.

(a) Take the individual accounts of the parent company and each subsidiary and **cancel out items** which appear as an asset in one company and a liability in another.

(b) Add together all the uncancelled assets and liabilities throughout the group.

Items requiring cancellation may include the following.

(a) The asset **'shares in subsidiary companies'** which appears in the parent company's accounts will be matched with the liability 'share capital' in the subsidiaries' accounts.

(b) There may be **intra group trading** within the group. For example, S Co may sell goods on credit to P Co. P Co would then be a receivable in the accounts of S Co, while S Co would be a payable in the accounts of P Co.

Part cancellation

An item may appear in the statements of financial position of a parent company and its subsidiary, but not at the same amounts.

(a)   The parent company may have acquired **shares in the subsidiary** at a price **greater or less than their par value**. The asset will appear in the parent company's accounts at cost, while the liability will appear in the subsidiary's accounts at par value. This raises the issue of **goodwill**, which is dealt with later in this chapter.

(b)   Even if the parent company acquired shares at par value, it **may not** have **acquired all the shares of the subsidiary** (so the subsidiary may be only partly owned). This raises the issue of **non-controlling interests**, which are also dealt with later in this chapter.

(c)   The inter company trading balances may be out of step because of **goods or cash in transit**.

(d)   One company may have **issued loan stock** of which a **proportion only** is taken up by the other company.

The procedure for items (c) and (d) is to **cancel as far as possible**. The remaining uncancelled amounts will appear in the consolidated statement of financial position.

(a)   **Uncancelled loan stock** will appear as a **liability of the group**.

(b)   **Uncancelled balances on intra group accounts** represent **goods or cash in transit**, which will appear in the consolidated statement of financial position.

2 Non-controlling interests – IFRS 3 (revised)

It was mentioned earlier that the total assets and liabilities of subsidiary companies are included in the consolidated statement of financial position, even in the case of subsidiaries which are only partly owned. A proportion of the net assets of such subsidiaries in fact belongs to investors from outside the group (**non-controlling interests**).

IFRS 3 allows two alternative ways of calculating non-controlling interest in the group statement of financial position. Non-controlling interest can be valued at:

(a)   Its proportionate share of the fair value of the subsidiary's net assets; or

(b)   Full (or fair) value (usually based on the market value of the shares held by the non-controlling interest).

The following example shows non-controlling interest calculated at its proportionate share of the subsidiary's net assets.

Example: non-controlling interest

P Co has owned 75% of the share capital of S Co since the date of S Co's incorporation. Their latest statements of financial position are given below.

P CO
STATEMENT OF FINANCIAL POSITION

	$	$
Assets		
Non-current assets		
Property, plant and equipment	50,000	
30,000 $1 ordinary shares in S Co at cost	30,000	
		80,000
Current assets		45,000
Total assets		125,000
Equity and liabilities		
Equity		
80,000 $1 ordinary shares	80,000	
Retained earnings	25,000	
		105,000
Current liabilities		20,000
Total equity and liabilities		125,000

S CO
STATEMENT OF FINANCIAL POSITION

	$	$
Assets		
Property, plant and equipment		35,000
Current assets		35,000
Total assets		70,000
Equity and liabilities		
Equity		
40,000 $1 ordinary shares	40,000	
Retained earnings	10,000	
		50,000
Current liabilities		20,000
Total equity and liabilities		70,000

Part
C

Group financial statements

The consolidated statement of financial positionwill be as follows.

P GROUP

CONSOLIDATED STATEMENT OF FINANCIAL POSITION

	$	$
Assets		
Property, plant and equipment		85,000
Current assets		80,000
Total assets		165,000
Equity and liabilities		
Equity attributable to owners of the present		
Share capital	80,000	
Retained earnings (25,000 + (75% × $10,000)	32,500	
		112,500
Non-controlling interest (50,000 × 25%)		12,500
		125,000
Current liabilities		40,000
Total equity and liabilities		165,000

3 Dividends paid by a subsidiary

When a subsidiary company pays a **dividend** during the year the accounting treatment is not difficult. Suppose S Co, a 60% subsidiary of P Co, pays a dividend of $1,000 on the last day of its accounting period. Its total reserves before paying the dividend stood at $5,000.

(a) $400 of the dividend is paid to non-controlling shareholders. The cash leaves the group and will not appear anywhere in the consolidated statement of financial position.

(b) The parent company receives $600 of the dividend, debiting cash and crediting profit or loss. This will be cancelled on consolidation.

(c) The remaining balance of retained earnings in S Co's statement of financial position ($4,000) will be consolidated in the normal way. The group's share (60% × $4,000 = $2,400) will be included in group retained earnings in the statement of financial position; the non-controlling interest share (40% × $4,000 = $1,600) is credited to the non-controlling interest account in the statement of financial position.

However, the situation is more complicated when a subsidiary pays a dividend shortly after acquisition and some of that dividend is deemed to been paid from pre-acquisition profits. This situation is considered later.

4 Goodwill arising on consolidation

When a company P Co wishes to **purchase shares** in a company S Co it must pay the previous owners of those shares. The most obvious form of payment would be in **cash**.

However, the previous shareholders might be prepared to accept some other form of consideration. For example, they might accept an agreed number of **shares** in P Co. P Co would then issue new shares in the agreed number and allot them to the former shareholders of S Co. This kind of deal might be attractive to P Co since it avoids the need for a heavy cash outlay. The former shareholders of S Co would retain an indirect interest in that company's profitability via their new holding in its parent company.

Suppose P Co. wishes to purchase all of the $40,000 shares in S Co. The shareholders of S Co agreed to accept one $1 ordinary share in P Co for every two $1 ordinary shares in S Co. P Co would then need to issue and allot 20,000 new $1 shares. How would this transaction be recorded in the books of P Co?

The 40,000 $1 shares acquired in S Co are thought to have a value of $60,000. The former shareholders of S Co have presumably agreed to accept 20,000 shares in P Co because they consider each of those shares to have a value of $3. The transaction is recorded as follows:

DEBIT	Investment in S Co at cost	$60,000	
CREDIT	Share capital		$20,000
	Share premium account		$40,000

The amount which P Co records in its books as the cost of its investment in S Co may be more or less than the book value of the assets it acquires. Suppose that S Co in the previous example has nil reserves and nil liabilities, so that its share capital of $40,000 is balanced by tangible assets with a book value of $40,000. For simplicity, assume that the book value of S Co's assets is the same as their market or fair value.

Now when the directors of P Co agree to pay $60,000 for a 100% investment in S Co they must believe that, in addition to its tangible assets of $40,000, S Co must also have intangible assets worth $20,000. This amount of $20,000 paid over and above the value of the tangible assets acquired is **goodwill arising on consolidation**.

Following the normal cancellation procedure the $40,000 share capital in S Co's statement of financial position could be cancelled against $40,000 of the 'investment in S Co' in the statement of financial position of P Co. This would leave a $20,000 debit uncancelled in the parent company's accounts and this $20,000 would appear in the consolidated statement of financial position under the caption 'Intangible non-current assets: goodwill arising on consolidation'.

Goodwill and pre acquisition profits

Up to now we have assumed that S Co had nil retained earnings when its shares were purchased by P Co. Assuming instead that S Co had earned profits of $8,000 in the period before acquisition, its statement of financial position just before the purchase would look as follows.

	$
Total assets	48,000
Share capital	40,000
Retained earnings	8,500
	48,000

If P Co now purchases all the shares in S Co it will acquire total assets worth $48,000 at a cost of $60,000. Clearly in this case S Co's intangible assets (goodwill) are being valued at $12,000. It should be apparent that any earnings retained by the subsidiary prior to its acquisition by the parent company must be **incorporated in the cancellation** process so as to arrive at a figure for goodwill arising on consolidation. In other words, not only S Co's share capital, but also its **pre acquisition** retained earnings, must be cancelled against the asset 'investment in S Co' in the accounts of the parent company. The uncancelled balance of $12,000 appears in the consolidated statement of financial position.

The consequence of this is that any **pre acquisition retained earnings of a subsidiary company are not aggregated with the parent company's retained earnings** in the consolidated statement of financial position. The figure of consolidated retained earnings comprises the retained earnings of the parent company plus the **post acquisition retained earnings only of subsidiary companies**. The post-acquisition retained earnings are simply retained earnings now less retained earnings at acquisition.

Example: goodwill and pre acquisition profits

P Co acquired the ordinary shares of S Co on 31 March when its draft statement of financial position was as follows:

		$
Current assets		60,000
Equity		
50,000 ordinary shares of $1 each		50,000
Retained earnings		10,000
		60,000
The goodwill is calculated as:	$	$
Consideration transferred		80,000
Net assets acquired as represented by:		
Ordinary share capital	50,000	
Retained earnings on acquisition	10,000	
		(60,000)
Goodwill		20,000

Goodwill and non-controlling interest

Not let us look at what would happen if P Co had obtained less than 100% of the shares of S Co.

If P Co had paid $80,000 for 40,000 shares in S Co, the goodwill working would be as follows:

	$
Consideration transferred	80,000
Non-controlling interest (60,000 × 20%)	12,000
Net assets acquired	(60,000)
Goodwill	32,000

The goodwill has been increased by the non-controlling interest – P Co has paid the same amount but acquired a smaller shareholding.

Non-controlling interest at fair value

IFRS 3 (revised) gives entities the option of valuing non-controlling interest at fair value. The thinking behind this is that the non-controlling interest, in purchasing their shares, also purchased goodwill in the subsidiary, and that the traditional method of consolidation does not show this goodwill.

IFRS 3 revised suggests that the closest approximation to fair value will be the market price of the shares held by non-controlling shareholders just before acquisition by the parent.

Continuing our example above, we will assume that the market price of the shares was $1.25. The goodwill calculation will then be as follows:

	$
Consideration transferred	80,000
Non-controlling interest (10,000 × $1.25)	12,500
Net assets acquired	(60,000)
Goodwill	32,500

Goodwill is $500 higher than goodwill calculated measuring non-controlling interest at its share of the net assets of the subsidiary. This $500 represents the **goodwill attributable to the non-controlling interest.**

Non-controlling interest at year end

Where the option is used to value non-controlling interest at fair value, this applies only to **non-controlling interest at acquisition**. At the year end, the non-controlling interest is measured at its share of the subsidiary's year end net assets, subject to adjustments for intra-group trading which we will cover later. However, **where the fair value option has been used**, goodwill at the year end will include the additional goodwill attributable to the non-controlling interest, in the example above $500. The other side of the entry is to **add the goodwill onto the non-controlling interest at the year end**.

Example: non-controlling interest at fair value

P acquired 75% of the shares in S on 1 January 2007 when S had retained earnings of $15,000. The market price of S's shares just before the date of acquisition was $1.60. P values non-controlling interest at fair value. Goodwill is not impaired.

The statements of financial position of P and S at 31 December 20X7 were as follows:

	P	S
	$	$
Property, plant and equipment	60,000	50,000
Shares in S	68,000	–
	128,000	50,000
Current assets	52,000	35,000
	180,000	85,000

Share capital – $1 shares	100,000	50,000
Retained earnings	70,000	25,000
	170,000	75,000
Current liabilities	10,000	10,000
	180,000	85,000

Now we will prepare the consolidated statement of financial position of the P Group.

CONSOLIDATED STATEMENT OF FINANCIAL POSITION

	$
Assets	
Non-current assets	
Property plant and equipment (60,000 + 50,000)	110,000
Goodwill (W1)	23,000
Current assets (52,000 + 35,000)	87,000
Total assets	220,000
Equity and liabilities	
Equity attributable to the owners of P	
Share capital	100,000
Retained earnings (W2)	77,500
	177,500
Non-controlling interest (W3)	22,500
Total equity	200,000
Current liabilities (10,000 + 10,000)	20,000
	220,000

Workings

1. *Goodwill*

	$
Consideration transferred	68,000
Non-controlling interest at acquisition (12,500 shares @ $1.60)	20,000
Net assets of S at acquisition (50,000 + 15,000)	(65,000)
Goodwill (parent and non-controlling interest)	23,000
Non-controlling interest at fair value (as above)	20,000
Non-controlling share of net assets at acquisition (65,000 × 25%)	(16,250)
Goodwill attributable to non-controlling interest	3,750

2.   Retained earnings

	P	S
	$	$
Per statement of financial position	70,000	25,000
Less pre acquisition		(15,000)
		10,000
Group share of S (10,000 × 75%)	7,500	
Group retained earnings	77,500	

3.   Non-controlling interest at year end

	$
Share of net assets of S (75,000 × 25%)	18,750
Goodwill (W1)	3,750
	22,500

Note that non-controlling interest at the year end can also be calculated as follows:

	$
Non-controlling interest at acquisition	20,000
Share of post-acquisition retained earnings (10,000 × 25%)	2,500
	22,500

Effect of non-controlling interest at fair value

You can see from the above example that the use of the fair value option increases goodwill and non-controlling interest by the same amount. That amount represents goodwill attributable to the shares held by non-controlling shareholders. It is not necessarily proportionate to the goodwill attributed to the parent. The parent may have paid more to acquire a controlling interest.

Impairment of goodwill

Goodwill arising on consolidation is subjected to an annual impairment review and impairment may be expressed as an amount or as a percentage.

However, when non-controlling interest is valued at **fair value** the goodwill in the statement of financial position includes goodwill attributable to the non-controlling interest. In this case the double entry will reflect the non-controlling interest proportion based on their shareholding.

In our solution above the non-controlling interest holds 25%. If the goodwill of $23,000 was impaired by 20% the double entry for this would be:

	$		$
DEBIT Retained earnings	3,450	CREDIT Goodwill	4,600
DEBIT Non-controlling interest	1,150		

Non-controlling interest at the year end would then be $21,350.

Gain on a bargain purchase

Goodwill arising on consolidation is one form of **purchased goodwill**, and is governed by IFRS 3. As explained in an earlier chapter IFRS 3 requires that goodwill arising on consolidation should be **capitalised in the consolidated statement of financial position** and **reviewed for impairment every year**.

Goodwill arising on consolidation is the difference between the cost of an acquisition and the value of the subsidiary's net assets acquired. This difference can be negative: the aggregate of the fair values of the separable net assets acquired may **exceed** what the parent company paid for them. IFRS 3 refers to this as a 'bargain purchase'. In this situation:

(a) An entity should first **re-assess** the amounts at which it has measured both the cost of the combination and the acquiree's identifiable net assets. This exercise should identify any errors.
(b) Any **excess remaining** should be **recognised immediately in profit or loss**.

Forms of consideration

The consideration paid by the parent for the shares in the subsidiary can take different forms and this will affect the calculation of goodwill. Here are some examples:

Contingent consideration

The parent acquired 60% of the subsidiary's $100m share capital on 1 January 20X6 for a cash payment of $150m and a further payment of $50m on 31 March 20X7 if the subsidiary's post acquisition profits have exceeded an agreed figure by that date.

In the financial statements for the year to 31 December 20X6 $50m will be added to the cost of the combination, discounted as appropriate.

IFRS 3 requires the acquisition-date **fair value** of contingent consideration to be recognised as part of the consideration for the acquiree. The acquirer may be required to pay contingent consideration in the form of equity or of a debt instrument or cash. A debt instrument should be presented as under IAS 32. Contingent consideration can also be an asset, if the consideration has already been transferred and the acquirer has the right to return of some of it, if certain considerations are met.

Note: The previous version of IFRS 3 only required contingent consideration to be recognised if it was **probable** that it would become payable. IFRS 3 revised dispenses with this requirement – **all contingent consideration is now recognised**.

Deferred consideration

The parent acquired 75% of the subsidiary's 80m $1 shares on 1 January 20X6. It paid $3.50 per share and agreed to pay a further $108m on 1 January 20X8.

The parent company's cost of capital is 8%.

In the financial statements for the year to 31 December 20X6 the cost of the combination will be as follows:

	$m
80m shares × 75% × $3.50	210
Deferred consideration:	
$108m × 1/1.08	100
Total consideration	310

At 31 December 20X7, the cost of the combination will be unchanged but $8m will be charged to finance costs, being the unwinding of the discount on the deferred consideration.

Share exchange

The parent has acquired 12,000 $1 shares in the subsidiary by issuing 5 of its own $1 shares for every 4 shares in the subsidiary. The market value of the parent company's shares is $6.

Cost of the combination:

	$m
12,000 × 5/4 × $6	90,000

Note that this is credited to the share capital and share premium of the parent company as follows:

	DR	CR
Investment in subsidiary	90,000	
Share capital ($12,000 × 5/4)		15,000
Share premium ($12,000 × 5/4 × 5)		75,000

Expenses and issue costs

Expenses of the combination, such as lawyers and accountants fees are written off as incurred. However, IFRS 3 requires that the costs of issuing equity are treated as a deduction from the proceeds of the equity issue. Share issue costs will therefore be debited to the share premium account. Issue costs of financial instruments are deducted from the proceeds of the financial instrument.

5 Intra-group trading

Unrealised profit

Any receivable/payable balances outstanding between the companies are cancelled on consolidation. No further problem arises if all such intra group transactions are **undertaken at cost**, without any mark up for profit.

However, each company in a group is a separate trading entity and may wish to treat other group companies in the same way as any other customer. In this case, a company (say A Co) may buy goods at one price and sell them at a higher price to another group company (B Co). The accounts of A Co will quite properly include the profit earned on sales to B Co; and similarly B Co's statement of financial position will include inventories at their cost to B Co, ie at the amount at which they were purchased from A Co.

This gives rise to two problems.

(a)   Although A Co makes a profit as soon as it sells goods to B Co, the group does not make a sale or achieve a profit until an outside customer buys the goods from B Co.

(b)   Any purchases from A Co which remain unsold by B Co at the year end will be included in B Co's inventory. Their value in the statement of financial position will be their cost to B Co, which is not the same as their cost to the group.

The objective of consolidated accounts is to present the financial position of several connected companies as that of a single entity, the group. This means that **in a** consolidated statement of financial position **the only profits recognised should be those earned by the group** in providing goods or services to outsiders; and similarly, inventory in the consolidated statement of financial position should be valued at cost to the group.

Suppose that a holding company P Co buys goods for $1,600 and sells them to a wholly owned subsidiary S Co for $2,000. The goods are in S Co's inventory at the year end and appear in S Co's statement of financial position at $2,000. In this case, P Co will record a profit of $400 in its individual accounts, but from the group's point of view the figures are:

Cost	$1,600
External sales	nil
Closing inventory at cost	$1,600
Profit/loss	nil

If we add together the figures for retained earnings and inventory in the individual statements of financial position of P Co and S Co the resulting figures for consolidated retained earnings and consolidated inventory will each be overstated by $400. A consolidation adjustment is therefore necessary as follows.

DEBIT   Group retained earnings

CREDIT   Group inventory (statement of financial position)

with the amount of profit **unrealised by the group.**

Non-controlling interests in unrealised intra-group profits

A further problem occurs where a subsidiary company which is not wholly owned is involved in **intra-group trading** within the group. If a subsidiary S Co is 75% owned and sells goods to the parent company for $16,000 cost plus $4,000 profit, ie for $20,000 and if these items are unsold by P Co at the end of the reporting period, the 'unrealised' profit of $4,000 earned by S Co and charged to P Co will be partly owned by the non-controlling interest of S Co. As far as the non-controlling interest of S Co is concerned, their share (25% of $4,000) amounting to $1,000 of profit on the sale of goods would appear to have been fully realised. It is only the group that has not yet made a profit on the sale.

However, best practice is to debit the non-controlling interest with its share, so the entries are:

DEBIT   Group retained earnings

DEBIT   Non-controlling interest

CREDIT   Group inventory (statement of financial position)

6 Intra group sales of non-current assets

Accounting treatment

In their individual accounts the companies concerned will treat the transfer just like a sale between unconnected parties: the selling company will record a profit or loss on sale, while the purchasing company will record the asset at the amount paid to acquire it, and will use that amount as the basis for calculating depreciation.

On consolidation, the usual **'group entity' principle applies**. The consolidated statement of financial position must show assets at their cost to the group, and any depreciation charged must be based on that cost. Two consolidation adjustments will usually be needed to achieve this.

(a) An adjustment to alter retained earnings and non-current assets cost so as to remove any element of unrealised profit or loss. This is similar to the adjustment required in respect of unrealised profit in inventory.

(b) An adjustment to alter retained earnings and accumulated depreciation is made so that consolidated depreciation is based on the asset's cost to the group.

In practice, these steps are combined so that the retained earnings of the entity making the unrealised profit are debited with the unrealised profit less the additional depreciation.

The double entry is as follows.

(a) Sale by parent

DEBIT   Group retained earnings

CREDIT Non-current assets

with the profit on disposal, less the additional depreciation.

(b) Sale by subsidiary

DEBIT   Group retained earnings (P's share of S)

DEBIT   Non-controlling interest (NCI's share of S)

CREDIT Non-current assets

with the profit on disposal, less additional depreciation

Example: intra group sale of non-current assets

P Co owns 60% of S Co and on 1 January 20X1 S Co sells plant costing $10,000 to P Co for $12,500. The companies make up accounts to 31 December 20X1 and the balances on their retained earnings at that date are:

P Co after charging depreciation of 10% on plant	$27,000
S Co including profit on sale of plant	$18,000

The working for consolidated retained earnings will be as follows:

	P Co $	S Co $
	27,000	18,000
Disposal of plant:		
Profit		(2,500)
Depreciation: 10% × $2,500		250
		15,750
Share of S Ltd: $15,750 × 60%	9,450	
	36,450	

7 Acquisition of a subsidiary during its accounting period

The subsidiary company's accounts to be consolidated will show the subsidiary's profit or loss for the whole year. For consolidation purposes, however, it will be necessary to distinguish between:

(a)   Profits earned before acquisition
(b)   Profits earned after acquisition

In practice, a subsidiary company's profit may not accrue evenly over the year. Nevertheless, the assumption can be made that **profits accrue evenly** whenever it is impracticable to arrive at an accurate split of pre and post acquisition profits.

Once the amount of pre acquisition profit has been established the appropriate consolidation workings (goodwill, retained earnings) can be produced.

Bear in mind that in calculating **non-controlling interests** at the year end, the distinction between pre and post acquisition profits is irrelevant. The non-controlling shareholders are simply credited with their share of the subsidiary's total net assets at the end of the reporting period.

It is worthwhile to summarise what happens on consolidation to the retained earnings figures extracted from a subsidiary's statement of financial position. Suppose the accounts of S Co, a 60% subsidiary of P Co, show retained earnings of $20,000 at the end of the reporting period, of which $14,000 were earned prior to acquisition. The figure of $20,000 will appear in the consolidated statement of financial position as follows.

	$
Non-controlling interests working: their share of total retained earnings at the end of the reporting period (40% × $20,000)	8,000
Goodwill working: group share of pre acquisition retained earnings (60% × $14,000)	8,400
Consolidated retained earnings working:group share of post-acquisition retained earnings (60% × $6,000)	3,600
	20,000

Example: pre acquisition losses of a subsidiary

As an illustration of the entries arising when a subsidiary has pre acquisition losses, suppose P Co acquired all 50,000 $1 ordinary shares in S Co for $20,000 on 1 January 20X1 when there was a debit balance of $35,000 on S Co's retained earnings. In the years 20X1 to 20X4 S Co makes profits of $40,000 in total, leaving a credit balance of $5,000 on retained earnings at 31 December 20X4. P Co's retained earnings at the same date are $70,000.

The consolidation workings would appear as follows.

1.   *Goodwill*

	$	$
Consideration transferred		20,000
Net assets acquired		
Ordinary share capital	50,000	
Retained earnings	(35,000)	
		(15,000)
Goodwill		5,000

2.   *Retained earnings*

	P Co	S Co
	$	$
At the end of the reporting period	70,000	5,000
Pre-acquisition loss		35,000
		40,000
S Co – share of post-acquisition retained earnings (40,000 × 100%)	40,000	
	110,000	

8 Dividends and pre-acquisition profits

The parent company, as a member of the subsidiary, is entitled to its share of the dividends paid but it is necessary to decide whether or not these dividends come out of the pre acquisition profits of the subsidiary.

If the dividends come from **post-acquisition** profits there is no problem. The holding company simply credits the relevant amount to its **own statement of comprehensive income**, as with any other dividend income. The dividend received by the parent and paid by the subsidiary are then cancelled upon consolidation. The double entry is quite different, however, if the dividend is paid from **pre-acquisition profits**, being as follows.

DEBIT   Cash

CREDIT   Investment in subsidiary

Where the dividend is paid from pre-acquisition profits, it **reduces** the cost of the parent company's investment.

Is the dividend paid from pre-acquisition profits?

We need next to consider how it is decided whether a dividend is paid from pre-acquisition profits. The simplest example is where a parent acquires a subsidiary on the first day of an accounting period and the dividend was in respect of the previous accounting period. Clearly, the dividend was paid from profits earned in the period before acquisition.

The position is less straightforward if shares are acquired **during the subsidiary's accounting period**. The usual method of dealing with this is by **time-apportionment**.

Example

P acquires a 60% interest in S on 1 September 20X0. S's year end is 31 December. On 10 January 20X1 S pays a dividend of $10,000 in respect of 20X0. P's share of the dividend is $6,000. However, as it relates to the year of acquisition, $2,000 (6,000 × 4/12 is treated as being from post-acquisition profits and $4,000 (6,000 × 8/12) is treated as being from pre-acquisition profits.

Why do we make this distinction? If we consider the situation of a holding company deciding whether to invest in a subsidiary, we can see the significance of a dividend paid from pre-acquisition profits. If the prospective subsidiary's financial statements disclose that it proposes to pay a dividend in the near future, the prospective holding company knows that if it invests in the shares some of its investment will be returned to it very soon. Also, a dividend paid out of pre-acquisition profits cannot be regarded as a return on the company's investment because it relates to the period before the investment was made. So we treat it as what it effectively is – a reduction in the cost of the investment.

Example

To continue the example of P and S above, P has paid $175,000 for its 60% shareholding in S. At the date of acquisition S had share capital of $100,000 and retained earnings of $70,000.

In 20X1 S pays a $10,000 dividend of which P receives $6,000. $4,000 is deemed to be from pre-acquisition profits. The goodwill calculation at 31 December 20X1 is as follows:

	$	$
Consideration transferred		175,000
Less pre-acquisition dividend		(4,000)
		171,000
Non-controlling interest (170,000 × 40%)		68,000
		239,000
Net assets acquired:		
Share capital	100,000	
Retained earnings	70,000	
		(170,000)
Goodwill		69,000

9 Fair values in acquisition accounting

To understand the importance of fair values in the acquisition of a subsidiary consider again what we mean by goodwill.

> **Goodwill.** Any excess of the consideration transferred over the acquirer's interest in the fair value of the identifiable assets and liabilities acquired as at the date of the exchange transaction. *(IFRS 3)*

The **statement of financial position of a subsidiary company** at the date it is acquired may not be a guide to the fair value of its net assets. For example, the market value of a freehold building may have risen greatly since it was acquired, but it may appear in the statement of financial position at historical cost less accumulated depreciation.

Fair value is defined as follows by IFRS 3 and various other standards – it is an important definition.

> **Fair value**. The amount for which an asset could be exchanged, or a liability settled, between knowledgeable, willing parties in an arm's length transaction.   *(IFRS 3)*

We will look at the requirements of IFRS 3 regarding fair value in more detail below. First let us look at some practical matters.

Fair value adjustment calculations

Until now we have calculated goodwill as the difference between the consideration transferred and the **carrying value** of net assets acquired by the group. If this calculation is to comply with the definition above we must ensure that the carrying value of the subsidiary's net assets is the same as their **fair value**.

There are two possible ways of achieving this.

(a)   The **subsidiary company** might **incorporate any necessary revaluations** in its own books of account. In this case, we can proceed directly to the consolidation, taking asset values and reserves figures straight from the subsidiary company's statement of financial position.

(b)   The **revaluations** may be made as a **consolidation adjustment without being incorporated** in the subsidiary company's books. In this case, we must make the necessary adjustments to the subsidiary's statement of financial position as a working. Only then can we proceed to the consolidation.

Note. Remember that when depreciating assets are revalued there may be a corresponding alteration in the amount of depreciation charged and accumulated.

IFRS 3 Fair values

IFRS 3 sets out **general principles** for arriving at the fair values of a subsidiary's assets and liabilities. The acquirer should recognise the acquiree's identifiable assets, liabilities and contingent liabilities at the acquisition date only if they satisfy the following criteria.

(a)   In the case of an **asset** other than an intangible asset, it is **probable** that any associated **future economic benefits** will flow to the acquirer, and its fair value can be **measured reliably**.

(b)   In the case of a liability other than a contingent liability, it is probable that an outflow of resources embodying economic benefits will be required to settle the obligation, and its fair value can be measured reliably.

(c)   In the case of an **intangible asset** or a **contingent liability**, its fair value can be **measured reliably**.

The acquiree's identifiable assets and liabilities might include assets and liabilities **not previously recognised** in the acquiree's financial statements. For example, a tax benefit arising from the acquiree's tax losses that was not recognised by the acquiree may be recognised by the group if the acquirer has future taxable profits against which the unrecognised tax benefit can be applied.

Restructuring and future losses

An acquirer **should not recognise liabilities for future losses** or other costs expected to be incurred as a result of the business combination.

IFRS 3 explains that a plan to restructure a subsidiary following an acquisition is not a present obligation of the acquiree at the acquisition date. Neither does it meet the definition of a contingent liability. Therefore an acquirer **should not recognise a liability for** such a **restructuring plan** as part of allocating the cost of the combination unless the subsidiary was already committed to the plan before the acquisition.

This **prevents creative accounting**. An acquirer cannot set up a provision for restructuring or future losses of a subsidiary and then release this to profit or loss in subsequent periods in order to reduce losses or smooth profits.

Intangible assets

The acquiree may have **intangible assets**, such as development expenditure. These can be recognised separately from goodwill only if they are **identifiable**. An intangible asset is identifiable only if it:

(a)   Is **separable**, ie capable of being separated or divided from the entity and sold, transferred, or exchanged, either individually or together with a related contract, asset or liability, or

(b)   Arises from contractual or other legal rights

Contingent liabilities

Contingent liabilities of the acquirer are **recognised** if their **fair value can be measured reliably**. This is a departure from the normal rules in IAS 37; contingent liabilities are not normally recognised, but only disclosed.

After their initial recognition, the acquirer should measure contingent liabilities that are recognised separately at the higher of:

(a)   The amount that would be recognised in accordance with IAS 37

(b)   The amount initially recognised

Cost of a business combination

The general principle is that the acquirer should measure the cost of a business combination as the total of the **fair values**, at the date of exchange, **of assets given**, liabilities incurred or assumed, and equity instruments issued by the acquirer, in exchange for control of the acquiree.

Sometimes all or part of the cost of an acquisition is deferred (ie, does not become payable immediately). The fair value of any deferred consideration is determined by **discounting** the amounts payable to their **present value** at the date of exchange.

Where equity instruments (eg, ordinary shares) of a quoted entity form part of the cost of a combination, the **published price** at the date of exchange normally provides the best evidence of the instrument's fair value and except in rare circumstances this should be used.

Future losses or other costs expected to be incurred as a result of a combination should not be included in the cost of the combination.

Costs **attributable** to the combination, for example professional fees and administrative costs, should not be included: they are recognised as an expense when incurred. **Costs of issuing debt instruments and equity shares** are covered by IAS 32 *Financial instruments: presentation*, which states that such costs should **reduce the proceeds from the debt issue or the equity issue**.

18

The consolidated statement of comprehensive income and statement of cash flows

1 The consolidated income statement

The consolidated statement of comprehensive income is the consolidated income statement with the addition of 'other comprehensive income' attributable to either the parent or one or more subsidiaries. The consolidation work is done in the income statement section, so that is where we begin.

Simple example: consolidated income statement

P Co acquired 75% of the ordinary shares of S Co on that company's incorporation in 20X3. The summarised income statements and movement on retained earnings of the two companies for the year ending 31 December 20X9 are set out below.

	P Co	S Co
	$	$
Sales revenue	75,000	38,000
Cost of sales	(30,000)	(20,000)
Gross profit	45,000	18,000
Administrative expenses	(14,000)	(8,000)
Profit before tax	31,000	10,000
Income tax expense	(10,000)	(2,000)
Profit for the year	21,000	8,000
Note: Movement on retained earnings		
Retained earnings brought forward	87,000	17,000
Profit for the year	21,000	8,000
Retained earnings carried forward	108,000	25,000

We will prepare the consolidated income statement and extract from the statement of changes in equity showing retained earnings and non-controlling interest.

P CO CONSOLIDATED INCOME STATEMENT FOR THE YEAR ENDED 31 DECEMBER 20X9

	$
Sales revenue (75 + 38)	113,000
Cost of sales (30 + 20)	(50,000)
Gross profit	63,000
Administrative expenses (14 + 8)	(22,000)
Profit before tax	41,000
Income tax expense	(12,000)
Profit for the year	29,000
Profit attributable to:	
Owners of the parent	27,000
Non-controlling interest ($8,000 × 25%)	2,000
	29,000

STATEMENT OF CHANGES IN EQUITY (EXTRACT)

	Retained Earnings $	Non-controlling Interest $	Total Equity $
Balance b/f	99,750	4,250	104,000
Profit for the year	27,000	2,000	29,000
	126,750	6,250	133,000

Notice how the non-controlling interest is dealt with.

(a) Down to the line **'profit for the year'** the **whole** of S Co's results is included without reference to group share or non-controlling share. A **one-line adjustment** is then inserted to deduct the non-controlling share of S Co's profit.

(b) The non-controlling share ($4,250) of S Co's retained earnings brought forward (17,000 × 25%) is **excluded** from group retained earnings. This means that the carried forward figure of $126,750 is the figure which would appear in the statement of financial position for group retained earnings.

Intra-group trading

Like the consolidated statement of financial position, the consolidated income statement should deal with the results of the group as those of a single entity. When one company in a group sells goods to another an identical amount is added to the sales revenue of the first company and to the cost of sales of the second. Yet as far as the entity's dealings with outsiders are concerned no sale has taken place.

The consolidated figures for sales revenue and cost of sales should represent **sales to**, and **purchases from, outsiders**. An adjustment is therefore necessary to reduce the sales revenue and cost of sales figures by the value of intra-group sales during the year.

Any unrealised profits on intra group trading should be excluded from the figure for group profits. This will occur whenever goods sold at a profit within the group remain in the inventory of the purchasing company at the year end. The best way to deal with this is to **calculate the unrealised profit on unsold inventories at the year end** and add this amount back to cost of sales, thereby reducing gross profit.

Example: intra-group trading

Suppose in our earlier example that S Co had recorded sales of $5,000 to P Co during 20X9. S Co had purchased these goods from outside suppliers at a cost of $3,000. One half of the goods remained in P Co's inventory at 31 December 20X9.

The consolidated income statement for the year ended 31 December 20X9 would now be as follows.

	$
Sales revenue (75 + 38 – 5)	108,000
Cost of sales (30 + 20 – 5 + 1*)	(46,000)
Gross profit	62,000
Administrative expenses	(22,000)
Profit before taxation	40,000
Income tax expense	(12,000)
Profit for the year	28,000
Profit attributable to:	
Owners of the parent	26,250
Non-controlling interest	1,750
	28,000
Note:	
Retained earnings brought forward	99,750
Profit for the year	26,250
Retained earnings carried forward	126,000

*Unrealised profit: ½ × ($5,000 – $3,000)

An adjustment will be made for the unrealised profit against the inventory figure in the consolidated statement of financial position.

Intra-group dividends

In our example so far we have assumed that S Co retains all of its after tax profit. It may be, however, that S Co distributes some of its profits as dividends. As before, the non-controlling interest in the subsidiary's profit should be calculated immediately after the figure of after tax profit. For this purpose, no account need be taken of how much of profit due to the **non-controlling interest** is to be distributed by S Co as dividend.

Note that group retained earnings are only adjusted for dividends paid to the parent company shareholders. Dividends paid by the subsidiary to the parent are cancelled on consolidation and dividends paid to the non-controlling interest are replaced by the allocation to the non-controlling interest of their share of the profit for the year of the subsidiary.

Pre-acquisition profits

As explained above, the figure for retained earnings carried forward must be the same as the figure for retained earnings in the consolidated statement of financial position. We have seen in previous chapters that retained earnings in the consolidated statement of financial position comprise:

(a)   The **whole of the parent company's** retained earnings

(b)   A **proportion of the subsidiary company's** retained earnings. The proportion is the **group's share of post acquisition retained earnings** in the subsidiary. From the total retained earnings of the subsidiary we must therefore **exclude** both the **non-controlling share** of total retained earnings and the **group's share of pre-acquisition** retained earnings.

A **similar procedure is necessary in the consolidated income statement** if it is to link up with the consolidated statement of financial position. Previous examples have shown how the non-controlling share of profits is excluded in the income statement. Their share of profits for the year is deducted from profit after tax, while the figure for profits brought forward in the consolidation schedule includes only the group's proportion of the subsidiary's profits.

In the same way, when considering examples which include pre acquisition profits in a subsidiary, the figure for profits brought forward should include only the group's share of the post acquisition retained profits. If the subsidiary is **acquired during the accounting year**, it is therefore necessary to apportion its profit for the year between pre-acquisition and post-acquisition elements. The part-year method is used.

With the part-year method, the entire income statement of the subsidiary is split between pre-acquisition and post-acquisition proportions. Only the post-acquisition figures are included in the consolidated income statement.

Example

P Co acquired 60% of the equity of S Co on 1 April 20X5. The income statements of the two companies for the year ended 31 December 20X5 are set out below.

	P Co	S Co	S co $(^9/_{12})$
	$	$	$
Sales revenue	170,000	80,000	60,000
Cost of sales	65,000	36,000	27,000
Gross profit	105,000	44,000	33,000
Other income – dividend received S Co	3,600		
Administrative expenses	43,000	12,000	9,000
Profit before tax	65,600	32,000	24,000
Income tax expense	23,000	8,000	6,000
Profit for the year	42,600	24,000	18,000

Note

Dividends (paid 31 December)	12,000	6,000
Profit retained	30,600	18,000

Retained earnings brought forward	81,000	40,000
Retained earnings carried forward	111,600	58,000

Now we will prepare the consolidated income statement and retained earnings extract from the statement of changes in equity.

The shares in S Co were acquired three months into the year. Only the post acquisition proportion (9/12ths) of S Co's income statement is included in the consolidated income statement. This is shown above for convenience.

P CO CONSOLIDATED INCOME STATEMENT
FOR THE YEAR ENDED 31 DECEMBER 20X5

	$
Sales revenue (170 + 60)	230,000
Cost of sales (65 + 27)	(92,000)
Gross profit	138,000
Administrative expenses (43 + 9)	(52,000)
Profit before tax	86,000
Income tax expense (23 + 6)	(29,000)
Profit for the year	57,000

Profit attributable to:	
Owners of the parent	49,800
Non-controlling interest (18 × 40%)	7,200
	57,000

STATEMENT OF CHANGES IN EQUITY	Retained earnings
	$
Balance brought forward*	81,000
Dividend paid (P)	(12,000)
Total comprehensive income for the year	49,800
Balance carried forward	118,800

* All of S Co's profits brought forward are pre-acquisition.

2 The consolidated statement of comprehensive income

A consolidated statement of comprehensive income is simple to produce once the income statement has been prepared. Any item of 'other comprehensive income' is attributable to either the parent or a subsidiary. If it is attributable to a subsidiary, part of it is allocated to the non-controlling interest.

Here is an example where an 80% subsidiary has 'other comprehensive income'.

CONSOLIDATED STATEMENT OF COMPREHENSIVE INCOME FOR THE YEAR TO 30 APRIL 20X7

	$'000
Sales revenue	1,600
Cost of sales	(930)
Gross profit	670
Administrative expenses	(255)
Profit before tax	415
Income tax expense	(75)
Profit for the year	340
Other comprehensive income:	
Gain on property revaluation	200
Total comprehensive income for the year	540
Profit attributable to:	
Owners of the parent	332
Non-controlling interest	8
	340
Total comprehensive income attributable to:	
Owners of the parent (332 + (200 × 80%))	492
Non-controlling interest (8 + (200 × 20%))	48
	540

Consolidated statement of changes in equity

These amounts would appear in the consolidated statement of changes in equity as follows:

	Retained earnings $'000	Revaluation surplus $'000	Total $'000	Non-controlling interest $'000	Total $'000
Total comprehensive income for the year	332	160	492	48	540

3 The consolidated statement of cash flows

The method of preparing the group statement of cash flows is the same as for the individual entity statement. The aim is to show the cash flows of the group with third parties. As the statement is based on the consolidated financial statements, any intra-group transactions will already have been eliminated.

However there are a number of additional issues to be considered.

Non-controlling interest

The non-controlling interest is not part of the group, so dividends paid to the non-controlling interest should be shown as a cash outflow under 'financing activities'.

Associates

We will be dealing with associates in the next chapter. For the statement of cash flows, it is important just to remember that an associate is also not part of the group.

Group 'profit before tax' in the consolidated statement of comprehensive income will include 'share of profit of associate'. This must be removed as part of the reconciliation to arrive at 'cash generated from operations'.

Dividends received from the associate are disclosed as a separate cash flow under 'cash flows from investing activities'.

Acquisition of a subsidiary

If a subsidiary is acquired during the reporting period, the net cash effect of the acquisition is shown separately under 'cash flows from investing activities'. The net cash flow will be the cash amount paid less any cash and cash equivalents acquired.

Example: P Co acquires 65% of S Co by issuing 200,000 $1 shares at $1.60 and paying $500,000.

S Co's statement of financial position at acquisition shows cash and cash equivalents of $75,000.

In the statement of cash flows this will appear as follows:

	$'000
Cash flows from investing activities	
Acquisition of S Co, net of cash acquired (500 – 75)	(425)

Note:

Because the cash balance of the acquired subsidiary has been taken into account as a one-line entry, the assets and liabilities of the subsidiary should be excluded when calculating movement on PPE, inventories, receivables etc. Otherwise the cash effect of the acquisition would be double-counted.

Disposal of a subsidiary

The same principle applies when a subsidiary is disposed of during the year. If P Co disposes of its interest in S Co a few years later for $700,000 when S Co has an overdraft of $30,000, the statement of cash flows will show:

	$'000
Cash flows from investing activities	
Disposal of S Co, net of cash disposed of (700 + 30)	730

Again, the assets and liabilities of S Co will be added back in for the purposes of calculating movements over the year, as the effect of the disposal has already been taken into account.

Where dividend paid to the NCI has to be calculated as a balancing figure using the equity balances and the attributable profit, these equity balances must also be adjusted for acquisitions and disposals, before the calculation is done. The NCI added on acquisition of a subsidiary acquired during the year should be deducted and the NCI deducted on disposal of a subsidiary should be added back. The correct amount of dividend paid will then be the balancing figure.

In a reporting period where both an acquisition and a disposal took place, the working would be as follows:

NON-CONTROLLING INTEREST

	$m		$m
NCI deducted on disposal	4	NCI b/f (consolidated SFP)	15
Dividend paid to NCI (bal figure)	3	NCI added on acquisition	5
NCI c/f (consolidated SFP)	20	Profit attributable to NCI	7
	27		27

Accounting for associates

19

1 IAS 28: Investments in associates

Here are the main definitions relating to associates:

> * **Associate**. An entity, including an unincorporated entity such as a partnership, over which an investor has significant influence and which is neither a subsidiary nor an interest in a joint venture.
> * **Significant influence** is the power to participate in the financial and operating policy decisions of the investee but is not control or joint control over those policies.
> * **Equity method**. A method of accounting whereby the investment is initially recorded at cost and adjusted thereafter for the post-acquisition change in the investor's share of net assets of the investee. The profit or loss of the investor includes the investor's share of the profit or loss of the investee.   *(IAS 28)*

IAS 28 requires all investments in associates to be accounted for in the consolidated accounts using the equity method, unless the investment is classified as 'held for sale' in accordance with IFRS 5 in which case it should be accounted for under IFRS 5 or the exemption below applies.

An investor is exempt from applying the equity method if:

(a)   It is a parent exempt from preparing consolidated financial statements under IAS 27, or

(b)   All of the following apply:

(i)   The investor is a **wholly-owned subsidiary** or it is a **partially owned subsidiary** of another entity and its other owners, including those not otherwise entitled to vote, have been informed about, and do not object to, the investor not applying the equity method;

(ii)   The investor's securities are **not publicly traded**

(iii)   It is **not in the process of issuing securities** in public securities markets; and

(iv)   The **ultimate or intermediate parent** publishes consolidated financial statements that comply with International Financial Reporting Standards.

The revised version of IAS 28 **no longer allows** an investment in an associate to be excluded from equity accounting when an investee operates under severe long-term restrictions that significantly impair its ability to transfer funds to the investor. Significant influence must be lost before the equity method ceases to be applicable.

The use of the equity method should be **discontinued** from the date that the investor **ceases to have significant influence**.

From that date, the investor shall account for the investment in accordance with IAS 39 *Financial instruments: recognition and measurement*. The carrying amount of the investment at the date that it ceases to be an associate shall be regarded as its cost on initial measurement as a financial asset under IAS 39.

Separate financial statements of the investor

If an investor **issues consolidated financial statements** (because it has subsidiaries), an investment in an associate should be *either*:

(a)   Accounted for at cost, or
(b)   In accordance with IAS 39 (at fair value)

in its separate financial statements.

If an investor that does **not issue consolidated financial statements** (ie it has no subsidiaries) but has an investment in an associate this should similarly be included in the financial statements of the investor either at cost, or in accordance with IAS 39.

2 The equity method

Many of the procedures required to apply the equity method are the same as are required for full consolidation. In particular, **intra-group unrealised profits** must be excluded.

Consolidated statement of comprehensive income/income statement

The basic principle is that the investing company (X Co) should take account of its **share of the earnings** of the associate, Y Co, whether or not Y Co distributes the earnings as dividends. X Co achieves this by adding to consolidated profit the group's share of Y Co's profit after tax.

Notice the difference between this treatment and the **consolidation** of a subsidiary company's results. If Y Co were a subsidiary X Co would take credit for the whole of its sales revenue, cost of sales etc and would then make a one line adjustment to remove any non-controlling share.

Under equity accounting, the associate's sales revenue, cost of sales and so on are **not amalgamated** with those of the group. Instead the group share only of the associate's profit before tax and tax charge for the year is added to the corresponding lines of the parent company and its subsidiaries.

Consolidated statement of financial position

A figure for **investment in associates** is shown which at the time of the acquisition must be stated at cost. This amount will increase (decrease) each year by the amount of the group's share of the associated company's profit (loss) for the year.

Example: associate

P Co, a company with subsidiaries, acquires 25,000 of the 100,000 $1 ordinary shares in A Co for $60,000 on 1 January 20X8. In the year to 31 December 20X8, A Co earns profits after tax of $24,000, from which it pays a dividend of $6,000.

How will A Co's results be accounted for in the individual and consolidated accounts of P Co for the year ended 31 December 20X8?

In the individual accounts of P Co, the investment will be recorded on 1 January 20X8 at cost. Unless there is an impairment in the value of the investment (see below), this amount will remain in the individual statement of financial position of P Co permanently. The only entry in P Co's individual income statement will be to record dividends received. For the year ended 31 December 20X8, P Co will:

DEBIT	Cash	$1,500	
CREDIT	Income from shares in associates		$1,500

In the **consolidated accounts** of P Co equity accounting principles will be used to account for the investment in A Co. Consolidated profit after tax will include the group's share of A Co's profit after tax (25% × $24,000 = $6,000). To the extent that this has been distributed as dividend, it is already included in P Co's individual accounts and will automatically be brought into the consolidated results. That part of the group's share of profit in the associate which has not been distributed as dividend ($4,500) will be brought into consolidation by the following adjustment.

DEBIT	Investment in associates	$4,500	
CREDIT	Income from associates		$4,500

The asset 'Investment in associates' is then stated at $64,500, being cost plus the group share of post acquisition retained profits.

3 Income statement and statement of financial position

The following is a **suggested layout** for the consolidated income statement for a company having subsidiaries as well as associated companies.

	$
Revenue	1,400
Cost of sales	(770)
Gross profit	630
Other income: interest receivable	30
Administrative expenses	(290)
Finance costs	(20)
Share of profit of associate (30 – 13)*	17
Profit before taxation	367
Income tax expense	(145)
Profit for the year	222
Profit attributable to:	
Owners of the parent	200
Non-controlling interest	22
	222

* Profit for the year less tax

Consolidated statement of financial position

The consolidated statement of financial position will contain an **asset 'Investment in associates'**. The amount at which this asset is stated will be its original cost plus the group's share of any **profits earned since acquisition** which have not been distributed as dividends.

Example: consolidated statement of financial position

On 1 January 20X6 the net tangible assets of A Co amount to $220,000, financed by 100,000 $1 ordinary shares and revenue reserves of $120,000. P Co, a company with subsidiaries, acquires 30,000 of the shares in A Co for $75,000. During the year ended 31 December 20X6 A Co's profit after tax is $30,000, from which dividends of $12,000 are paid.

How will P Co's investment in A Co would appear in the consolidated statement of financial position at 31 December 20X6?

CONSOLIDATED STATEMENT OF FINANCIAL POSITION AS AT 31 DECEMBER 20X6 (extract)

	$
Non-current assets	
Investment in associated company	
Cost	75,000
Group share of post acquisition retained profits	
(30% × $18,000)	5,400
	80,400

The following points are also relevant and are similar to a parent-subsidiary consolidation situation.

(a) Use financial statements drawn up to the **same reporting date**.
(b) If this is impracticable, adjust the financial statements for **significant transactions/ events** in the intervening period. The difference between the reporting date of the associate and that of the investor must be no more than three months.
(c) Use **uniform accounting policies** for like transactions and events in similar circumstances, adjusting the associate's statements to reflect group policies if necessary.

'Upstream' and 'downstream' transactions

'Upstream' transactions are, for example, sales from an associate to the investor. 'Downstream' transactions are, for example, sales from the investor to an associate.

Unrealised profits resulting from 'upstream' and 'downstream' transactions between an investor (including its consolidated subsidiaries) and an associate are eliminated to the extent of the investor's interest in the associate. This is very similar to the procedure for eliminating unrealised profit between a parent and a subsidiary. The important thing to remember is that **only the group's share is eliminated**.

Example: downstream transaction

A Co, a parent with subsidiaries, holds 25% of the equity shares in B Co. During the year, A Co makes sales of $1,000,000 to B Co at cost plus a 25% mark-up. At the year-end, B Co has all these goods still in inventories.

A Co has made an unrealised profit of $200,000 (1,000,000 × 25/125) on its sales to the associate. The group's share (25%) of this must be eliminated:

DEBIT	Cost of sales (consolidated income statement)	$50,000
CREDIT	Investment in associate (consolidated statement of financial position)	$50,000

Because the sale was made to the associate, the group's share of the unsold inventory forms part of the investment in the associate at the year-end. If the associate had made the sale to the parent, the adjustment would have been:

DEBIT	Cost of sales (consolidated income statement)	$50,000
CREDIT	Inventories (consolidated statement of financial position)	$50,000

Associate's losses

When the equity method is being used and the investor's share of losses of the associate equals or exceeds its interest in the associate, the investor should discontinue including its share of further losses. The investment is reported at nil value. The interest in the associate is normally the carrying amount of the investment in the associate, but it also includes any other long-term interests, for example, long term receivables or loans.

After the investor's interest is reduced to nil, additional losses should only be recognised where the investor has incurred obligations or made payments on behalf of the associate (for example, if it has guaranteed amounts owed to third parties by the associate).

Impairment losses

IAS 39 sets out a list of indications that a financial asset (including an associate) may have become impaired. Any impairment loss is recognised in accordance with IAS 36 *Impairment of assets* for each associate individually.

In the case of an associate, any impairment loss will be deducted from the carrying amount in the statement of financial position.

The working would be as follows.

	$
Cost of investment	X
Share of post-acquisition retained earnings	X
	X
Impairment loss	(X)
Investment in associate	X

Part
C

Group financial statements

Accounting for joint ventures

20

1 IAS 31: Interests in joint ventures

Two or more persons may decide to enter into a business venture together without wishing to form a formal long-term partnership. Usually the venturers agree to place limitations on their activities, for example, a joint venture to manufacture and sell 'total eclipse of the sun' souvenirs could be limited by time, while a joint venture to buy and sell a bankrupt's inventory (a fairly common occurrence in practice) comes to an end when all the inventory has been sold.

Joint ventures are often found when each party can **contribute in different ways** to the venture. For example, one venturer may provide finance, another purchases or manufactures goods, while a third offers his marketing skills.

Joint ventures generally have the following characteristics.

* They are **limited by time and/or activity**
* The venturers usually **carry on their principal businesses** at the same time
* **Separate books** for the venture are not normally maintained
* The venturers usually agree to a **profit/loss sharing** ratio for the purpose of the venture

IAS 31 Interests in joint ventures covers all types of joint ventures. It is not concerned with the accounts of the joint venture itself (if separate accounts are maintained), but rather **how the interest in a joint venture is accounted for by each joint venturer** (ie each 'partner' in the joint venture).

The assets and liabilities, income and expenses of the joint venture must be reported in the financial statements of the venturers and investors, whatever the form of the joint venture.

IAS 31 looks at the various forms of joint venture which may be undertaken and then looks at how joint ventures are dealt with in the **individual financial statements** of the venturer and the **group financial statements**.

The IAS begins by listing some important definitions.

Joint venture. A contractual arrangement whereby two or more parties undertake an economic activity which is subject to joint control.

Control. The power to govern the financial and operating policies of an economic activity so as to obtain benefits from its activities.

Joint control. The contractually agreed sharing of control over an economic activity.

Significant influence. The power to participate in the financial and operating policy decisions of an economic activity but is not control or joint control over those policies.

Venturer. A party to a joint venture that has joint control over that joint venture.

Proportionate consolidation. A method of accounting whereby a venturer's share of each of the assets, liabilities, income and expenses of a jointly controlled entity is combined line-by-line with similar items in the venturer's financial statements or reported as separate line items in the venturer's financial statements.

Equity method. A method of accounting whereby an interest in a jointly controlled entity is initially recorded at cost and adjusted thereafter for the post acquisition change in the venturer's share of net assets of the jointly controlled entity. The income statement reflects the venturer's share of the profit or loss of the jointly controlled entity.

(IAS 31)

Forms of joint venture

The form and structure of joint ventures can vary enormously. There are, however, three main types identified by the standard.

- **Jointly controlled operations**
- **Jointly controlled assets**
- **Jointly controlled entities**

We will look at each of these below. They are all usually described as joint ventures and fulfil the definition of a joint venture given above.

Whatever the form and structure, every joint venture will have **two characteristics**.

- Two (or more) venturers are bound by a **contractual arrangement**.
- The contractual relationship establishes **joint control**.

Contractual arrangement

The existence of a contractual agreement distinguishes a joint venture from an investment in an associate. **If there is no contractual arrangement, then a joint venture does not exist.**

Evidence of a contractual arrangement could be in one of several forms.

- **Contract** between the venturers
- **Minutes** of discussion between the venturers
- Incorporation in the **articles or by-laws** of the joint venture

The contractual arrangement is usually **in writing**, whatever its form, and it will deal with the following issues surrounding the joint venture.

- **Its activity, duration and reporting obligations**
- The appointment of its **board of directors** (or equivalent) and the **voting rights** of the venturers
- **Capital contributions** to it by the venturers
- How its output, income, expenses or results are **shared** between the venturers

It is the contractual arrangement which establishes **joint control** over the joint venture, so that no single venturer can control the activity of the joint venture on its own.

One venturer, identified by the contractual agreement, may be the **operator of the joint venture**. This does *not* mean that the operator controls the joint venture, the operator must act within the policies (financial and operation) agreed by all the venturers as laid out in the contractual arrangement. If this is not the case, if the operator effectively controls the joint venture rather than only acting within the arrangements delegated to it, then the activity is *not* a joint venture.

SIC 13 – Jointly controlled entities – non-monetary contributions by venturers

The SIC states that, in applying IAS 31 to non-monetary contributions to a jointly controlled entity (JCE), **a venturer should recognise in profit or loss for the period the portion of a gain or loss attributed to the equity interests of the other venturers except** in certain circumstances.

(a)   The significant risks and rewards of ownership of the contributed non-monetary asset(s) have not been transferred to the JCE.

(b)   The gain or loss on the non-monetary contributions cannot be measured reliably.

(c)   The non-monetary assets contributed are similar to those contributed by the other venturers.

Jointly controlled operations

In this type of joint venture, there is no separate entity set up to deal with the joint venture, whether in the form of a corporation, partnership or other entity. Instead, the venturers **use their own assets and resources** for the joint venture, ie their own property, plant and equipment is used and they carry their own inventories.

The venturers also incur their own expenses and liabilities, and raise their own finance which then represent their own obligations. In these situations, the activities of the joint venture will often be performed by the venturers' staff alongside the venturers' **other similar activities**. The way that income and expenses are shared between the venturers is usually laid out in the joint venture agreement.

IAS 31 uses the example of building an aircraft. Say that Boeing is to build the body of the aircraft and the engines are to be built by Rolls Royce as specified by the airline customer for the aircraft. You can see that different parts of the manufacturing process are carried out by each of the venturers. In the Rolls Royce factory, workers will work on the engines for the Boeing plane alongside others working on engines for different aircraft.

Each venturer, Boeing and Rolls Royce, bears its own costs and takes a share of revenue from the aircraft sale. That share is decided in the contractual arrangement between the venturers.

Accounting treatment

When a joint venture in the nature of jointly controlled operations exists, IAS 31 requires a venturer to recognise the following in its financial statements.

(a)   The **assets** it controls and the **liabilities** it incurs

(b)   The **expenses** it incurs and the **income** it earns from the sale of goods or services by the joint venture

Separate accounts for the joint venture are not required, although the venturers may prepare management accounts for the joint venture, in order to assess its performance.

Jointly controlled assets

In this type of joint venture, the venturers have **joint control**, and often **joint ownership** of some or all of the assets in the joint venture. These assets may have been contributed to the joint venture or purchased for the purpose of the joint venture, but in any case they are **dedicated to the activities of the joint venture**. These assets are used to produce benefits for the venturers; each venturer takes a share of the output and bears a share of the incurred expenses.

As with jointly controlled operations, this type of joint venture does not involve setting up a corporation, partnership or any other kind of entity. The venturers **control their share of future economic benefits** through their share in the jointly controlled asset.

IAS 31 gives examples in the oil, gas and mineral extraction industries. In such industries companies may, say, jointly control and operate on oil or gas pipeline. Each company transports its own products down the pipeline and pays an agreed proportion of the expenses of operating the pipeline (perhaps based on volume).

A further example is a property which is jointly controlled, each venturer taking a share of the rental income and bearing a portion of the expense.

Accounting treatment

IAS 31 requires each venturer to recognise (ie include in their financial statements) the following in respect of its interest in jointly controlled assets.

(a) Its **share of the jointly controlled assets**, classified by their nature, eg a share of a jointly controlled oil pipeline should be classified as property, plant and equipment

(b) Any **liabilities** it has incurred, eg in financing its share of the assets

(c) Its share of any **liabilities incurred jointly** with the other venturers which relate to the joint venture

(d) Any **income** from the sale or use of its share of the joint venture's output, together with its share of any **expenses** incurred by the joint venture

(e) Any **expenses** which it has incurred in respect of its interest in the joint venture, eg those relating to financing the venturer's interest in the assets and selling its share of the output

This treatment of jointly controlled assets reflects the **substance and economic reality**, and (usually) the legal form of the joint venture. Separate accounting records need not be kept for the joint venture and financial statements for the joint venture need not be prepared. Management accounts may be produced, however, in order to monitor the performance of the joint venture.

Jointly controlled entities

This type of joint venture involves the setting up of a corporation, partnership or other entity. This **operates in the same way as any other entity**, except that the venturers have a contractual arrangement establishing their joint control over the economic activity of the entity.

A jointly controlled entity effectively operates as a **separate entity**: it controls the joint venture's assets, incurs liabilities and expenses and earns income. It can, as a separate entity, enter into contracts in its own name and raise finance to fund the activities of the joint venture. The venturers share the results of the jointly controlled entity, and in some cases they may also share the output of the joint venture.

Part C

Group financial statements

A common situation is where two or more entities transfer the relevant assets and liabilities to a jointly controlled entity in order to combine their activities in a particular line of business.

In other situations, an entity wishing to start operations in a foreign country will set up a jointly controlled entity with the government of the foreign country (or an agency of it).

The **substance** of jointly controlled entities are often similar in substance to the joint ventures discussed above (jointly controlled assets/operations). In the case of the oil/gas pipeline mentioned in IAS 31, the asset might be transferred to a jointly controlled entity for tax or similar reasons. In other circumstances, a jointly controlled entity may be set up to deal with only certain aspects of the jointly controlled operations, eg marketing or after-sales service, design or distribution.

As a separate entity, the jointly controlled entity must maintain its **own accounting records** and will **prepare financial statements** according to national requirements and IASs. The accounting treatment for jointly controlled entities is discussed in the next section.

Transactions between a venturer and a joint venture

A venturer may **sell or contribute assets** to a joint venture. The value attributed to such assets may create a gain or loss. However, any such gain or loss should only be recognised to the extent that it reflects the substance of the transaction.

What this means is that only the **gain** attributable to the interest of the other venturers should be recognised. However, the full amount of any **loss** should be recognised when the transaction shows evidence that the net realisable value of current assets is less than cost, or that there is an impairment loss (determined by applying IAS 36).

Example

K Co contributes inventories to a 50:50 joint venture it has undertaken with L Co. The recorded historical cost of the inventories is $2m.

What gain or loss should K Co recognise in its financial statements when the fair value (net realisable value) of the inventories is estimated at the date of transfer and recorded by the joint venture as:

(a) $2.2m?
(b) $1.8m?

(a) K Co has made a profit of $0.2m, but only 50% of this can be considered as realised, ie that part attributable to the other venturer. K Co should therefore recognise a gain of $0.1m.
(b) A loss of $0.2m has been made on the inventories, the entire amount of which should be recognised by K Co. It is known that the loss will be made, even though the inventories have not yet been sold, and so prudence requires that the full loss should be recognised.

A venturer may **purchase assets** from a joint venture. When it does so, the venturer should not recognise its share of the profit made by the joint venture on the transaction in question until it resells the assets to an independent third party, ie until the profit is realised. Losses should be treated in the same way, except losses should be recognised immediately if they represent a reduction in the net realisable value of current assets, or a permanent decline in the carrying amount of non-current assets.

Investors in joint ventures

There may be investors in joint ventures who **do not have joint control**. Such interests should be reported in accordance with IAS 39 or IAS 28 *Investments in associates*, depending on the circumstances.

Operators of joint ventures

Operators of joint ventures will often **receive fees** for their work in directly managing the joint venture. Such fees should be accounted for according to IAS 18 *Revenue*. Such management fees will be treated by the joint venture as an expense.

Special purpose entities

These are dealt with here because they do not fit in readily anywhere else! An entity may be created to accomplish a specific, defined objective. Examples include research and development, or securitisation of financial assets. Such special purpose entities (SPE) may be incorporated or unincorporated. Often there are strict and permanent limits on the decision-making powers of their governing board or other management. They operate on 'autopilot', ie the policy guiding their activities cannot be modified other than perhaps by their sponsor. The sponsor frequently transfers assets to the SPE or performs services for it.

SPEs are dealt with in SIC 12 *Consolidation – special purpose entities*. The SIC states that **an SPE should be consolidated** when the **substance of the relationship between an entity and the SPE indicates that the SPE is controlled by that entity**.

2 Accounting treatment of jointly controlled entities

Separate financial statements of a venturer

IAS 31 states that where a venturer prepares separate financial statements (as a single company), investments in jointly controlled entities should be either:

(a)   accounted for at **cost**, or
(b)   in accordance with **IAS 39**.

The same accounting treatment must be applied consistently to all jointly controlled entities.

Consolidated financial statements of a venturer

IAS 31 requires all interests in jointly controlled entities to be accounted for using *either* proportionate consolidation or the equity method.

However, several exemptions are available and neither of these methods need be applied where:

(a)   The interest is classified as held for sale in accordance with IFRS 5, or
(b)   The venturer is a parent exempt from preparing consolidated financial statements under IAS 27, or
(c)   All of the following apply:
    (i)   The venturer is a **wholly-owned subsidiary** or it is a **partially owned subsidiary** of another entity and its other owners, including those not otherwise entitled to vote, have been informed about, and do not object to, the investor not applying proportionate consolidation or the equity method.
    (ii)   Its securities are **not publicly traded**.

(iii) It is **not in the process of issuing securities** in public securities markets; and
(iv) The **ultimate or intermediate parent** publishes consolidated financial statements that comply with International Financial Reporting Standards.

Where an interest is classified as held for sale it should be accounted for in accordance with IFRS 5.

Proportionate consolidation

A venturer should report its interest in a jointly controlled entity in its consolidated financial statements using one of the two reporting formats for **proportionate consolidation**.

IAS 31 maintains that this treatment reflects the **substance and economic reality** of the arrangement, ie the control the venturer has over its share of future economic benefits through its share of the assets and liabilities of the venture.

The proportionate consolidation method differs from normal consolidation in that only the group share of assets and liabilities, income and expenses are brought into account. There is therefore **no non-controlling interest**.

There are **two different formats** with which the proportionate consolidation method can be used.

(a) **Combine on a line-by-line basis** the venturer's share of each of the assets, liabilities, income and expenses of the jointly controlled entity with the similar items in the venturer's consolidated financial statements.
(b) Include in the venturer's consolidated financial statements **separate line items** for the venturer's share of the assets and liabilities, income and expenses of the jointly controlled entity.

Example: Proportionate consolidation

Both of the above methods produce exactly the same results and they are demonstrated in this example. Set out below are the draft accounts of Parent Co and its subsidiaries and of Joint Venture Co. Parent Co acquired 50% of the equity capital of Joint Venture Co three years ago when the latter's retained earnings stood at $40,000.

SUMMARISED STATEMENTS OF FINANCIAL POSITION

	Parent Co & subsidiaries $'000	Joint Venture Co $'000
Tangible non-current assets	220	170
Investment in joint venture	75	–
Current assets	100	50
Loan to Joint Venture	20	–
	415	220
Share capital ($1 shares)	250	100
Retained earnings	165	100
Loan from Parent Co	–	20
	415	220

SUMMARISED INCOME STATEMENTS

	Parent Co & subsidiaries $'000	Joint Venture Co $'000
Profit before tax	95	80
Income tax expense	(35)	(30)
	60	50
Dividends paid	(50)	(10)
Profit for the year	10	40

Parent Co has taken credit for the dividend paid by Joint Venture Co.

Now we will prepare the summarised consolidated statement of financial position of Parent Co, under both the formats of proportionate consolidation recommended by IAS 31.

Line-by-line format

PARENT CO

CONSOLIDATED STATEMENT OF FINANCIAL POSITION

	$'000
Goodwill (W1)	5
Tangible non-current assets (220 + (50% × 170))	305
Current assets (100 + (50% × 50))	125
Loan to joint venturer (note)	10
	445
Share capital	250
Retained earnings (W2)	195
	445

Note. The loan is the proportion of the $20,000 lent to the other venturer.

Workings

1. *Goodwill*

	$'000
Consideration transferred	75
Share of net assets acquired (50% × 140)	(70)
Goodwill	5

2. *Retained earnings*

	Parent Co & subsidiaries $'000	Joint Venture Co $'000
Per individual SFP	165	100
Pre-acquisition		(40)
Post-acquisition		60
Group share in joint venture		
($60 × 50%)	30	
Group retained earnings	195	

Separate line method

PARENT CO

CONSOLIDATED STATEMENT OF FINANCIAL POSITION

	$'000	$'000
Goodwill (as above)		5
Tangible non-current assets		
Group	220	
Joint venture (170 × 50%)	85	
		305
Current assets		
Group	100	
Joint venture (50% × 50)	25	
		125
Loan to joint venturer		10
		445
Share capital		250
Retained earnings (as above)		195
		445

In both these cases the **consolidated income statements** would be shown in the same way.

The use of the proportionate consolidation method should be **discontinued** from the date the venturer ceases to have joint control over the entity.

Equity method

A venturer can report its interest in a joint venture in its consolidated financial statements under the **equity method**. The argument for this method is that it is misleading to combine controlled items with jointly controlled items. It is also felt by some that venturers have significant influence over the entity, not merely joint control.

IAS 31 does not agree with this approach, preferring the proportionate consolidation method for the reasons given above, but it allows the equity method, **as laid out in IAS 28**, to be used.

The use of the equity method should be **discontinued** from the date on which the venturer ceases to have joint control over, or have significant influence on, a jointly controlled entity.

1 IFRS 2: Share-based payment

Transactions whereby entities purchase goods or services from other parties, such as suppliers and employees, by **issuing shares or share options** to those other parties are **increasingly common**. Share schemes are a common feature of director and executive remuneration and in some countries the authorities may offer tax incentives to encourage more companies to offer shares to employees. Companies whose shares or share options are regarded as a valuable 'currency' commonly use share-based payment to obtain employee and professional services.

The increasing use of share-based payment has raised questions about the accounting treatment of such transactions in company financial statements.

Share options are often granted to employees at an exercise price that is equal to or higher than the market price of the shares at the date the option is granted. Consequently the options have no intrinsic value and so **no transaction is recorded in the financial statements**.

This leads to an **anomaly**: if a company pays its employees in cash, an expense is recognised in profit or loss, but if the payment is in share options, no expense is recognised.

There are a number of arguments **against** recognition. The IASB has considered and rejected the arguments below.

(a) **No cost therefore no charge**

There is no cost to the entity because the granting of shares or options does not require the entity to sacrifice cash or other assets. Therefore a charge should not be recognised.

This argument is unsound because it ignores the fact that a transaction has occurred. The employees have provided valuable services to the entity in return for valuable shares or options.

(b) **Earnings per share is hit twice**

It is argued that the charge to profit or loss for the employee services consumed reduces the entity's earnings, while at the same time there is an increase in the number of shares issued.

However, the dual impact on earnings per share simply reflects the two economic events that have occurred.

(i) The entity has issued shares or options, thus increasing the denominator of the earnings per share calculation.

(ii) It has also consumed the resources it received for those shares or options, thus reducing the numerator.

(c) **Adverse economic consequences**

It could be argued that entities might be discouraged from introducing or continuing employee share plans if they were required to recognise them in the financial statements. However, if this happened, it might be because the requirement for entities to account properly for employee share plans had revealed the economic consequences of such plans.

A situation where entities are able to obtain and consume resources by issuing valuable shares or options without having to account for such transactions could be perceived as a distortion.

IFRS 2 requires an entity to **reflect the effects of share-based payment transactions** in its profit or loss and financial position.

IFRS 2 applies to all share-based payment transactions. There are three types.

(a) **Equity-settled share-based payment transactions**, in which the entity receives goods or services in exchange for equity instruments of the entity (including shares or share options)

(b) **Cash-settled share-based payment transactions**, in which the entity receives goods or services in exchange for amounts of cash that are based on the price (or value) of the entity's shares or other equity instruments of the entity

(c) Transactions in which the entity receives or acquires goods or services and either the entity or the supplier has a **choice** as to whether the entity settles the transaction in cash (or other assets) or by issuing equity instruments

Certain transactions are **outside the scope** of the IFRS:

(a) Transactions with employees and others in their capacity as a holder of equity instruments of the entity (for example, where an employee receives additional shares in a rights issue to all shareholders)

(b) The issue of equity instruments in exchange for control of another entity in a business combination

These are the main definitions used in IFRS 2

Share-based payment transaction A transaction in which the entity receives goods or services as consideration for equity instruments of the entity (including shares or share options), or acquires goods or services by incurring liabilities to the supplier of those goods or services for amounts that are based on the price of the entity's shares or other equity instruments of the entity.

Share-based payment arrangement An agreement between the entity and another party (including an employee) to enter into a share-based payment transaction, which thereby entitles the other party to receive cash or other assets of the entity for amounts that are based on the price of the entity's shares or other equity instruments of the entity, or to receive equity instruments of the entity, provided the specified vesting conditions, if any, are met.

Equity instrument A contract that evidences a residual interest in the assets of an entity after deducting all of its liabilities.

Equity instrument granted The right (conditional or unconditional) to an equity instrument of the entity conferred by the entity on another party, under a share-based payment arrangement.

Share option A contract that gives the holder the right, but not the obligation, to subscribe to the entity's shares at a fixed or determinable price for a specified period of time.

Fair value The amount for which an asset could be exchanged, a liability settled, or an equity instrument granted could be exchanged, between knowledgeable, willing parties in an arm's length transaction.

Grant date The date at which the entity and another party (including an employee) agree to a share-based payment arrangement, being when the entity and the other party have a shared understanding of the terms and conditions of the arrangement. At grant date the entity confers on the other party (the counterparty) the right to cash, other assets, or equity instruments of the entity, provided the specified vesting conditions, if any, are met. If that agreement is subject to an approval process (for example, by shareholders), grant date is the date when that approval is obtained.

Intrinsic value The difference between the fair value of the shares to which the counterparty has the (conditional or unconditional) right to subscribe or which it has the right to receive, and the price (if any) the other party is (or will be) required to pay for those shares. For example, a share option with an exercise price of $15 on a share with a fair value of $20, has an intrinsic value of $5.

Measurement date The date at which the fair value of the equity instruments granted is measured. For transactions with employees and others providing similar services, the measurement date is grant date. For transactions with parties other than employees (and those providing similar services), the measurement date is the date the entity obtains the goods or the counterparty renders service.

Vest To become an entitlement. Under a share-based payment arrangement, a counterparty's right to receive cash, other assets, or equity instruments of the entity vests upon satisfaction of any specified vesting conditions.

Vesting conditions The conditions that must be satisfied for the counterparty to become entitled to receive cash, other assets or equity instruments of the entity, under a share-based payment arrangement. Vesting conditions include service conditions, which require the other party to complete a specified period of service, and performance conditions, which require specified performance targets to be met (such as a specified increase in the entity's profit over a specified period of time).

Vesting period The period during which all the specified vesting conditions of a share-based payment arrangement are to be satisfied. *(IFRS 2)*

Recognition: the basic principle

An entity should **recognise goods or services received or acquired in a share-based payment transaction when it obtains the goods or as the services are received**. Goods or services received or acquired in a share-based payment transaction **should be recognised as expenses unless they qualify for recognition as assets**. For example, services are normally recognised as expenses (because they are normally rendered immediately), while goods are recognised as assets.

If the goods or services were received or acquired in an **equity-settled** share-based payment transaction the entity should recognise **a corresponding increase in equity** (reserves).

If the goods or services were received or acquired in a **cash-settled** share-based payment transaction the entity should recognise a **liability**.

Equity-settled share-based payment transactions

Measurement

The issue here is how to measure the 'cost' of the goods and services received and the equity instruments (eg, the share options) granted in return.

The general principle in IFRS 2 is that when an entity recognises the goods or services received and the corresponding increase in equity, it should measure these at the **fair value of the goods or services received**. Where the transaction is with **parties other than employees**, there is a rebuttable presumption that the fair value of the goods or services received can be estimated reliably.

If the fair value of the goods or services received cannot be measured reliably, the entity should measure their value by reference to the **fair value of the equity instruments granted**.

Where the transaction is with a party other than an employee fair value should be measured at the date the entity obtains the goods or the counterparty renders service.

Where shares, share options or other equity instruments are granted to **employees** as part of their remuneration package, it is not normally possible to measure directly the services received. For this reason, the entity should measure the **fair value of the employee services received by reference to the fair value of the equity instruments granted**. The fair value of those equity instruments should be measured at **grant date**.

Determining the fair value of equity instruments granted

Where a transaction is measured by reference to the fair value of the equity instruments granted, fair value is based on **market prices** if available, taking into account the terms and conditions upon which those equity instruments were granted.

If market prices are not available, the entity should estimate the fair value of the equity instruments granted using a **valuation technique**, such as an option pricing model.

Transactions in which services are received

The issue here is **when** to recognise the transaction. When equity instruments are granted they may vest immediately, but often the counterparty has to meet specified conditions first. For example, an employee may have to complete a specified period of service. This means that the effect of the transaction normally has to be allocated over more than one accounting period.

If the equity instruments granted **vest immediately**, (ie, the counterparty is not required to complete a specified period of service before becoming unconditionally entitled to the equity instruments) it is presumed that the services have already been received (in the absence of evidence to the contrary). The entity should **recognise the services received in full**, with a corresponding increase in equity, **on the grant date**.

If the equity instruments granted do not vest until the counterparty completes a specified period of service, the entity should account for those services **as they are rendered** by the counterparty during the vesting period. For example if an employee is granted share options on condition that he or she completes three years' service, then the services to be rendered by the employee as consideration for the share options will be received in the future, over that three-year vesting period.

The entity should recognise an amount for the goods or services received during the vesting period based on the **best available estimate** of the **number of equity instruments** expected to vest. It should **revise** that estimate if subsequent information indicates that the number of equity instruments expected to vest differs from previous estimates. On **vesting date**, the entity should revise the estimate to **equal the number of equity instruments that actually vest**.

Once the goods and services received and the corresponding increase in equity have been recognised, the entity should make no subsequent adjustment to total equity after the vesting date.

Example: Equity-settled share-based payment transaction

On 1 January 20X1 an entity grants 100 share options to each of its 400 employees. Each grant is conditional upon the employee working for the entity until 31 December 20X3. The fair value of each share option is $20.

During 20X1 20 employees leave and the entity estimates that 20% of the employees will leave during the three year period.

During 20X2 a further 25 employees leave and the entity now estimates that 25% of its employees will leave during the three year period.

During 20X3 a further 10 employees leave.

What is the remuneration expense that will be recognised in respect of the share-based payment transaction for each of the three years ended 31 December 20X3?

IFRS 2 requires the entity to recognise the remuneration expense, based on the fair value of the share options granted, as the services are received during the three year vesting period.

In 20X1 and 20X2 the entity estimates the number of options expected to vest (by estimating the number of employees likely to leave) and bases the amount that it recognises for the year on this estimate.

In 20X3 it recognises an amount based on the number of options that actually vest. A total of 55 employees left during the three year period and therefore 34,500 options $(400 - 55 \times 100)$ vested.

The amount recognised as an expense for each of the three years is calculated as follows:

		Cumulative expense at year-end $	Expenses for year $
20X1	40,000 × 80% × 20 × 1/3	213,333	213,333
20X2	40,000 × 75% × 20 × 2/3	400,000	186,667
20X3	34,500 × 20	690,000	290,000

Example

On 1 January 20X9 an entity grants 250 share options to each of its 200 employees. The only condition attached to the grant is that the employees should continue to work for the entity until 31 December 20Y2. Five employees leave during the year.

The market price of each option was $12 at 1 January 20X9 and $15 at 31 December 20X9.

How will this transaction be reflected in the financial statements for the year ended 31 December 20X9?

The remuneration expense for the year is based on the fair value of the options granted at the grant date (1 January 20X9). As five of the 200 employees left during the year it is reasonable to assume that 20 employees will leave during the four year vesting period and that therefore 45,000 options (250 × 180) will actually vest.

Therefore the entity recognises a remuneration expense of $135,000 (45,000 × 12 × ¼) in the profit or loss and a corresponding increase in equity of the same amount.

Cash-settled share-based payment transactions

Examples of this type of transaction include:

(a) **Share appreciation rights** granted to employees: the employees become entitled to a future cash payment (rather than an equity instrument), based on the increase in the entity's share price from a specified level over a specified period of time, or

(b) An entity might grant to its employees a right to receive a future cash payment by granting to them a **right to shares that are redeemable**

The basic principle is that the entity measures the goods or services acquired and the liability incurred at the **fair value of the liability**.

The entity should **remeasure** the fair value of the liability **at each reporting date** until the liability is settled **and at the date of settlement**. Any **changes** in fair value are recognised in **profit or loss** for the period.

The entity should recognise the services received, and a liability to pay for those services, **as the employees render service**. For example, if share appreciation rights do not vest until the employees have completed a specified period of service, the entity should recognise the services received and the related liability, over that period.

Example: cash-settled share-based payment transaction

On 1 January 20X1 an entity grants 100 cash share appreciation rights (SARS) to each of its 500 employees, on condition that the employees continue to work for the entity until 31 December 20X3.

During 20X1 35 employees leave. The entity estimates that a further 60 will leave during 20X2 and 20X3.

During 20X2 40 employees leave and the entity estimates that a further 25 will leave during 20X3.

During 20X3 22 employees leave.

At 31 December 20X3 150 employees exercise their SARs. Another 140 employees exercise their SARs at 31 December 20X4 and the remaining 113 employees exercise their SARs at the end of 20X5.

The fair values of the SARs for each year in which a liability exists are shown below, together with the intrinsic values at the dates of exercise.

	Fair value $	Intrinsic value $
20X1	14.40	
20X2	15.50	
20X3	18.20	15.00
20X4	21.40	20.00
20X5		25.00

Now we will calculate the amount to be recognised in profit or loss for each of the five years ended 31 December 20X5 and the liability to be recognised in the statement of financial position at 31 December for each of the five years.

For the three years to the vesting date of 31 December 20X3 the expense is based on the entity's estimate of the number of SARs that will actually vest (as for an equity-settled transaction). However, the fair value of the liability is **re-measured** at each year-end.

The intrinsic value of the SARs at the date of exercise is the amount of cash actually paid.

		Liability at year-end $	$	Expense for year $
20X1	Expected to vest (500 – 95):			
	405 × 100 × 14.40 × 1/3	194,400		194,400
20X2	Expected to vest (500 – 100):			
	400 × 100 × 15.50 × 2/3	413,333		218,933
20X3	Exercised:			
	150 ×100 × 15.00		225,000	
	Not yet exercised (500 – 97 – 150):			
	253 × 100 × 18.20	460,460	47,127	
				272,127
20X4	Exercised:			
	140 × 100 × 20.00		280,000	
	Not yet exercised (253 – 140):			
	113 × 100 × 21.40	241,820	(218,640)	
				61,360
20X5	Exercised:			
	113 × 100 × 25.00		282,500	
		Nil	(241,820)	
				40,680
				787,500

Transactions which either the entity or the other party has a choice of settling in cash or by issuing equity instruments.

If the entity has incurred a liability to settle in cash or other assets it should account for the transaction as a cash-settled share-based payment transaction.

If no such liability has been incurred the entity should account for the transaction as an equity-settled share-based payment transaction.

2 Deferred tax implications

An entity may receive a tax deduction that differs from related cumulative remuneration expense, and may arise in a later accounting period.

Eg: an entity recognises an expense for share options granted under IFRS 2, but does not receive a tax deduction until the options are exercised and receives the tax deduction at the share price on the exercise date.

Measurement

The deferred tax asset temporary difference is measured as:

Carrying amount of share-based payment expense	0
Less: tax base of share-based payment expense	
(estimated amount tax authorities will permit as a deduction in	
future periods, based on year end information))	(X)
Temporary difference	(X)
Deferred tax asset at X%	X

If the amount of the tax deduction (or estimated future tax deduction) exceeds the amount of the related cumulative remuneration expense, this indicates that the tax deduction relates also to an equity item.

The excess is therefore recognised directly in equity.

Example: Deferred tax implications of share-based payment

On 1 January 20X2, a company granted 5,000 share options to an employee vesting two years later on 31 December 20X3. The fair value of each option measured at the grant date was $3.

Tax law in the jurisdiction in which the entity operates allows a tax deduction of the intrinsic value of the options on exercise. The intrinsic value of the share options was $1.20 at 31 December 20X2 and $3.40 at 31 December 20X3 on which date the options were exercised.

We will assume a tax rate of 30%.

The deferred tax accounting treatment of the above transaction at 31 December 20X2, 31 December 20X3 (before exercise), and on exercise will be:

	31/12/20X2	31/12/20X3 before exercise
	$	$
Carrying amount of share-based payment expense	0	0
Less: Tax base of share-based payment expense		
(5,000 × $1.2 × ½)/(5,000 × $3.40)	(3,000)	(17,000)
Temporary difference	(3,000)	(17,000)
Deferred tax asset @ 30%	900	5,100
Deferred tax (Cr I/S) (5,100 – 900 – (Working) 600)	900	3,600
Deferred tax (Cr Equity) (Working)	0	600

On exercise, the deferred tax asset is replaced by a current tax one. The double entry is:

Debit deferred tax (I/S)	4,500	
Debit deferred tax (equity)	600	reversal
Credit deferred tax asset	5,100	
Debit current tax asset	5,100	
Credit current tax (I/S)	4,500	
Credit current tax (equity)	600	

Working

Accounting expense recognised		
(5,000 × $3 × ½)/(5,000 × $3)	7,500	15,000
Tax deduction	(3,000)	(17,000)
Excess temporary difference	0	(2,000)
Excess deferred tax asset to equity @ 30%	0	600

3 Recent developments

Amendment to IFRS 2

The ED *Amendment to IFRS 2 Share-based payment: vesting conditions and cancellations* was issued in January 2008.

IFRS 2 was amended to define vesting conditions and clarify the accounting treatment of cancellations by parties other than the entity. The amendment restricts vesting conditions to service conditions and performance conditions.

The amendment additionally requires cancellations by the employee to be treated in the same way as cancellations by the employer, resulting in an **accelerated charge to profit or loss of the unamortised balance of the options granted**.

Proposed amendment to IFRS 2

In December 2007, the IASB issued an ED of an amendment to IFRS 2 Share-based payment – Group cash-settled share-based payment transactions.

The proposed amendment gives guidance on how a group entity that receives goods or services from its suppliers (including employees) should account for the following arrangements:

(a) **Arrangement 1** – the entity's suppliers will receive cash payments that are linked to the price of the equity instruments of the entity.

(b) **Arrangement 2** – the entity's suppliers will receive cash payments that are linked to the price of the equity instruments of the entity's parent.

Under either arrangement, the entity's parent has an obligation to make the required cash payments to the entity's suppliers. The entity itself does not have any obligation to make such payments.

The proposed amendment to IFRS 2 clarifies that **IFRS 2 applies to arrangements such as those described above** even if the entity that receives goods or services from its suppliers has no obligation to make the required share-based cash payments.

Employee benefits

22

1 IAS 19: Employee benefits

IAS 19 (revised) *Employee benefits* replaced the previous IAS 19 *Retirement benefit costs*. The new standard covers **all employee benefit costs**, except share-based payment, not only retirement benefit (pension) costs. Before we look at IAS 19, we should consider the nature of employee benefit costs and why there is an accounting problem which must be addressed by a standard.

When a company or other entity employs a new worker, that worker will be offered a **package of pay and benefits**. Some of these will be short-term and the employee will receive the benefit at about the same time as he or she earns it, for example basic pay, overtime etc. Other employee benefits are **deferred**, however, the main example being retirement benefits (ie a pension).

The cost of these deferred employee benefits to the employer can be viewed in various ways. They could be described as **deferred salary** to the employee. Alternatively, they are a **deduction** from the employee's true gross salary, used as a tax-efficient means of saving. In some countries, tax efficiency arises on retirement benefit contributions because they are not taxed on the employee, but they are allowed as a deduction from taxable profits of the employer.

Accounting for employee benefit costs

Accounting for **short-term employee benefit costs** tends to be quite straightforward, because they are simply recognised as an expense in the employer's financial statements of the current period.

Accounting for the cost of **deferred employee benefits** is much more difficult. This is because of the large amounts involved, as well as the long time scale, complicated estimates and uncertainties. In the past, entities accounted for these benefits simply by charging the income statements of the employing entity on the basis of actual payments made. This led to substantial variations in reported profits of these entities and disclosure of information on these costs was usually sparse.

IAS 19 is intended to prescribe the following.

(a)   **When** the cost of employee benefits should be **recognised as a liability or an expense**

(b)   The **amount** of the liability or expense that should be recognised

As a basic rule, the standard states the following.

(a)   A **liability** should be recognised when an employee has provided a service in exchange for benefits to be received by the employee at some time in the future.

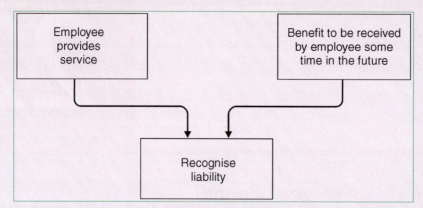

(b)   An **expense** should be recognised when the entity enjoys the economic benefits from a service provided by an employee regardless of when the employee received or will receive the benefits from providing the service.

The basic problem is therefore fairly straightforward. An entity will often enjoy the **economic benefits** from the services provided by its employees in advance of the employees receiving all the employment benefits from the work they have done, for example they will not receive pension benefits until after they retire.

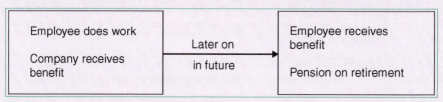

Categories of employee benefits

The standard recognises four categories of employee benefits, and proposes a different accounting treatment for each. These four categories are as follows.

1   **Short-term benefits** including:

- Wages and salaries
- Social security contributions
- Paid annual leave
- Paid sick leave
- Paid maternity/paternity leave
- Profit shares and bonuses paid within 12 months of the year end
- Paid jury service
- Paid military service
- Non-monetary benefits, eg medical care, cars, free goods

2   **Post-employment benefits**, eg pensions and post-employment medical care

3   **Other long-term benefits**, eg profit shares, bonuses or deferred compensation payable later than 12 months after the year end, sabbatical leave, long-service benefits

4   **Termination benefits**, eg early retirement payments and redundancy payments

Benefits may be paid to the employees themselves, to their dependants (spouses, children, etc) or to third parties.

Definitions

Employee benefits are all forms of consideration given by an entity in exchange for service rendered by employees.

Short-term employee benefits are employee benefits (other than termination benefits) which fall due wholly within twelve months after the end of the period in which the employees render the related service.

Post-employment benefits are employee benefits (other than termination benefits) which are payable after the completion of employment.

Post-employment benefit plans are formal or informal arrangements under which an entity provides post-employment benefits for one or more employees.

Defined contribution plans are post-employment benefit plans under which an entity pays fixed contributions into a separate entity (a fund) and will have no legal or constructive obligation to pay further contributions if the fund does not hold sufficient assets to pay all employee benefits relating to employee service in the current and prior periods.

Defined benefit plans are post-employment benefit plans other than defined contribution plans.

Multi-employer plans are defined contribution plans (other than state plans) or defined benefit plans (other than state plans) that:

(a) pool the assets contributed by various entities that are not under common control, and

(b) use those assets to provide benefits to employees of more than one entity, on the basis that contribution and benefit levels are determined without regard to the identity of the entity that employs the employees concerned.

Other long-term employee benefits are employee benefits (other than post-employment benefits and termination benefits) which do not fall due wholly within twelve months after the end of the period in which the employees render the related service.

Termination benefits are employee benefits payable as a result of either:

(a) an entity's decision to terminate an employee's employment before the normal retirement date, or

(b) an employee's decision to accept voluntary redundancy in exchange for those benefits.

Vested employee benefits are employee benefits that are not conditional on future employment.

The **present value of a defined benefit** obligation is the present value, without deducting any plan assets, of expected future payments required to settle the obligation resulting from employee service in the current and prior periods.

Current service cost is the increase in the present value of the defined benefit obligation resulting from employee service in the current period.

Interest cost is the increase during a period in the present value of a defined benefit obligation which arises because the benefits are one period closer to settlement.

Plan assets comprise:

(a) Assets held by a long-term employee benefit fund; and
(b) Qualifying insurance policies

The **return on plan assets** is interest, dividends and other revenue derived from the plan assets, together with realised and unrealised gains or losses on the plan assets, less any cost of administering the plan and loess any tax payable by the plan itself.

Actuarial gains and losses comprise:

(a) Experience adjustments (the effects of differences between the previous actuarial assumptions and what has actually occurred), and
(b) The effects of changes in actuarial assumptions.

Past service cost is the increase in the present value of the defined benefit obligation for employee service in prior periods, resulting in the current period from the introduction of, or changes to, post-employment benefits or other long-term employee benefits. Past service cost may be either positive (where benefits are introduced or improved) or negative (where existing benefits are reduced).

(IAS 19)

Asset ceiling test

The revisions to IAS 19 in May 2002 seek to prevent what the IASB regards as a 'counter-intuitive' result produced by the interaction of two aspects of the existing IAS 19.

(a) Permission to defer recognition of actuarial gains and losses
(b) Imposition of an upper limit on the amount that can be recognised as an asset (the asset ceiling)

The issue affects only those entities that have, at the beginning or end of the accounting period, a surplus in a defined benefit plan that, based on the current terms of the plan, the entity cannot fully recover through refunds or reductions in future contributions.

The issue is the impact of the wording of the asset ceiling.

(a) Sometimes a gain is recognised when a pension plan is in surplus only because of the deferring and amortising of an actuarial loss or added past service cost in the current period.
(b) Conversely, a loss may be recognised because of a deferral of actuarial gains.

The revisions to IAS 19 introduce a limited amendment that would prevent gains (losses) from being recognised solely as a result of past service cost or actuarial losses (gains) arising in the period. No change is currently proposed to the general approach of allowing deferral of actuarial gains and losses. During its deliberations on the amendments to IAS 19, the IASB concluded that there were further conceptual and practical problems with these provisions. The IASB intends to conduct a comprehensive review of these aspects of IAS 19 as part of its work on convergence of accounting standards across the world.

2 Short-term employee benefits

The rules for short-term benefits are essentially an application of **basic accounting principles and practice**.

(a) **Unpaid short-term employee benefits** as at the end of an accounting period should be recognised as an accrued expense. Any short-term benefits **paid in advance** should be recognised as a prepayment (to the extent that it will lead to, eg a reduction in future payments or a cash refund).

(b) The **cost of short-term employee benefits** should be recognised as an **expense** in the period when the economic benefit is given, as employment costs (except insofar as employment costs may be included within the cost of an asset, eg property, plant and equipment).

Short-term absences

There may be **short-term accumulating compensated absences**. These are absences for which an employee is paid, and if the employee's entitlement has not been used up at the end of the period, they are carried forward to the next period. An example is paid holiday leave, where any unused holidays in one year are carried forward to the next year. The cost of the benefits of such absences should be **charged as an expense** as the employees render service that increases their entitlement to future compensated absences.

There may be **short-term non-accumulating compensated absences**. These are absences for which an employee is paid when they occur, but an **entitlement to the absences does not accumulate**. The employee can be absent, and be paid, but only if and when the circumstances arise. Examples are maternity/paternity pay, (in most cases) sick pay, and paid absence for jury service.

Profit sharing or bonus plans

Profit shares or bonuses payable within 12 months after the end of the accounting period should be recognised as an expected cost when the entity has a **present obligation to pay** it, ie when the employer has no real option but to pay it. This will usually be when the employer recognises the profit or other performance achievement to which the profit share or bonus relates.

3 Post-employment benefits

Many employers provide post-employment benefits for their employees after they have stopped working. **Pension schemes** are the most obvious example, but an employer might provide post-employment death benefits to the dependants of former employees, or post-employment medical care.

Post-employment benefit schemes are often referred to as '**plans**'. The 'plan' receives regular contributions from the employer (and sometimes from current employees as well) and the money is invested in assets, such as stocks and shares and other investments. The post-employment benefits are paid out of the income from the plan assets (dividends, interest) or from money from the sale of some plan assets.

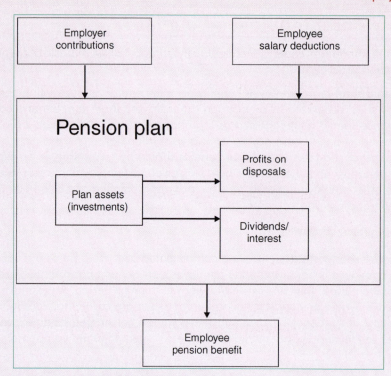

There are two types or categories of post-employment benefit plan, as given in the definitions in Section 1 above.

(a)   **Defined contribution plans**. With such plans, the employer (and possibly current employees too) pay regular contributions into the plan of a given or 'defined' amount each year. The contributions are invested, and the size of the post-employment benefits paid to former employees depends on how well or how badly the plan's investments perform. If the investments perform well, the plan will be able to afford higher benefits than if the investments performed less well.

(b)   **Defined benefit plans**. These are defined very simply as 'other than defined contribution plans'. But behind that simple definition is a complex and expensive arrangement from which many companies are now seeking to extricate themselves. With these plans, the size of the post-employment benefits is determined in advance, ie the benefits are 'defined'. The employer (and possibly current employees too) pay contributions into the plan, and the contributions are invested. The size of the contributions is set at an amount that is expected to earn enough investment returns to meet the obligation to pay the post-employment benefits. If, however, it becomes apparent that the assets in the fund are insufficient, the employer will be required to make additional contributions into the plan to make up the expected shortfall. On the other hand, if the fund's assets appear to be larger than they need to be, and in excess of what is required to pay the post-employment benefits, the employer may be allowed to take a 'contribution holiday' (ie stop paying in contributions for a while).

It is important to make a clear distinction between the following.

(a)   **Funding** a defined benefit plan, ie paying contributions into the plan
(b)   **Accounting** for the cost of funding a defined benefit plan

Before we examine accounting for both these types of scheme, we need to mention a couple of other issues addressed by the standard.

Multi-employer plans

These were defined above. IAS 19 requires an entity to **classify** such a plan as a defined contribution plan or a defined benefit plan, depending on its terms (including any constructive obligation beyond those terms).

For a multi-employer plan that is a **defined benefit plan**, the entity should account for its proportionate share of the defined benefit obligation, plan assets and cost associated with the plan in the same way as for any other defined benefit plan and make full disclosure.

When there is **insufficient information** to use defined benefit accounting, then the multi-employer plan should be accounted for as a defined contribution plan and additional disclosures made (that the plan is in fact a defined benefit plan and information about any known surplus or deficit).

Insurance benefits

Insurance premiums paid by an employer to fund an employee post-employment benefit plan should be accounted for as **defined contributions** to the plan, unless the employer, has a legal or constructive obligation to pay the employee benefits directly when they fall due, or to make further payments in the event that the insurance company does not pay all the post-employment benefits (relating to service given in prior years and the current period) for which insurance has been paid.

Examples: Insurance benefits

For example, Employer A pays insurance premiums to fund post-employment medical care for former employees. It has no obligation beyond paying the annual insurance premiums. The premium paid each year should be accounted for as a defined contribution.

Employer B similarly pays insurance premiums for the same purpose, but retains the liability to pay for the medical benefits itself. In the case of Employer B, the rights under the insurance policy should be recognised as an asset, and it should account for the obligation to employees as a liability as if there were no insurance policy.

4 Defined contribution plans

Accounting for payments into defined contribution plans is straightforward.

(a)   The **obligation** is determined by the amount paid into the plan in each period.
(b)   There are no actuarial assumptions to make.
(c)   If the obligation is settled in the current period (or at least no later than 12 months after the end of the current period) there is no **requirement for discounting**.

IAS 19 requires the following.

(a)   **Contributions** to a defined contribution plan should be recognised as an **expense** in the period they are payable (except to the extent that labour costs may be included within the cost of assets).
(b)   Any liability for **unpaid contributions** that are due as at the end of the period should be recognised as a **liability** (accrued expense).

(c)   Any **excess contributions** paid should be recognised as an asset (prepaid expense), but only to the extent that the prepayment will lead to, eg a reduction in future payments or a cash refund.

In the (unusual) situation where contributions to a defined contribution plan do not fall due entirely within 12 months after the end of the period in which the employees performed the related service, then these should be **discounted**. The discount rate to be used is discussed below.

Disclosure requirements

(a)   A **description** of the plan

(b)   The amount recognised as an **expense** in the period

5 Defined benefit plans: recognition and measurement

Accounting for defined benefit plans is much more complex. The complexity of accounting for defined benefit plans stems largely from the following factors.

(a)   The future benefits (arising from employee service in the current or prior years) cannot be estimated exactly, but whatever they are, the employer will have to pay them, and the liability should therefore be recognised now. To estimate these future obligations, it is necessary to use actuarial assumptions.

(b)   The obligations payable in future years should be valued, by discounting, on a present value basis. This is because the obligations may be settled in many years' time.

(c)   If actuarial assumptions change, the amount of required contributions to the fund will change, and there may be actuarial gains or losses. A contribution into a fund in any period is not necessarily the total for that period, due to actuarial gains or losses.

Most of the definitions given in the standard (shown in Section 1) are to do with defined benefit plans.

Outline of the method

Step 1   Actuarial assumptions should be used to make a reliable estimate of the amount of future benefits employees have earned from service in relation to the current and prior years. Assumptions include, for example, assumptions about employee turnover, mortality rates, future increases in salaries (if these will affect the eventual size of future benefits such as pension payments).

Step 2   These future benefits should be attributed to service performed by employees in the current period, and in prior periods, using the Projected Unit Credit Method. This gives a total present value of future benefit obligations arising from past and current periods of service.

Step 3   The fair value of any plan assets should be established.

Step 4   The size of any actuarial gains or losses should be determined, and the amount of these that will be recognised.

Step 5   If the benefits payable under the plan have been improved, the extra cost arising from past service should be determined.

Step 6 If the benefits payable under the plan have been reduced or cancelled, the resulting gain should be determined.

Constructive obligation

IAS 19 makes it very clear that it is not only its legal obligation under the formal terms of a defined benefit plan that an entity must account for, but also any constructive obligation that it may have. A **constructive obligation**, which will arise from the entity's informal practices, exists when the entity has no realistic alternative but to pay employee benefits, for example if any change in the informal practices would cause unacceptable damage to employee relationships.

We will look at all the steps in due course, but we will begin by covering the mathematics involved in the Projected Unit Credit Method.

The Projected Unit Credit Method

With this method, it is assumed that each period of service by an employee gives rise to an **additional unit of future benefits**. The present value of that unit of future benefits can be calculated, and attributed to the period in which the service is given. The units, each measured separately, build up to the overall obligation. The accumulated present value of (discounted) future benefits will incur interest over time, and an interest expense should be recognised.

In practice, the mathematics will be complex. Here is a simplified example, using figures rounded to whole numbers.

Example: Projected unit credit method

An employer pays a lump sum to employees when they retire. The lump sum is equal to 1% of their salary in the final year of service, for every year of service they have given.

(a) An employee is expected to work for 5 years (actuarial assumption)
(b) His salary is expected to rise by 8% pa (actuarial assumption)
(c) His salary in 20X1 is $10,000
(d) The discount rate applied is 10% pa

What are the amounts chargeable to each of years 20X1 to 20X5 and the closing obligation each year, assuming no change in actuarial assumptions?

Since his salary in 20X1 is $10,000, his salary in 20X5 is expected to be $13,605. His lump sum entitlement is therefore expected to be $136 for each year's service, ie $680 in total.

Using the Projected Unit Credit Method, and assuming that the actuarial assumptions do not change over any of 20X1 to 20X5, and that the employees do leave at the end of 20X5, the calculations are as follows.

Future benefit attributable	20X1	20X2	20X3	20X4	20X5
	$	$	$	$	$
Prior years	0	136	272	408	544
Current year					
(1% of final salary)	136	136	136	136	136
Prior and current years total	136	272	408	544	680

The future benefit builds up to $680 over the five years, at the end of which the employee is expected to leave and the benefit is payable.

These figures, however, are not discounted. The benefit attributable to the current year should be discounted, in this example at 10%, from the end of 20X5.

	20X1	20X2	20X3	20X4	20X5
	$	$	$	$	$
Opening obligation (note 1)	–	93	204	336	494
Interest (note 2)	–	9	20	34	50*
Current service cost (note 3)	93	102	112	124	136
Closing obligation (note 4)	93	204	336	494	680

* There is a rounding error of $1 in the calculations. To make the total add up to $680, the interest of $49.4 has therefore been rounded up to $50 in compensation.

Notes

1   The opening obligation is the closing obligation of the previous period, brought forward.
2   Interest is charged on this opening obligation to the current year.
3   The current service cost is the future obligation attributed to the current period (in this example $136 in each year).
4   The closing obligation is the total of the opening obligation brought forward, the interest charge on that amount and the current year service cost.
5   The calculations in the example above assume that actuarial forecasts are exactly correct. If these were to prove incorrect (which is likely in practice), there could be an adjustment to make, resulting in an actuarial gain or an actuarial loss.

Interest cost

The interest cost in the income statement is the **present value of the defined benefit obligation** as at the start of the year **multiplied by the discount rate**.

Note that the interest charge is not the opening statement of financial position liability multiplied by the discount rate, because the liability is stated after deducting the market value of the plan assets and after making certain other adjustments, for example for actuarial gains or losses. Interest is the obligation multiplied by the discount rate.

The statement of financial position

In the statement of financial position, the amount recognised as a **defined benefit liability** (which may be a negative amount, ie an asset) should be the total of the following.

(a)   The **present value of the defined obligation** at the reporting date, **plus**
(b)   Any **actuarial gains** or minus any actuarial losses that have not yet been recognised, **minus**
(c)   Any **past service cost** not yet recognised (if any), **minus**
(d)   The **fair value of the assets of the plan** as at the reporting date (if there are any) out of which the future obligations to current and past employees will be directly settled

If this total is a **negative amount**, there is a statement of financial position asset and this should be shown in the statement of financial position as the **lower** of (a) and (b) below.

(a)   The figure as calculated above

(b)   The total of the present values of:
    (i)   Any unrecognised actuarial losses and past service costs
    (ii)   Any refunds expected from the plan
    (iii) Any reductions in future contributions to the plan because of the surplus

The determination of a discount rate is covered below.

The statement of comprehensive income

The **expense** that should be recognised in the income statement for post-employment benefits in a defined benefit plan is the total of the following.

(a)   The **current service cost**
(b)   **Interest**
(c)   The **expected return on any plan assets**
(d)   The actuarial gains or losses, to the extent that they are recognised
(e)   **Past service cost** to the extent that it is recognised
(f)   The effect of any **curtailments** or **settlements**

Attributing benefit to periods of service

Consider a situation where a defined benefit plan provides for annual pensions for former employees on retirement. The size of the pension is 2.5% of the employee's salary in his/her final year, for each full year of service. The pension is payable from the age of 65.

The post-employment benefit for each employee is an annual pension of 2.5% of his/her final year's salary for every full year of service. This annual payment obligation should first be converted to a present 'lump sum' value as at the retirement date, using actuarial assumptions. Having established an obligation as at the expected retirement date, the **current service cost** is calculated as the present value of that obligation, ie the present value of monthly pension payments of 2.5% of final salary, multiplied by the number of years of service up to the reporting date.

For example, if an employee is expected to earn $10,000 in his final year of employment, and is expected to live for 15 years after retirement, the benefit payable for each year of employment would be calculated as the discounted value, as at retirement date, of $250 per annum for 15 years. This should then be converted to a present value (as at the reporting date) to determine the current service cost for the year for that employee.

Probabilities should be taken into consideration in the calculations. Suppose that a benefit of $1,000 for every year of service is payable to employees when they retire at the age of 60, provided that they remain with the employer until they retire (ie that they don't leave to work for someone else). Suppose also that an employee joins the firm at the age of 40, with 20 years to work to retirement.

The benefit attributable to each year of service is $1,000 **multiplied by the probability** that the employee will remain with the employer until he/she is 60. Since the benefit is payable at retirement as a lump sum, it should be discounted to a present value as at the reporting date to determine the current service cost for a given year. The obligation should be calculated as the present value of $40,000 (40 years × $1,000) **multiplied by the same probability**.

No added obligations arise **after all significant post-employment benefits have vested**; in other words, no extra post-benefit obligations arise after an employee has already done everything necessary to qualify in full for the post-employment benefit. Suppose for example that employees have an entitlement to a lump sum payment on retirement of $2,000 for every year they have worked, up to a maximum of 10 years, ie a maximum lump sum payment of $20,000. The benefit vests after 10 years.

In accounting for this **lump sum benefit on retirement**, a benefit of $2,000 should be attributed to each of the first ten years of an employee's service. The current service cost in each of the ten years should be the present value of $2,000. If an employee has 25 years to go to retirement from the time he/she joins the firm, there should be a service cost in each of the first ten years, and none in the 15 years thereafter (other than the interest cost on the obligation).

Example

Under X Co's plan, all employees are paid a lump sum retirement benefit of $100,000. They must be still employed aged 55 after 20 years' service, or still employed at the age of 65, no matter what their length of service.

How should this benefit should be attributed to service periods?

There are three aspects to consider.

(a) In the case of those employees joining before age 35, service first leads to benefits under this plan at the age of 35, because an employee could leave at the age of 30 and return at the age of 33, with no effect on the amount/timing of benefits. In addition, service beyond age 55 will lead to no further benefits. Therefore, for these employees X Co should allocate $100,000 ÷ 20 = $5,000 to each year between the ages of 35 and 55.

(b) In the case of employees joining between the ages of 35 and 45, service beyond 20 years will lead to no further benefit. For these employees, X Co should allocate $100,000 ÷ 20 = $5,000 to each of the first 20 years.

(c) Employees joining at 55 exactly will receive no further benefit past 65, so X Co should allocate $100,000 ÷ 10 = $10,000 to each of the first 10 years.

The current service cost and the present value of the obligation for all employees reflect the probability that the employee may not complete the necessary period of service.

Actuarial assumptions

Actuarial assumptions are needed **to estimate the size of the future (post-employment) benefits** that will be payable under a defined benefits scheme. The main categories of actuarial assumptions are as follows.

Demographic assumptions	Financial assumptions
• Mortality rates before and after retirement	• Discount rates to apply
• Rate of employee turnover	• Expected return on plan assets
• Early retirement	• Future salary levels (allowing for seniority and promotion as well as inflation)
• Claim rates under medical plans for former employees	• Future rate of increase in medical costs (not just inflationary cost rises, but also cost rises specific to medical treatments and to medical treatments required given the expectations of longer average life expectancy)

The standard requires actuarial assumptions to be neither too cautious nor too imprudent: they should be '**unbiased**'. They should also be based on '**market expectations**' at the reporting date, over the period during which the obligations will be settled.

The discount rate adopted should be determined by reference to **market yields** (at the reporting date) on high quality fixed-rate corporate bonds. In the absence of a 'deep' market in such bonds, the yields on comparable government bonds should be used as reference instead. The maturity of the corporate bonds that are used to determine a discount rate should have a term to maturity that is consistent with the expected maturity of the post-employment benefit obligations, although a single weighted average discount rate is sufficient.

The guidelines comment that there may be some difficulty in obtaining a **reliable yield for long-term maturities**, say 30 or 40 years from now. This should not, however, be a significant problem: the present value of obligations payable in many years time will be relatively small and unlikely to be a significant proportion of the total defined benefit obligation. The total obligation is therefore unlikely to be sensitive to errors in the assumption about the discount rate for long-term maturities (beyond the maturities of long-term corporate or government bonds).

Actuarial gains or losses

Actuarial gains or losses arise because of the following.

- **Actual events** (eg employee turnover, salary increases) differ from the actuarial assumptions that were made to estimate the defined benefit obligations.
- **Actuarial assumptions are revised** (eg a different discount rate is used, or a different assumption is made about future employee turnover, salary rises, mortality rates, and so on)
- **Actual returns on plan assets** differ from expected returns

Since actuarial assumptions are rarely going to be exact, some actuarial gains or losses are inevitable. The proposed standard suggests that, given the inevitability of actuarial gains or losses, they **should not be recognised unless they appear 'significant'**. They are not sufficient to warrant recognition if they fall within a tolerable range or 'corridor'.

The standard requires the following.

(a) An entity should, as a **general rule**, recognise actuarial gains and losses as an item of income or expense (profit or loss), and as part of the deferred benefit liability (statement of financial position).

(b) However, only a portion of such actuarial gains or losses (as calculated above) should be recognised if the **net cumulative actuarial gains/losses exceed** the *greater* of:

 (i) 10% of the present value of the opening defined benefit obligation (ie before deducting plan assets), and

 (ii) 10% of the fair value of the opening plan assets.

A separate calculation should be made for each defined benefit plan: two or more plans should not be aggregated.

The excess calculated above should be **divided by the expected average remaining working lives of participating employees** to give the portion of actuarial gains and losses to be recognised.

However, IAS 19 allows any systematic method to be adopted if it results in **faster recognition** of actuarial gains and losses. The same basis must be applied to both gains and losses and applied consistently between periods.

Immediate recognition – amendment to IAS 19

In December 2004, the IASB issued an amendment to IAS 19. This allows an entity to **recognise actuarial gains and losses immediately** in the period in which it arises, outside profit and loss. These gains and losses need to be presented in the **statement of comprehensive income** as 'other comprehensive income'. If the entity adopts this approach, it must do so:

*   For all of its defined benefits plans
*   For all of its actuarial gains and losses

This makes IAS 19 more convergent with the UK standard, FRS 17.

In addition, the amendment requires improved disclosures, including many also required by FRS 17, and slightly eases the methods whereby the amounts recognised in the consolidated financial statements have to be allocated to individual group companies for the purposes of their own reporting under IFRSs.

Past service cost

A past service cost arises when an entity either introduces a defined benefits plan or **improves the benefits payable** under an existing plan. As a result, the entity has taken on additional obligations that it has not hitherto provided for. For example, an employer might decide to introduce a medical benefits scheme for former employees. This will create a new defined benefit obligation, that has not yet been provided for. How should this obligation be accounted for?

A past service cost may be in respect of either **current employees or past employees**. IAS 19 has introduced a different accounting treatment for past service costs, according to whether they relate to **current employees or past employees**.

Current employees	Past employees
The **past service cost** should be **recognised** as a **part** of the **defined benefit liability** in the statement of financial position. In the income statement, the past service cost should be **amortised** on a **straight line basis** over the **average period** until the **benefits become vested**.	If the changes affect them, the past service cost should be recognised in full immediately the plan is introduced or improved (ie because they are immediately 'vested'), as part of the defined benefit liability and as an expense (in full) to the financial period.

Example

Y Co operates a pension plan that provides a pension of 2% of final salary for every year of service and the benefits become vested after five years' service. On 1 January 20X6 Y Co improved the pension to 2.5% of final salary for every year of service starting from 1 January 20X2.

At the date of improvement, the present value of the additional benefits for service from

1 January 20X2 to 1 January 20X6 is as follows.

	$m
Employees with more than 5 years' service at 1/1/X6	300
Employees with less than 5 years' service at 1/1/X6	
(average period until vesting = 3 years)	240
	540

What will be the correct accounting treatment for past service costs?

Y Co should recognise $300m immediately, because these benefits are already vested. $240m should be recognised on a straight-line basis over three years from 1 January 20X6.

Plan assets

The contributions into a plan by the employer (and employees) are invested, and the plan builds up assets in the form of stocks and shares, etc. The **fair value of these plan assets** are deducted from the defined benefits obligation, in calculating the liability in the statement of financial position. This makes sense, because the employer is not liable to the defined benefits scheme to the extent that the assets of the fund are sufficient to meet those obligations.

The standard includes the following specific requirements.

(a) The fair value of the plan assets should be **net of any transaction costs** that would be incurred in selling them.
(b) The plan assets should **exclude any contributions** due from the employer but not yet paid.

Return on plan assets

It is also necessary to recognise the distinction between:

(a) The **expected return** on the plan assets, which is an actuarial assumption, and
(b) The **actual return** made by the plan assets in a financial period.

The **expected return** on the plan assets is a component element in the income statement, not the actual returns. The **difference between the expected return and the actual return** may also be included in the income statement, but within the actuarial gains or losses. This difference will only be reported if the actuarial gains or losses are outside the 10% corridor for these gains or losses, otherwise they will not be included in the expense item because they are not regarded as significant.

Example: plan assets

At 1 January 20X2 the fair value of the assets of a defined benefit plan were valued at $1m. Net cumulative actuarial gains and losses were $76,000.

On 31 December 20X2, the plan received contributions from the employer of $490,000 and paid out benefits of $190,000.

After these transactions, the fair value of the plan's assets at 31 December 20X2 were $1.5m. The present value of the defined benefit obligation was $1,479,200 and actuarial losses on the obligation for 20X2 were $6,000.

The reporting entity made the following estimates at 1 January 20X2, based on market prices at that date.

	%
Dividend/interest income (after tax payable by fund)	9.25
Realised and unrealised gains (after tax) on plan assets	2.00
Administration costs	(1.00)
	10.25

The expected and actual return for 20X2 are as follows.

	$
Return on $1m held for 12 months at 10.25%	102,500
Return on $(490,000 – 190,000) = $300,000	
for 6 months at 5% (ie 10.25% annually compounded every 6 months)	15,000
Expected return on plan assets	117,500

	$
Fair value of plan assets at 31/12/X2	1,500,000
Less fair value of plan assets at 1/1/X2	(1,000,000)
Less contributions received	(490,000)
Add benefits paid	190,000
Actual return on plan assets	200,000

Actuarial gain = $(200,000 – 117,500) = $82,500.

∴ Cumulative net unrecognised actuarial gains = $(76,000 + 82,500 – 6,000)
= $152,500.

The limits of the corridor are set at the *greater* of:

(a)   10% × $1,500,000 = $150,000, and
(b)   10% × $1,479,200 = $147,920.

In 20X3 the entity should recognise an actuarial gain of $(152,500 – 150,000) = $2,500, divided by the expected average remaining working life of the relevant employees.

For 20X3, the expected return on plan assets will be based on market expectations at 1/1/X3 for returns over the entire life of the obligation.

The following accounting treatment is required

Statement of comprehensive income	Statement of financial position
In the **statement of comprehensive income**, an expected return on fund assets of $117,500 will be recognised, together with an actuarial gain of $2,500 divided by the expected average remaining useful life of the employees.	In the **statement of financial position**, the defined benefit liability will adjust the defined benefit obligation as at 31 December 20X2. The recognised actuarial gain (ie the gain within the 10% corridor) should be added, and the market value of the plan assets as at that date should be subtracted.

6 Defined benefit plans: other matters

Curtailments and settlements

A **curtailment** occurs when an entity cuts back on the benefits available under a defined benefit scheme, so that there is either a significant reduction in the number of employees eligible for the post-employment benefits (eg because a large number of staff have been made redundant due to a plant closure), or there is a reduction in the post-employment benefits that will be given for the future service of current employees.

A **settlement** occurs either when an employer pays off its post-employment benefit obligations in exchange for making a lump sum payment, or when an employer reduces the size of post-employment benefits payable in the future in respect of **past service**.

A curtailment and settlement might **happen together**, for example when an employer brings a defined benefit plan to an end by settling the obligation with a one-off lump sum payment and then scrapping the plan.

Gains or losses arising from the curtailment or settlement of a defined benefit plan should be **recognised in full in the financial year that they occur**. These gains or losses will comprise the following.

*   Any **change in the present value of the future obligations** of the entity as a result of the curtailment or settlement
*   Any **change in the fair value of the plan assets** as a consequence of the curtailment or settlement
*   Any related **actuarial gains/losses** and **past service cost** that had not previously been recognised

An entity should **remeasure the obligation** (and the related plan assets, if any) using current actuarial assumptions, before determining the effect of a curtailment or settlement.

Example

Z Co discontinues a business segment. Employees of the discontinued segment will earn no further benefits (ie this is a curtailment without a settlement). Using current actuarial assumptions (including current market interest rates and other current market prices) immediately before the curtailment, Z Co had a defined benefit obligation with a net present value of $500,000, plan assets with a fair value of $410,000 and net cumulative unrecognised actuarial gains of $25,000. The entity had first adopted IAS 19 (revised) one year before. This increased the net liability by $50,000, which the entity chose to recognise over five years (this is permitted under the transitional provisions). The curtailment reduces the net present value of the obligation by $50,000 to $450,000.

What is the required treatment for the curtailment?

Of the previously unrecognised actuarial gains and transitional amounts, 10% ($50,000/$500,000) relates to the part of the obligation that was eliminated through the curtailment. Therefore, the effect of the curtailment is as follows.

	Before curtailment	Curtailment gain	After curtailment
	$'000	$'000	$'000
Net present value of obligation	500.0	(50.0)	450.0
Fair value of plan assets	(410.0)	–	(410.0)
	90.0	(50.0)	40.0
Unrecognised actuarial gains	25.0	(2.5)	22.5
Unrecognised transitional amount ($50,000 × 4/5)	(40.0)	4.0	(36.0)
Net liability recognised in statement of financial position	75.0	(48.5)	26.5

Presentation and disclosure

The standard states that an entity **should not offset** an asset relating to one plan against a liability relating to a different plan, unless the entity has a legally enforceable right of offset and intends to use it.

A reporting entity should disclose the following information about post-retirement defined benefit plans.

- **Accounting policy** for recognising actuarial gains and losses
- **General description** of the type of plan
- **Reconciliation** of the assets and liabilities recognised in the statement of financial position, showing the following as a minimum.
  - Present value at the reporting date of defined benefit obligations that are wholly unfunded
  - Present value (before deducting the fair value of plan assets) at the reporting date of defined benefit obligations that are wholly or partly funded
  - Fair value of any plan assets at the reporting date
  - Net actuarial gains or losses not recognised in the statement of financial position
  - Past service cost not yet recognised in the statement of financial position
  - Any amount not recognised as an asset, because of the limit
  - Amounts recognised in the statement of financial position
- Amounts included in the **fair value** of plan assets for:
  - Each category of the reporting entity's own financial instruments, and
  - Any property occupied by, or other assets used by, the reporting entity
- Reconciliation showing the movements during the period in the net liability (or asset) recognised in the **statement of financial position**
- Total expense recognised in the **statement of comprehensive income** for each of the following, and the line item(s) of the statement of comprehensive income in which they are included
  - Current service cost
  - Interest cost
  - Expected return on plan assets
  - Actuarial gains and losses
  - Past service cost
  - Effect of any curtailment or settlement

- Actual return on plan assets
- Principal actuarial assumptions used as at the statement of financial position date, including, where applicable:
  - Discount rates
  - Expected rates of return on any plan assets for the periods presented in the financial statements
  - Expected rates of salary increases (and of changes in an index or other variable specified in the formal or constructive terms of a plan as the basis for future benefit increases
  - Medical cost trend rates
  - Any other material actuarial assumptions used

Disclose each actuarial assumption in **absolute terms** (eg as an absolute percentage) and not just as a margin between different percentages or other variables.

7 Special cases

We have now covered the major parts of IAS 19 (revised), but the standard goes on to discuss certain other matters which we will cover briefly here. The transitional arrangements are quite important due to the **long-term effect** of post-retirement benefits and we will look at these at the end of the section.

Other long-term employment benefits

There may be other long-term employment benefits, in addition to post-employment benefits. These include **bonuses** and **profit shares** payable 12 months or more after the reporting date, and **long-term sabbatical leave**.

The standard requires these benefits to be accounted for **in the same way as post-employment defined benefits**, but with two major differences.

(a) **Actuarial gains or losses** should be recognised in full immediately in the financial year they become apparent, and there should be no 10% corridor.
(b) All **past service cost** for current as well as past employees should be recognised as an expense in full immediately.

There are no specific disclosure requirements with respect to these benefits.

Termination benefits

Termination benefits are benefits to employees arising as a consequence of **termination of their employment**. An example is the payment of a lump sum to an employee who volunteers for early retirement.

The standard recommends that these costs should be recognised in full as a liability and an expense in the financial period when the entity recognises a **demonstrable obligation** to pay those benefits at some time in the future. Evidence of a demonstrable obligation would be a formal plan (eg a plan for voluntary redundancy) drawn up and communicated to the people affected.

If the termination is to take place over 12 months after the reporting date, the termination benefits should be **discounted**. The discount rate should be found as detailed elsewhere in the standard.

Where an offer is made to encourage **voluntary redundancy**, the calculation should be based on the number of employees expected to accept.

8 Other issues and recent developments

Problems with IAS 19

Accounting for employee benefits, particularly retirement benefits, has been seen as problematic in the following respects:

(a) **Income statement (statement of comprehensive income) treatment**. It has been argued that the complexity of the presentation makes the treatment hard to understand and the splitting up of the various components is arbitrary.

(b) **Fair value and volatility**. The fair value of plan assets may be volatile, and values in the statement of financial position may fluctuate. However, not all those fluctuations are recognised in the statement of financial position.

(c) **Fair value and economic reality**. Fair value, normally market value, is used to value plan assets. This may not reflect economic reality, because fair values fluctuate in the short term, while pension scheme assets and liabilities are held for the long term. It could be argued that plan assets should be valued on an actuarial basis instead.

(d) **Problems in determining the discount rate used in measuring the defined benefit obligation**. Guidance is contradictory.

Discussion Paper

In March 2008, the IASB issued a Discussion Paper *Preliminary Views on Amendments to IAS 19 Employee Benefits*. The purpose of the Discussion Paper is to improve accounting in the short-term for employee benefits in the light of criticisms of the current IAS 19 by users and preparers of financial statements, including the US SEC and the EU's European Financial Reporting Advisory Group (that approves IFRS for use in the EU). In the long term, the IASB intends to produce a common IASB-FASB standard, but recognises that this will take many years to complete.

Because the Paper is a short-term measure, its scope is limited to the following areas.

(a) Deferred recognition of some gains and losses arising from defined benefit plans
(b) Presentation of changes in value of the defined benefit obligation and assets
(c) Accounting for benefits that are based on contributions and a promised return
(d) Accounting for benefit promises with a 'higher of' option.

However, the IASB recognises that the scope could be expanded to include items such as:

(a) **Recognition of the obligation based on the 'benefit' formula**. This current approach means that unvested benefits are recognised as a liability which is inconsistent with other IFRSs.

(b) **Measurement of the obligation**. The 'projected unit credit method' (as defined before) is used which is based on expected benefits (including salary increases). Alternative approaches include accumulated benefit, projected benefit, fair value and settlement value.

(c) **Presenting of a net defined benefit obligation**. Defined benefit plan assets and liabilities are currently presented net on the grounds that the fund is not controlled (which would require consolidation of the fund).

(d) **Multi-employer plans**. Current accounting is normally for the entity's proportionate share of the obligation, plan assets and costs as for a single-employer plan, but an exemption is currently provided where sufficient information is not available, and defined contribution accounting can be used instead. Should the exemption be removed?

Preliminary discussions

(a) **Deferred recognition**

(i) This (ie the corridor method) is to be eliminated. Actuarial gains and losses to be recognised in the period incurred.

(ii) The actual return on assets would not be divided into expected return and actuarial gain/loss.

(iii) Past service costs would be recognised in the period of plan amendment.

(b) **Presentation of changes in value of the defined benefit obligation and assets**
Possible options are as follows:

(i) Show all in profit or loss in the period incurred

(ii) Include all costs of service in profit or loss, all other changes in other comprehensive income

(iii) Re-measurements arising from changes in financial assumptions (that is, changes in the discount rate for liabilities and changes in plan assets) in other comprehensive income, all other changes in profit or loss.

(c) **Benefits based on contributions plus a promised return on assets**

(i) Arguably these are not faithfully represented under current approach

(ii) It is proposed to measure the liability for contribution-based promises at fair value (as a separate category; as consideration of the projected unit credit method approach to measuring the defined benefit liability itself deferred to a later date)

(iii) Changes are to be disaggregated into a service cost and other value changes (but both recognised in profit or loss).

(d) **Benefit promises with a 'higher of' option**

(i) These occur where a plan member will receive the higher of a defined benefit pension or contributions plus a promised return on assets.

(ii) In substance there is an embedded option/guarantee.

(iii) The liability may be underestimated under the current IAS 19 approach.

(iv) It is proposed to separate out the 'higher of' option and separately measure it at fair value assuming the terms of the benefit promise do not change (with all changes in the option value recognised in profit or loss).

Exposure draft

Following review of comments received on the Discussion Paper, the IASB aims to publish an Exposure Draft on recognition and presentation of changes in the defined benefit obligation and in plan assets and disclosures early in 2010. A final standard is expected in the first half of 2011.

Part
D

Specialised standards

1 Foreign currency

If a company trades overseas, it will buy or sell assets in **foreign currencies**. For example, an Indian company might buy materials from Canada, and pay for them in US dollars, and then sell its finished goods in Germany, receiving payment in Euros, or perhaps in some other currency. If the company owes money in a foreign currency at the end of the accounting year, or holds assets which were bought in a foreign currency, those liabilities or assets must be translated into the local currency (in this text $), in order to be shown in the books of account.

A company might have a subsidiary abroad (ie a foreign entity that it owns), and the subsidiary will trade in its own local currency. The subsidiary will keep books of account and prepare its annual accounts in its own currency. However, at the year end, the holding company must 'consolidate' the results of the overseas subsidiary into its group accounts, so that somehow, the assets and liabilities and the **annual profits of the subsidiary must be translated from the foreign currency into $.**

If foreign currency exchange rates remained constant, there would be no accounting problem. As you will be aware, however, foreign exchange rates are continually changing, and it is not inconceivable for example, that the rate of exchange between the Polish zloty and sterling might be Z6.2 to £1 at the start of the accounting year, and Z5.6 to £1 at the end of the year (in this example, a 10% increase in the relative strength of the zloty).

There are two distinct types of foreign currency transaction, **conversion and translation**.

Conversion gains and losses

Conversion is the process of exchanging amounts of one foreign currency for another. For example, suppose a local company buys a large consignment of goods from a supplier in Argentina. The order is placed on 1 May and the agreed price is 124,250 pesos. At the time of delivery the rate of foreign exchange was 3.50 pesos to $1. The local company would record the amount owed in its books as follows.

DEBIT	Inventory account (124,250 ÷ 3.5)	$35,500	
CREDIT	Payables account		$35,500

When the local company comes to pay the supplier, it needs to obtain some foreign currency. By this time, however, if the rate of exchange has altered to 3.55 pesos to $1, the cost of raising 124,250 pesos would be (÷ 3.55) $35,000. The company would need to spend only $35,000 to settle a debt for inventories 'costing' $35,500. Since it would be administratively difficult to alter the value of the inventories in the company's books of account, it is more appropriate to record a profit on conversion of $500.

DEBIT	Payables account	$35,500	
CREDIT	Cash		$35,000
CREDIT	Profit on conversion		$500

Profits (or losses) on conversion would be included in the income statement for the year in which conversion (whether payment or receipt) takes place.

Suppose that another home company sells goods to a Chinese company, and it is agreed that payment should be made in Chinese Yuan at a price of Y116,000. We will further assume that the exchange rate at the time of sale is Y10.74 to $1, but when the debt is eventually paid, the rate has altered to Y10.79 to $1. The company would record the sale as follows.

| DEBIT | Receivables account (116,000 ÷ 10.74) | $10,800 | |
| CREDIT | Sales account | | $10,800 |

When the Y116,000 are paid, the local company will convert them into $, to obtain (÷ 10.79) $10,750. In this example, there has been a loss on conversion of $50 which will be written off to the income statement:

DEBIT	Cash	$10,750	
DEBIT	Loss on conversion	$50	
CREDIT	Payables account		$10,800

There are **no accounting difficulties** concerned with foreign currency conversion gains or losses, and the procedures described above are uncontroversial.

Translation

Foreign currency translation, as distinct from conversion, does not involve the act of exchanging one currency for another. **Translation is required at the end of an accounting period when a company still holds assets or liabilities in its statement of financial position which were obtained or incurred in a foreign currency.**

These assets or liabilities might consist of any of the following.

(a) An individual home company holding individual **assets** or **liabilities** originating in a foreign currency 'deal'.

(b) An individual home company with a separate **branch** of the business operating abroad which keeps its own books of account in the local currency.

(c) A home company which wishes to consolidate the **results of a foreign subsidiary**.

There has been great **uncertainty** about the method which should be used to translate the following.

- Value of assets and liabilities from a foreign currency into $ for the year end statement of financial position
- Profits of an independent foreign branch or subsidiary into $ for the annual statement of comprehensive income

Suppose, for example, that an Albanian subsidiary purchases a piece of property for Leks 2,100,000 on 31 December 20X7. The rate of exchange at this time was L70 to $1. During 20X8, the subsidiary charged depreciation on the building of L16,800, so that at 31 December 20X8, the subsidiary recorded the asset as follows.

	L
Property at cost	2,100,000
Less accumulated depreciation	(16,800)
Carrying amount	2,083,200

At this date, the rate of exchange has changed to L60 to $1.

The local holding company must translate the asset's value into $, but there is a choice of exchange rates.

(a) Should the rate of exchange for translation be the rate which existed at the date of purchase, which would give a net book value of 2,083,200 ÷ 70 = $29,760?

(b) Should the rate of exchange for translation be the rate existing at the end of 20X8 (the closing rate of L60 to $1)? This would give a net book value of $34,720.

Similarly, should depreciation be charged in the group income statement at the rate of L70 to $1 (the historical rate), L60 to $1 (the closing rate), or at an average rate for the year (say, L64 to $1)?

Consolidated accounts

If a parent has a subsidiary whose accounts are presented in a foreign currency, those accounts must be translated into the local currency before they can be included in the consolidated financial statements.

- Should the subsidiary's accounts be translated as if the subsidiary is an extension of the parent?
- Or should they be translated as if the subsidiary is a separate business?

Where the affairs of a foreign operation are very closely interlinked with those of the investing company, it should be included in the consolidated financial statements as if the transactions had been entered into by the investing company in its own currency. Non-monetary assets and depreciation are translated at **historical rate** and sales, purchase and expenses at **average rate**. **Exchange differences** arising on retranslation are reported as part of **profit or loss** on ordinary activities.

Where a foreign operation is effectively a separate business, the **closing rate** is used for most items in the financial statements. **Exchange differences** are taken **directly to equity**.

2 IAS 21: The effects of changes in foreign exchange rates

The questions discussed above are addressed by IAS 21. We will examine those matters which affect single company accounts here.

These are some of the definitions given by IAS 21.

- **Foreign currency**. A currency other than the functional currency of the entity.
- **Functional currency**. The currency of the primary economic environment in which the entity operates.
- **Presentation currency**. The currency in which the financial statements are presented.
- **Exchange rate**. The ratio of exchange for two currencies.
- **Exchange difference**. The difference resulting from translating a given number of units of one currency into another currency at different exchange rates.

- **Closing rate**. The spot exchange rate at the reporting date.
- **Spot exchange rate**. The exchange rate for immediate delivery.
- **Monetary items**. Units of currency held and assets and liabilities to be received or paid in a fixed or determinable number of units of currency.   *(IAS 21)*

Each entity – whether an individual company, a parent of a group, or an operation within a group (such as a subsidiary, associate or branch) – should determine its **functional currency** and **measure its results and financial position in that currency**.

For most individual companies the functional currency will be the currency of the country in which they are located and in which they carry out most of their transactions. Determining the functional currency is much more likely to be an issue where an entity operates as part of a group. IAS 21 contains detailed guidance on how to determine an entity's functional currency and we will look at this in more detail.

An entity can present its financial statements in any currency (or currencies) it chooses. IAS 21 deals with the situation in which financial statements are presented in a currency other than the functional currency.

Again, this is unlikely to be an issue for most individual companies. Their presentation currency will normally be the same as their functional currency (the currency of the country in which they operate). A company's presentation currency may be different from its functional currency if it operates within a group and we will look at this further on.

Foreign currency transactions: initial recognition

IAS 21 states that a foreign currency transaction should be recorded, on initial recognition in the functional currency, by applying the exchange rate between the reporting currency and the foreign currency **at the date of the transaction** to the foreign currency amount.

An **average rate** for a period may be used if exchange rates do not fluctuate significantly.

Reporting at subsequent reporting dates

The following rules apply at each subsequent reporting date.
(a)   Report foreign currency **monetary items** using the **closing rate**.
(b)   Report **non-monetary items** (eg non-current assets, inventories) which are carried at **historical cost** in a foreign currency using the **exchange rate at the date of the transaction** (historical rate).
(c)   Report **non-monetary items** which are carried at **fair value** in a foreign currency using the exchange rates that existed **when the values were determined**.

Recognition of exchange differences

Exchange differences occur when there is a **change in the exchange rate** between the transaction date and the date of settlement of monetary items arising from a foreign currency transaction.

Exchange differences arising on the settlement of monetary items (receivables, payables, loans, cash in a foreign currency) or on translating an entity's monetary items at rates different from those at which they were translated initially, or reported in previous financial statements, should be **recognised in profit or loss** in the period in which they arise.

There are two situations to consider.

(a) The transaction is **settled in the same period** as that in which it occurred: all the exchange difference is recognised in that period.

(b) The transaction is **settled in a subsequent accounting period**: the exchange difference recognised in each intervening period up to the period of settlement is determined by the change in exchange rates during that period.

In other words, where a monetary item has not been settled at the end of a period, it should be **restated using the closing exchange rate** and any gain or loss taken to the income statement.

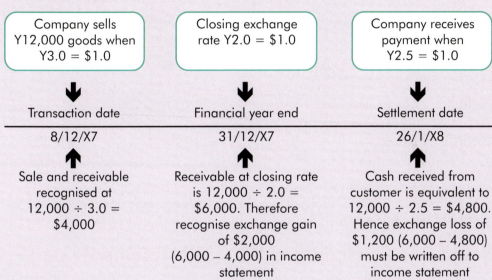

Company sells Y12,000 goods when Y3.0 = $1.0	Closing exchange rate Y2.0 = $1.0	Company receives payment when Y2.5 = $1.0
↓	↓	↓
Transaction date	Financial year end	Settlement date
8/12/X7	31/12/X7	26/1/X8
↑	↑	↑
Sale and receivable recognised at 12,000 ÷ 3.0 = $4,000	Receivable at closing rate is 12,000 ÷ 2.0 = $6,000. Therefore recognise exchange gain of $2,000 (6,000 – 4,000) in income statement	Cash received from customer is equivalent to 12,000 ÷ 2.5 = $4,800. Hence exchange loss of $1,200 (6,000 – 4,800) must be written off to income statement

Example

R Co, whose year end is 31 December, buys some goods from SA of France on 30 September. The invoice value is €40,000 and is due for settlement in equal instalments on 30 November and 31 January. The exchange rate moved as follows.

	€= $1
30 September	1.60
30 November	1.80
31 December	1.90
31 January	1.85

What are the accounting entries in the books of R Co?

The purchase will be recorded in the books of R Co using the rate of exchange ruling on 30 September.

| DEBIT | Purchases | $25,000 | |
| CREDIT | Trade payables | | $25,000 |

Being the $ cost of goods purchased for €40,000 (€40,000 ÷ €1.60/$1)

On 30 November, R Co must pay €20,000. This will cost €20,000 ÷ €1.80/$1 = $11,111 and the company has therefore made an exchange gain of $12,500 – $11,111 = $1,389.

DEBIT	Trade payables	$12,500	
CREDIT	Exchange gains: Profit or loss		$1,389
CREDIT	Cash		$11,111

On 31 December, the reporting date, the outstanding liability will be recalculated using the rate applicable to that date: €20,000 ÷ €1.90/$1 = $10,526. A further exchange gain of $1,974 has been made and will be recorded as follows.

| DEBIT | Trade payables | $1,974 | |
| CREDIT | Exchange gains: Profit or loss | | $1,974 |

The total exchange gain of $3,363 will be included in the operating profit for the year ending 31 December.

On 31 January, R Co must pay the second instalment of €20,000. This will cost them $10,811 (€20,000 ÷ €1.85/$1).

DEBIT	Trade payables	$10,526	
	Exchange losses: Profit or loss	$285	
CREDIT	Cash		$10,811

When a gain or loss on a non-monetary item is recognised **directly in equity** (for example, where property is revalued), any **related exchange differences** should also be **recognised directly in equity**.

3 IAS 21: Consolidated financial statements stage

The following definitions are relevant here.

> **Foreign operation**. A subsidiary, associate, joint venture or branch of a reporting entity, the activities of which are based or conducted in a country or currency other than those of the reporting entity.
>
> **Net investment in a foreign operation**. The amount of the reporting entity's interest in the net assets of that operation. *(IAS 21)*

Determining functional currency

A holding or parent company with foreign operations must **translate the financial statements** of those operations into its own reporting currency before they can be consolidated into the group accounts. There are two methods: **the method used depends upon whether** the foreign operation has the **same functional currency as the parent**.

IAS 21 states that an entity should consider the following factors in determining its functional currency:

(a)   The currency that mainly **influences sales prices** for goods and services (often the currency in which prices are denominated and settled)

(b)   The currency of the **country whose competitive forces and regulations** mainly determine the sales prices of its goods and services

(c)   The currency that mainly **influences labour, material and other costs** of providing goods or services (often the currency in which prices are denominated and settled)

Sometimes the functional currency of an entity is not immediately obvious. Management must then exercise judgement and may also need to consider:

(a)   The currency in which **funds from financing activities** (raising loans and issuing equity) are generated

(b)   The currency in which **receipts from operating activities** are usually retained

Where a parent has a foreign operation a number of factors are considered:

(a)   Whether the activities of the foreign operation are carried out as an **extension of the parent**, rather than being carried out with a **significant degree of autonomy**.

(b)   Whether **transactions with the parent** are a high or a low proportion of the foreign operation's activities.

(c)   Whether cash flows from the activities of the foreign operation directly affect the cash flows of the parent and are readily available for remittance to it.

(d)   Whether the activities of the foreign operation are **financed from its own cash flows** or by **borrowing from the parent**.

To sum up: in order to determine the functional currency of a foreign operation it is necessary to consider the **relationship** between the foreign operation and its parent:

*   If the foreign operation carries out its business as though it were an **extension of the parent's operations**, it almost certainly has the **same functional currency** as the parent.

*   If the foreign operation is semi-autonomous it almost certainly has **a different functional currency** from the parent.

The translation method used has to reflect the economic reality of the relationship between the reporting entity (the parent) and the foreign operation.

Same functional currency as the reporting entity

In this situation, the foreign operation normally carries on its business as though it were an **extension of the reporting entity's operations**. For example, it may only sell goods imported from, and remit the proceeds directly to, the reporting entity.

Any **movement in the exchange rate** between the reporting currency and the foreign operation's currency will have an **immediate impact** on the reporting entity's cash flows from the foreign operations. In other words, changes in the exchange rate affect the **individual monetary items** held by the foreign operation, not the reporting entity's net investment in that operation.

Different functional currency from the reporting entity

In this situation, although the reporting entity may be able to exercise control, the foreign operation normally operates in a **semi-autonomous** way. It accumulates cash and other monetary items, generates income and incurs expenses, and may also arrange borrowings, all in its own local currency.

A change in the exchange rate will produce **little or no direct effect on the present and future cash flows** from operations of either the foreign operation or the reporting entity. Rather, the change in exchange rate affects the reporting entity's **net investment** in the foreign operation, not the individual monetary and non-monetary items held by the foreign operation.

Accounting treatment: different functional currency from the reporting entity

The financial statements of the foreign operation must be translated to the functional currency of the parent. Different procedures must be followed here, because the functional currency of the parent is the **presentation currency** of the foreign operation.

(a)   The **assets and liabilities** shown in the foreign operation's statement of financial position are translated at the **closing rate** at the year end, regardless of the date on which those items originated. The balancing figure in the translated statement of financial position represents the reporting entity's net investment in the foreign operation.

(b)   Amounts in the **statement of comprehensive income** should be translated at the rate ruling at the date of the transaction (an **average rate** will usually be used for practical purposes).

(c)   **Exchange differences** arising from the re translation at the end of each year of the parent's net investment should be **taken to equity**, not through the profit or loss for the year, until the disposal of the net investment.

Example: different functional currency from the reporting entity

A dollar-based company, set up a foreign subsidiary on 30 June 20X7. It subscribed €24,000 for share capital when the exchange rate was €2 = $1. The subsidiary, borrowed €72,000 and bought a non monetary asset for €96,000. The parent prepared its accounts on 31 December 20X7 and by that time the exchange rate had moved to €3 = $1. As a result of highly unusual circumstances, the subsidiary sold its asset early in 20X8 for €96,000. It repaid its loan and was liquidated. The parent's capital of €24,000 was repaid in February 20X8 when the exchange rate was €3 = $1.

From the above it can be seen that the parent will record its initial investment at $12,000 which is the starting cost of its shares. The statement of financial position of the subsidiary at 31 December 20X7 is summarised below.

	€'000
Non monetary asset	96
Share capital	24
Loan	72
	96

This may be translated as follows.

	$'000
Non monetary asset (€3 = $1)	32
Share capital and reserves (retained earnings) (balancing figure)	8
Loan (€3 = $1)	24
	32
Exchange gain/(loss) for 20X7	(4)

The exchange gain and loss are the differences between the value of the original investment ($12,000) and the total of share capital and reserves (retained earnings) as disclosed by the above statements of financial position.

On liquidation, the parent will receive $8,000 (€24,000 converted at €3 = $1). No gain or loss will arise in 20X8.

Analysis of exchange differences

The exchange differences in the above exercise could be reconciled by splitting them into their component parts.

The exchange difference consists of those exchange gains/losses arising from:

- Translating **income/expense items** at the exchange rates at the date of transactions, whereas **assets/liabilities** are translated at the closing rate.
- Translating the **opening net investment** (opening net assets) in the foreign entity at a closing rate different from the closing rate at which it was previously reported.

Further matters relating to foreign operations

Goodwill and fair value adjustments

Goodwill and fair value adjustments arising on the acquisition of a foreign operation should be treated as assets and liabilities of the acquired entity. This means that they should be expressed in the functional currency of the foreign operation and translated at the **closing rate**.

This means that goodwill is restated at the end of each repoting period and the resulting foreign exchange gain or loss is recognised.

Consolidation procedures

Follow normal consolidation procedures, except that where an exchange difference arises on **long– or short-term intra-group monetary items**, these cannot be offset against other intra-group balances. This is because these are commitments to convert one currency into another, thus exposing the reporting entity to a gain or loss through currency fluctuations.

If the foreign operation's **reporting date** is different from that of the parent, it is acceptable to use the accounts made up to that date for consolidation, as long as adjustments are made for any significant changes in rates in the interim.

Hyperinflationary economies

We will look at IAS 29 *Financial reporting in hyperinflationary economies* later in this chapter. The financial statements of a foreign operation operating in a hyperinflationary economy must be adjusted under IAS 29 before they are translated into the parent's reporting currency and then consolidated. When the economy **ceases to be hyperinflationary**, and the foreign operation ceases to apply IAS 29, the amounts restated to the price level at the date the entity ceased to restate its financial statements should be used as the historical costs for translation purposes.

Disposal of foreign entity

When a parent disposes of a foreign entity, the cumulative amount of deemed exchange differences relating to that foreign entity should be **recognised as an income or expense** in the same period in which the gain or loss on disposal is recognised. Effectively, this means that these exchange differences are recognised once by taking them to reserves and then are recognised for a second time ('recycled') by transferring them to the income statement on disposal of the foreign operation.

In the parent's financial statements

In the parent company's own financial statements, exchange differences arising on a **monetary item** that is effectively part of the parent's net investment in the foreign entity should be recognised **in profit or loss** in the separate financial statements of the reporting entity or the individual financial statements of the foreign operation, as appropriate.

Change in functional currency

The functional currency of an entity can be changed only if there is a change to the underlying transactions, events and conditions that are relevant to the entity. For example, an entity's functional currency may change if there is a change in the currency that mainly influences the sales price of goods and services.

Where there is a change in an entity's functional currency, the entity translates all items into the new functional currency **prospectively** (ie, from the date of the change) using the exchange rate at the date of the change.

Tax effects of exchange differences

IAS 12 *Income taxes* should be applied when there are tax effects arising from gains or losses on foreign currency transactions and exchange differences arising on the translation of the financial statements of foreign operations.

Foreign associates

Foreign associates will be companies with substantial autonomy from the group and so their **functional currency will be different** from that of the parent.

Disclosure

IAS 21 requires disclosure of the following.

(a) Amount of exchange differences recognised in profit or loss
(b) Net exchange differences (classified as equity) as a separate component of equity, and a reconciliation of the amount of such exchange differences at the beginning and end of the period

In addition, when the **presentation currency is different** from the functional currency, that fact should be stated and the functional currency should be disclosed. The reason for using a different presentation currency should also be disclosed.

Where there is a **change in the functional currency** of either the reporting entity or a significant foreign operation, that fact and the reason for the change in functional currency should be disclosed.

An entity may present its financial statements or other financial information in a currency that is different from either its functional currency or its presentation currency. For example, it may convert selected items only, or it may use a translation method that does not comply with IFRSs in order to deal with hyperinflation. In this situation the entity must:

(a) Clearly identify the information as supplementary information to distinguish it from information that complies with IFRSs
(b) Disclose the currency in which the supplementary information is displayed; and
(c) Disclose the entity's functional currency and the method of translation used to determine the supplementary information.

4 IAS 29: Financial reporting in hyperinflationary economies

In a hyperinflationary economy, **money loses its purchasing power very quickly**. Comparisons of transactions at different points in time, even within the same accounting period, are misleading. It is therefore considered inappropriate for entities to prepare financial statements without making adjustments for the **fall in the purchasing power of money over time**.

IAS 29 *Financial reporting in hyperinflationary economies* applies to the **primary financial statements** of entities (including consolidated accounts and statements of cash flows) whose functional currency is the currency of a hyperinflationary economy. In this section, we will identify the hyperinflationary currency as $H.

The standard does not define a **hyperinflationary economy** in exact terms, although it indicates the characteristics of such an economy, for example, where the cumulative inflation rate over three years approaches or exceeds 100%.

What other factors might indicate a hyperinflationary economy?

These are examples, but the list is not exhaustive.

(a) The population prefers to retain its wealth in non-monetary assets or in a relatively stable foreign currency. Amounts of local currency held are immediately invested to maintain purchasing power.

(b) The population regards monetary amounts not in terms of the local currency but in terms of a relatively stable foreign currency. Prices may be quoted in that currency.

(c) Sales/purchases on credit take place at prices that compensate for the expected loss of purchasing power during the credit period, if that period is short.

(d) Interest rates, wages and prices are linked to a price index.

The reported value of **non-monetary assets**, in terms of current measuring units, increases over time. For example, if a fixed asset is purchased for $H1,000 when the price index is 100, and the price index subsequently rises to 200, the value of the asset in terms of current measuring units (ignoring accumulated depreciation) will rise to $H2,000.

In contrast, the value of **monetary assets and liabilities**, such as a debt for 300 units, is unaffected by changes in the prices index, because it is an actual money amount payable or receivable. If a debtor owes $H300 when the price index is 100, and the debt is still unpaid when the price index has risen to 150, the debtor still owes just $H300. The purchasing power of monetary assets, however, will decline over time as the general level of prices goes up.

Requirement to restate financial statements in terms of measuring units current at the year end

In most countries, financial statements are produced on the basis of either:

(a) **historical cost**, except to the extent that some assets (eg property and investments) may be revalued, or

(b) **current cost**, which reflects the changes in the values of specific assets held by the entity.

In a hyperinflationary economy, neither of these methods of financial reporting are meaningful unless adjustments are made for the fall in the purchasing power of money.

IAS 29 therefore requires that the **primary financial statements** of entities in a hyperinflationary economy should be produced by restating the figures prepared on either a historical cost basis or a current cost basis in terms of **measuring units current at the year end**.

> **Measuring unit current at the year end date.** This is a unit of local currency with a purchasing power as at the date of the statement of financial position, in terms of a general prices index.

Financial statements that are not restated (ie that are prepared on a historical cost basis or current cost basis without adjustments) may be presented as **additional statements** by the entity, but this is discouraged. The primary financial statements are those that have been restated.

After the assets, liabilities, equity and statement of comprehensive income of the entity have been restated, there will be a **net gain or loss on monetary assets and liabilities (the 'net monetary position')** and this should be recognised separately in profit or loss for the period.

Making the adjustments

IAS 29 recognises that the resulting financial statements, after restating all items in terms of measuring units current at the year end, will **lack precise accuracy**. However, it is more important that certain procedures and judgements should be applied consistently from year to year. The implementation guidelines to the Standard suggest what these procedures should be.

Statement of financial position: historical cost

Where the entity produces its accounts on a historical cost basis, the following procedures should be applied.

(a) Items that are not already expressed in terms of measuring units current at the year end should be restated, using a **general prices index**, so that they are valued in measuring units current at the year end.

(b) **Monetary assets and liabilities** are not restated, because they are already expressed in terms of measuring units current at the year end.

(c) Assets that are **already stated at market value or net realisable value** need not be restated, because they too are already valued in measuring units current at the year end.

(d) Any assets or liabilities **linked by agreement to changes in the general level of prices**, such as indexed-linked loans or bonds, should be adjusted in accordance with the terms of the agreement to establish the amount outstanding as at the year end.

(e) All **other non-monetary assets**, ie tangible long-term assets, intangible long-term assets (including accumulated depreciation/amortisation) investments and inventories, should be restated in terms of measuring units as at the year end, by applying a general prices index.

The **method of restating** these assets should normally be to multiply the original cost of the assets by a factor: [prices index at year end /prices index at date of acquisition of the asset]. For example, if an item of machinery was purchased for $H2,000 units when the prices index was 400 and the prices index at the year end is 1,000, the restated value of the long-term asset (before accumulated depreciation) would be:

$$\$H2,000 \times [1,000/400] = \$H5,000$$

If, in the above example, the non current asset has been held for half its useful life and has no residual value, the **accumulated depreciation** would be restated as $H2,500. (The depreciation charge for the year should be the amount of depreciation based on historical cost, multiplied by the same factor as above: 1,000/400.)

If an asset has been **revalued** since it was originally purchased (eg a property), it should be restated in measuring units at the year end date by applying a factor: (prices index at year end/prices index at revaluation date) to the revalued amount of the asset.

If the restated amount of a non-monetary asset **exceeds its recoverable value** (ie its net realisable value or market value), its value should be reduced accordingly.

The **owners' equity** (all components) as at the start of the accounting period should be restated using a general prices index from the beginning of the period.

Statement of comprehensive income: historical cost

In the statement of comprehensive income, all amounts of income and expense should be **restated in terms of measuring units current at the year end**. All amounts therefore need to be restated by a factor that allows for the change in the prices index since the item of income or expense was first recorded.

Gain or loss on net monetary position

In a period of inflation, an entity that holds monetary assets (cash, receivables) will suffer a fall in the purchasing power of these assets. By the same token, in a period of inflation, the value of monetary liabilities, such as a bank overdraft or bank loan, declines in terms of current purchasing power.

(a)   If an entity has an **excess of monetary assets over monetary liabilities**, it will suffer a loss over time on its net monetary position, in a period of inflation, in terms of measuring units as at 'today's date'.

(b)   If an entity has an **excess of monetary liabilities over monetary assets**, it will make a gain on its net monetary position, in a period of inflation.

Example: Hyperinflationary accounts

An entity maintains an unchanged position over time. At 1 January, when the general prices index was 100, its statement of financial position was as follows.

	$H
Assets	
Non-monetary assets	2,000
Monetary assets	2,000
	4,000
Liabilities and equity	
Monetary liabilities	1,000
Equity	3,000
	4,000

Suppose that the general prices index rises to 150 at 31 December.

What are the adjustments required in the statement of financial position?

Restating this statement of financial position in terms of measuring units when the prices index is 50% higher gives the following.

	$H
Assets	
Non-monetary assets (× 150/100)	3,000
Monetary assets	2,000
	5,000
Liabilities and equity	
Monetary liabilities	1,000
Equity (× 150/100)	4,500
	5,500

The entity has suffered a loss on its net monetary position of $H500, in terms of measuring units at the current date $H(5,500 – 5,000). This is because it has held net monetary assets of $H1,000 during the period.

In the financial statements of an entity reporting in the currency of a hyperinflationary economy, the gain or loss on the net monetary position:

(a) may be derived as the **difference between total assets and total equity and liabilities**, after restating the non-monetary assets, owners' equity, statement of comprehensive income items and index-linked items, or

(b) may be estimated by **applying the change in the general prices index** for the period to the weighted average of the net monetary position of the entity in the period.

The gain or loss on the net monetary position should be **included in net income** and disclosed separately. (Any adjustment that was made to index-linked items can be set off against this net monetary gain or loss.)

Current cost accounts: restating the accounts

A similar procedure is required to restate the accounts of an entity that prepares its accounts using a current cost basis.

(a) Items stated in the statement of financial position at current cost do not need to be restated. Other items should be restated in the same way as for adjusting accounts prepared on a historical cost basis.

(b) In the **statement of comprehensive income**, cost of sales and depreciation are generally reported at current costs at the time of consumption and sales and other expenses at money amounts at the time they occurred. These items will need to be restated in terms of measuring units as at the year end by making a prices index adjustment.

(c) There will be a **gain or loss on the net monetary position**, which will be established in the same way as for accounts based on historical cost.

Economies ceasing to be hyperinflationary economies

When an economy ceases to be a hyperinflationary economy, entities reporting in the currency of the economy are no longer required to produce financial statements in compliance with IAS 29.

Suppose for example that in 20X4 an entity reports in compliance with IAS 29, but in 20X5 it reverts to historical cost accounting because the economy is no longer a hyperinflationary economy. As a starting point for reverting to historical cost accounts reporting, the entity should use the amounts expressed in terms of measuring units as at the end of 20X4 as the basis for its carrying amounts in 20X5 and subsequent years.

Disclosures

IAS 29 calls for the following disclosures.

*   The fact that the **financial statements have been restated** for the changes in general purchasing power.
*   Whether the financial statements as shown are based on **historical cost or current cost**.
*   The **identity of the prices index** used to make the restatements, its level at the year end the movement in the index during the current and the previous reporting periods.

In financial statements prepared under IAS 29, corresponding figures for the previous year should be **restated using the general prices index**.

Hyperinflation and changes in foreign exchange rates

IAS 21 *The effects of changes in foreign exchange rates* was covered earlier. A parent may have a foreign operation whose functional currency is the currency of a hyperinflationary economy. When the parent prepares consolidated financial statements it should:

(a)   **restate the financial statements** of the foreign operation in accordance with IAS 29; before

(b)   **translating all amounts** from the foreign operation's functional currency to the presentation currency **at the closing rate**.

The following example is a simple illustration of the problems that can arise where a foreign subsidiary operates in a hyperinflationary economy.

Example: 'Disappearing assets'

A company has a subsidiary in a country which suffers from hyperinflation. On 31 December 20X2 the subsidiary acquired freehold land for $H1,000,000. At that date the exchange rate was $H4 = $1 and the relevant price index was 100.

At 31 December 20X3 the exchange rate was $H10 = $1 and the price index was 300.

At what value will the freehold land be included in the consolidated financial statements of the parent at 31 December 20X3 if the subsidiary's financial statements:

(a)   are not restated to reflect current price levels;
(b)   are restated to reflect current price levels?

(a)   **Without restatement**

Assuming that the subsidiary has a different functional currency ($H) from that of its parent ($) the statement of financial position is translated at the closing rate.

At 31 December 20X3 the land is included at $100,000 ($H1,000,000 @ 10).

At 31 December 20X2 (the date of purchase) its was stated at $250,000 ($H1,000,000 @ 4). Therefore there has been an exchange loss of $150,000 (which may significantly reduce equity) and the land appears to have fallen to only 40% of its original value.

(b)   **With restatement**

At 31 December 20X3 the land is included at $300,000 ($H1,000,000 × 300/100 @ 10).

The value of the land is now adjusted so that it reflects the effect of inflation over the year and the 'disappearing assets' problem is overcome.

Where the financial statements of an entity whose functional currency is that of a hyperinflationary economy are translated into a different presentation currency, **comparative amounts** should be those that were presented as current year amounts in the relevant prior year financial statements (ie, **not adjusted** for subsequent changes in the price level or subsequent changes in exchange rates).

Accounting for agriculture and mineral resources

1 IAS 41: Agriculture

IAS 41 was issued by the old IASC in 2001, and is an instance of the IASC/IASB developing standards that are specific to individual industries where the accounting issues involved are of sufficient substance and significance.

IAS 41 has contributed to the international harmonisation of accounting standards, because agriculture in particular was characterised by a **great diversity in accounting treatments**. Cows, for instance, were accounted for as 'stocks' in Ireland but as 'fixed assets' in the UK. IAS 41 has helped to foster increased comparability between accounts produced in these different regions.

Perhaps more interestingly, it is quite difficult to apply **traditional accounting methods** to agricultural activities, which explains why agriculture is excluded from many IASs.

(a)   When and how do you account for the **critical events** associated with biological transformation (growth, procreation, production and degeneration), which alter the substance of biological assets?

(b)   **Statement of financial position classification** is made difficult by the variety and characteristics of the living assets of agriculture.

(c)   The nature of the management of agricultural activities also causes problems, particularly determination of the **unit of measurement**, ie whether biological assets are a perpetual group of assets or a number of limited life assets.

The standard has improved and harmonised practice in accounting for agriculture, which demonstrates fundamental **differences in its nature and characteristics** to other business activities.

Definitions

The following definitions are used in IAS 41.

- **Agricultural activity** is the management by an entity of the biological transformation of biological assets for sale, into agricultural produce or into additional biological assets.
- **Agricultural produce** is the harvested product of an entity's biological assets.
- A **biological asset** is a living animal or plant.
- **Biological transformation** comprises the processes of growth, degeneration, production and procreation that cause qualitative and quantitative changes in a biological asset.

- A **group of biological assets** is an aggregation of similar living animals or plants.

> - **Harvest** is the detachment of produce from a biological asset or the cessation of a biological asset's life processes
> - **Fair value** is the amount for which an asset could be exchanged, or a liability settled, between knowledgeable, willing parties in an arm's length transaction.
> - **Carrying amount** is the amount at which an asset is recognised in the statement of financial position.   *(IAS 41)*

Note the key parts of the definition of agriculture.

(a) **Biological**: agriculture relates to 'life phenomena', living animals and plants with an innate capacity of biological transformation which are dependent upon a combination of natural resources (sunlight, water, etc).

(b) **Transformation**: agriculture involves physical transformation, whereby animals and plants undergo a change in biological quantity (fat cover, density, etc) and/or quantity (progeny, live weight etc) over time, which is measured and monitored (increasingly objectively) as part of management control.

(c) **Management**: biological transformation is managed.
 (i) Conditions are stabilised or enhanced
 (ii) The transparency of the relationship between inputs and outputs is determined by the degree of control (intensive versus extensive)
 (iii) It is different from exploitation through extraction, where no attempt is made to facilitate the transformation
 (iv) Biological assets are managed in groups of plant or animal classes, using individual assets to ensure the sustainability of the group
 (v) Sustainability of an agricultural activity is a function of quality and quantity

(d) **Produce**: agricultural produce is diverse and may require further processing before ultimate consumption.

The standard applies to the three elements that form part of, or result from, agricultural activity.

- Biological assets
- Agricultural produce at the point of harvest
- Government grants

The standard does not apply to agricultural land (IASs 16 and 40) or intangible assets related to agricultural activity (IAS 38). After harvest, IAS 2 is applied.

Biological assets

Biological assets are the core income-producing assets of agricultural activities, held for their transformative capabilities. **Biological transformation** leads to various **different outcomes.**

- **Asset changes:**
 – Growth: increase in quantity and or quality
 – Degeneration: decrease in quantity and/or quality
- **Creation of new assets:**
 – Production: producing separable non-living products
 – Procreation: producing separable living animals

We can distinguish between the importance of these by saying that asset changes are **critical to the flow of future economic benefits** both in and beyond the current period, but the relative importance of new asset creation will depend on the purpose of the agricultural activity.

The IAS distinguishes therefore between two broad categories of agricultural production system.

(a) **Consumable**: animals/plants themselves are harvested
(b) **Bearer**: animals/plants bear produce for harvest

A few further points are made.

(a) Biological assets are usually managed in groups of animal or plant classes, with characteristics (eg male/female ratio) which allow sustainability in perpetuity.
(b) **Land often forms an integral part** of the activity itself in pastoral and other land-based agricultural activities.

The Standard then goes on to look at the principal issues in accounting for biological assets.

Recognition of biological assets

The recognition criteria are very **similar to those for other assets**, in that animals or plants should be recognised as assets in the following circumstances.

(a) The entity **controls** the asset as a result of past events
(b) It is probable that the **future economic benefits** associated with the asset will flow to the entity
(c) The fair value or cost of the asset to the entity can be **measured reliably**

The significant physical attributes of biological assets can be measured using various methods (which are used by markets to measure value) and generally indicate the source of future economic benefits. The **certainty** of the flow of rewards can be determined by formal ownership records, eg land title, branding. The availability of both cost and value for biological assets indicates the reliability aspect of the measurement criteria is fulfilled.

Measurement of biological assets

The IAS provides for a benchmark treatment and an allowed alternative treatment.

Benchmark treatment	Allowed alternative treatment
Fair value less estimated point of sale costs	Cost less accumulated depreciation and impairment losses

The alternative method is allowed, if a fair value cannot be determined because market-determined prices or values are not available.

This alternative basis is only allowed on **initial recognition**.

The **measurement basis** used to depict the fair value of a biological asset will differ depending on the existence of an active market, market efficiency and the use made of the asset.

In summary, it is felt that **fair value**, when compared to historical cost, has greater relevance, reliability, comparability and understandability as a measure of future economic benefits.

Determining fair value

The standard states that the primary indicator of fair value should be **net market value**. This is reasonable as efficient markets exist for most biological assets in most locations, and net market value is usually considered as providing the best evidence of fair value where an active market exists. Markets will generally differentiate between differing **qualities and quantities**. Market value is not generally predicted on management's intended use, however, but recognises alternative uses.

An active and efficient market may not be available for a class of biological assets in a specific location, or there may be imperfections in the market. The standard goes into some detail about **how fair value should be estimated** in such circumstances, but in summary, the valuation techniques should be consistent with the objectives of measuring fair value and should attain an appropriate balance between relevance and reliability.

Recognition

This is an important principle, whereby the change in the carrying amount for a group of biological assets should be allocated between:

(a)   The change attributable to **differences in fair value**, and
(b)   The **physical change** in biological assets held.

The total change in carrying value between the beginning and end of the period thus consists of two components. Although the separation of these two components might appear impractical, the Standard states that separate disclosure of each is **fundamental to appraising current period performance and future prospects**. This is because they will not be reported in the same way in the financial statements.

(a)   The change in carrying amount attributable to the **physical change in biological assets** must be recognised as income or expense and described as the change in biological assets. This allows management's performance to be evaluated in relation to the production from, and maintenance and renewal of, biological assets. This is the 'operating' part of the change in carrying amount.
(b)   The change in carrying amount attributable to **differences in fair value** should be recognised in the statement of non-owner movements in equity and presented in equity under the heading of surplus/(deficit) on fair valuation of biological assets. This is the 'holding' part of the change in carrying amount.

In the **statement of financial position** the biological assets must be shown at fair value, incorporating the consequences of all biological transformations. These assets, with their differing risk and return characteristics, should be identified clearly.

The recommended **method of separating the above components** is to calculate the change attributable to the differences in fair value by restating biological assets on hand at the opening reporting date using end of period fair values and comparing this with the closing carrying amount. The biological assets on hand at the beginning and end of the period will then be expressed in a common measurement unit, ie period-end fair value. This allows the relative significance of sales, disposals, purchases, additions and biological transformations to be evaluated in relation to the overall change in substance of the biological assets held during the period.

There are **exceptions to this approach** in certain situations. For example, in some agricultural systems the predominant activity has a production cycle of less than a year (eg broiler chickens, mushroom growing, cereal crops). In such cases the total change in carrying amount is reported in the income statement as a single item of income or expense.

Any other events giving rise to a change in biological assets of such a **size, nature or incidence** that their disclosure is relevant to explain the entity's performance (as defined in IAS 8) should be included in the change in biological assets recognised as income or expense. They should, however, be shown as a separate item in the reconciliation required to determine the change attributable to biological transformation.

Presentation and disclosure

In the **statement of financial position** biological assets should be classified as a separate class of assets falling under neither current nor non-current classifications. This reflects the view of such assets as having an unlimited life on a collective basis; it is the total exposure of the entity to this type of asset that is important.

Biological assets should also be **sub-classified** (either on the face of the statement of financial position or as a note to the accounts).
(a)   Class of animal or plant
(b)   Nature of activities (consumable or bearer)
(c)   Maturity or immaturity for intended purpose

Where activities are **consumable**, the maturity criterion will be attainment of harvestable specifications, whereas in **bearer** activities, it will be attainment of sufficient maturity to sustain economic harvests.

In the **statement of comprehensive income**, entities with significant agricultural activity are encouraged to provide, on the face of the statement of comprehensive income, an analysis of the income and expenses used in determining profit from operating activities based on the nature of income and expenses (ie rather than the cost of sales method).

The IAS also lists some detailed disclosure requirements including the measurement base used for fair value, the details of the reconciliation of the change in carrying value for the year and so on.

Agricultural produce

This was defined in the key terms above. It is **recognised at the point of harvest** (eg detachment from the biological asset). Agricultural produce is either incapable of biological process or such processes remain dormant (eg stored grain). **Recognition ends** once the produce enters trading activities or production processes within integrated agribusinesses, although processing activities that are incidental to agricultural activities and that do not materially alter the form of the produce (eg drying or cleaning) are not counted as processing. Following harvest, the provisions of IAS 2 apply.

Measurement and presentation

Following the treatment of biological assets above, the IAS states that agricultural produce should be **measured at each reporting date at fair value** less estimated point of-sale costs, to the extent that it is sourced from an entity's biological assets, which are also valued at fair value. This is logical when you consider that, until harvest, the agricultural produce was valued at fair value anyway as part of the biological asset.

The **change in the carrying amount** of the agricultural produce held at two reporting dates should be recognised as **income or expense** in the income statement. This will be rare as such produce is usually sold or processed within a short time, so that produce held over two reporting dates is being held for a specific management purpose and the consequences of that should be reflected in the current period.

Agricultural produce that is harvested for **trading or processing activities** within integrated agricultural/ agribusiness operations should be measured at **fair value** at the date of harvest and this amount is deemed cost for application of IAS 2 to consequential inventories.

Presentation in the statement of financial position

Agricultural produce should be classified as inventory in the statement of financial position and disclosed separately either in the statement of financial position or in the notes.

Government grants

An unconditional government grant related to a biological asset measured at its fair value less estimated point-of-sale costs should be recognised as income when, and only when, the grant becomes receivable.

If a government grant requires an entity not to engage in specified agricultural activity (eg the EU's set aside grant), an entity should only recognise the grant as income when, and only when, the conditions are met.

IAS 20 does not apply to a government grant on biological assets measured at fair value less estimated point-of-sale costs. However if a biological asset is measured at cost less accumulated depreciation and accumulated impairment losses then IAS 20 does apply.

The following should be disclosed.

*   The nature and extent of government grants recognised in the financial statements.
*   Unfulfilled conditions and other contingencies attaching to government grants.
*   Significant decreases expected in the level of government grants.

2   IFRS 6: Exploration for and evaluation of mineral resources

IFRS 6 is an interim standard. It is only a short-term solution to the problems of accounting in this area, and was issued so that entities had at least some guidance until a complete standard is issued in the future. Before IFRS, accounting practices varied greatly between national standard-setters, so it was important that, with more and more entities switching to IFRS, there was at least some IFRS guidance in the area. Since it had had to be specifically excluded from IAS 16 and IAS 38, the IASB developed and issued IFRS 6.

IFRS 6 is related to IAS 38's distinction between research and development phases, where research costs are expensed and development costs are capitalised. The problem is that the exploration for and evaluation of mineral resources is not quite research and not quite development – hence the need for IFRS 6.

The scope of IFRS 6 is intentionally very narrow. Entities must apply IFRS 6 to all exploration and evaluation expenditure incurred, but it does not address other aspects of their accounting.

IFRS 6 only applies **after** the entity has obtained legal rights to explore in a specific area and **before** technical feasibility and commercial viability of extraction have been demonstrated.

> **Exploration and evaluation expenditures** are expenditures incurred by an entity in connection with the exploration for and evaluation of mineral resources before the technical feasibility and commercial viability of extracting a mineral resource are demonstrable.
>
> **Exploration and evaluation assets** are exploration and evaluation expenditures recognised as assets in accordance with the entity's accounting policy.
>
> **Exploration for and evaluation of mineral resources** is the search for mineral resources, including minerals, oil, natural gas and similar non-regenerative resources after the entity has obtained legal rights to explore in a specific area, as well as the determination of the technical feasibility and commercial viability of extracting the mineral resource. *(IFRS 6)*

Recognition

Expenditure is recognised as an asset for IFRS 6 up to the point where the technical feasibility and commercial viability of extracting resources can be demonstrated. Note that this also means that the entity must have the necessary technical and financial means to extract the resources.

An entity can then choose its own accounting policy as long as it is line with IAS 8. Specifically, it must conform to IAS 8 paragraph 10, which states that **management should use its judgement** in developing an **accounting policy** that results in information that is **relevant** and **reliable**. After choosing their policy, entities must then **apply their policy consistently**.

Note that expenditure related to the **development** of mineral resources must not be recognised as exploration and evaluation assets under IFRS 6, as it comes under IAS 38.

Measurement at recognition

At recognition, exploration and evaluation **assets must be measured at cost**.

The following are examples of expenditures an entity might incur in the initial measurement of exploration and evaluation assets:

(a) Acquisition of rights to explore
(b) Topographical geological, geochemical and geophysical studies
(c) Exploratory drilling
(d) Trenching
(e) Sampling
(f) Activities in relation to evaluating the technical feasibility and commercial viability of extracting a mineral resource

An entity should also recognise the cost of any obligations for removal and restoration, in line with IAS 37.

Measurement after recognition

Entities must apply either the cost model or the revaluation model (taking the revaluation model either from IAS 16 or IAS 38).

Classification and reclassification

Exploration and evaluation assets are classified as **tangible or intangible according to the nature** of the assets acquired. For example, drilling rights would be intangible; vehicles or drilling rigs would be tangible. The classification must be applied consistently.

They should no longer be classified as exploration and evaluation assets when the technical feasibility and commercial viability of extracting a mineral resource are demonstrable. Any impairment loss on the assets must be recognised before classification.

Impairment

Exploration and evaluation assets must be **assessed for impairment when facts and circumstances suggest that the carrying amount of an asset may exceed its recoverable amount. Any resulting impairment loss must be measured, presented and disclosed in accordance with IAS 36.**

The following **factors** suggest exploration and evaluation assets should be tested for impairment:

(a) The period for which the entity has **exploration rights has expired** or is due to expire in the near future and is not expected to be reviewed.

(b) **Substantive expenditure** on further exploration in the specific area is **not budgeted** or planned.

(c) Exploration in a specific area has **not** led to the discovery of **commercially viable quantities** of mineral resources, and the entity has decided to discontinue activities in this area.

(d) Sufficient data indicates that whilst a development in a specific area may proceed, the **carrying value of the exploration and evaluation asset is unlikely to be recovered** from successful development and sale.

For impairment purposes, each cash generating unit or group of units to which an exploration and evaluation asset is allocated must not be larger than a segment as determined by IFRS 8 *Operating segments*.

Disclosures

These must identify and explain the amounts recognised in the accounts. Specifically, entities must explain:

* Accounting policies
* The amounts of assets, liabilities, income and expenses, and operating and investing cash flows

Index

A

B

C

D

G

H

I

J

K

L

M

N